The Successful Family

Everything You Need to Know to Build a Stronger Family

Resource Guides in *The Successful Family* series

Before the Ring
Marriage Enhancement
Family Planning and Children
The Secret to a Happy Family
Making a Go of It
Life on the Edge

Other products in *The Successful Family* series

Kidz Faith Confessions
Family Confessions

Ask for them at your local bookstore or visit us on the web:
www.creflodollarministries.org

The Successful Family

Everything You Need to Know to Build a Stronger Family

Dr. Creflo A. Dollar and Taffi L. Dollar

The Successful Family: Everything You Need to Know to Build a Stronger Family
ISBN 1-59089-468-5
Copyright © 2002 by Dr. Creflo A. Dollar and Taffi L. Dollar

Published by Creflo Dollar Ministries
P.O. Box 490124
College Park, GA 30349

CONTENTS

Part IV — The Secret to a Happy Family

Part V — Making a Go of It

Part VI — Life on the Edge

PREFACE

"Except the Lord builds the house, they labour in vain who build it…"
(Psalm 127:1, *The Amplified Bible*).

Lifelong success…that is everyone's dream. We all desire to prosper and excel in all that we do. For some, success seems to come instantaneously. The media saturates us with the overnight success stories of athletes, businessmen, actors, writers and artists. Unfortunately, this only serves to reinforce the fairytale mentality of someone being plucked from obscurity and launched into fame and fortune. As a result, many people wait for success to fall into their laps instead of achieving their goals and attaining their dreams through hard work, determination and wisdom.

The world is in a constant state of turmoil and change. Economic recessions, company layoffs, terrorist attacks, wars, crime and scandals are part of our everyday lives and do much to paint a bleak picture of the future. Doubt, insecurity and fear of the unknown can discourage even the most positive and upbeat person. As a result, lasting success seems harder to come by and almost not worth the effort.

What impact should this have on the family unit? None whatsoever. Strong individuals make strong families. And strong families have nothing to fear. Whenever there is darkness in the world, there is also light and hope. The two live side by side. As long as there is a chance things can change for the better, there is nothing to worry or be discouraged about. This expectation leads to the fact that God, our Omnipotent Creator and loving Father, is always with us. Our paths in life are illuminated by His love. He is ready and willing to show us His goodness so we can mature as individuals and lay a solid foundation of integrity, unity and high moral standards for the future success of our families.

The Successful Family: Everything You Need to Know to Build a Stronger Family is a beacon of light in this dark world. It was written for people like you who desire to maximize their family's potential by enhancing their interpersonal relationships and adding to their knowledge of how to properly invest in the future. Whether you are single, married, divorced or simply interested in family dynamics, this reference guide contains a wealth of ideas and basic, commonsense principles. Everyone can benefit from it. That is what makes it unique.

This book is designed to help people succeed, regardless of their past history or present circumstances. It is a solution-oriented guide to help you resolve those "impossible" issues and improve your relationships with family members. Just as doctors, lawyers, teachers and mechanics are unable to operate efficiently without the tools of their trade, so are you unable to effectively manage your home life without the proper guidance and reference materials.

Wisdom From Experience

Taffi and I have collaborated on this work with the desire to give you the answers you need to build a family that will go the distance. Over the past 20 years, we have had our share of triumphs, challenges, disagreements and

The willingness to change is the secret to a happy home.

memorable moments that prove it *is* possible to strengthen yourself and your family through the *consistent* application of biblical principles.

Our lives have been marked by success and victory. Through trial and error (and much prayer and practical application) we have discovered the secret to a happy home life: a willingness to change. By aligning our actions with what the Word of God has to say regarding this subject, we have seen our family evolve into a beautiful coalition. We want your family to experience this same joy as well. That's why, as transparent people, we share with you personal information about our lives over the years. Allow our stories of success to encourage and motivate you. Giving up has never been an option in the Dollar household, and it shouldn't be an option for your family either.

To be successful, you must have the right mindset. Just as an athlete is unable to win a competition without first focusing on the task at hand, you are also unable to build a strong family without a practical understanding of what it is, how it should work and the purpose behind it. Knowledge is power. Determination is necessary. Passivity is not an option. To be successful, you must implement success principles. These can be found in the Word of God. By allowing Scripture to order, or direct, your steps (Psalm 119:133), you guarantee positive, long-lasting results.

A Wonderful Design

Doing things God's way enables us to fulfill His original plan for the family structure, which includes wholeness and total life prosperity. By *total life prosperity* we mean that you have a biblical right to succeed financially, socially, mentally, physically and spiritually—basically in every area of your life! In fact, your life should be a never-ending series of victories and successes instead of struggles and failures.

Our idea of what a family is must be the same as God's. After all, He is the Creator and ultimate authority on the subject. If anyone should know about what true family is, it would be Him. As far as God is concerned, your family is not just a web of interpersonal relationships or a group of people living together. Instead, it is a tool designed to carry His power, presence and love to the world. When a family is healthy and operating according to the Word of God, it becomes a powerful force that can tear down walls and break through barriers. It can heal, restore, inspire and motivate others.

God intended for the family unit to be a dominant force in the earth. It is supposed to dominate sin and temptation, sickness and disease, poverty and insufficiency. Just as God rules in the spirit realm, His earthly family is designed to rule in the natural realm. As beings created in His image, we carry inside us the capacity to create, destroy and rebuild. We are able to think, speak and act just as He would in any given situation. In fact, as born-again Christians, we carry His power and presence with us wherever we go.

Ruling in life as a family starts with understanding family from God's perspective. It begins with an individual's singleness—the state of being where he or she realizes his or her self-worth and uniqueness—and continues with the bond of matrimony. Together, a man and woman form a *covenant*, which is "an agreement between two or more parties to carry out terms agreed on." The Bible provides a detailed outline of the terms of marriage; therefore, it stands to reason that the Word of God should be the  final authority in how we conduct our lives and relationships. All arguments must end with the Word.

Strong individuals make strong families.

The same is true where raising children is concerned. In fact, throughout God's Word we see that children play a major role in our relationships. They are gifts from heaven and must be taught how to fulfill His purpose for their lives.

That is why you must be able to provide spiritual training without breaking a child's spirit—destroying his or her dreams and aspirations for the future. There's nothing worse than a child whose hopes have been destroyed.

Together with your children and God's guidance, you can fulfill your purpose of dominating in the earth. Nothing should stop us from living like kings and queens in the earth. Adam and Eve once knew what it meant to live the good life (Genesis 2-3). Before sin entered the picture, they had everything they could have ever wanted, including dominion over all creation. Even their relationships with each other and God were perfect.

Unfortunately, Adam's disobedience cost them everything they had, and humanity has suffered ever since. Think of the most beautiful place on earth and imagine how it must have been before sin entered the world. It's almost hard to believe that there was such a perfect place as the Garden of Eden. But that's exactly what God intended for *all* families, including yours, to enjoy—Paradise on earth.

As the result of sin, many families experience less than God's best in their lives. Instead of living like kings and queens, they either content themselves with substandard living or struggle all of their lives for a little piece of heaven. God's original plan for the family has been perverted. Poverty, debt, divorce and separation were never part of His plan for the family, and neither was homosexuality, drug addiction, anorexia or physical abuse. Difficulties such as these were born of Adam's disobedience all those centuries ago.

Press Toward the Goal

Remember, the best thing you can do for your family is the best that you can do.

The family structure of today is very different from what it was 50, 10, or even five years ago. There are tough issues that must be dealt with head-on in order to begin the journey to success. Divorce, adultery, single-parenting, remarriage and infertility are just a few of the issues that touch us on a daily basis, whether we watch them on television, read them in the paper or experience them in our own lives.

The goal of this book is to challenge you to do *whatever it takes* to fulfill God's original plan for your life and family. The greatest challenge facing you is the challenge to *change*. Change is never easy. You may be tempted to try to change your spouse, children and other family members first, but it won't make your circumstances or relationships any better. Success comes when *you* change *you*. Your decision to change will encourage others to do the same. It's contagious!

But it won't happen overnight. Permanent change takes time. You must be willing and determined to live God's way. We all have certain roles and responsibilities within our family structure. It's only by owning up to those responsibilities that we can begin enjoying God's best in our homes. As you read this book, examine your life and ask yourself some tough questions: *Is my lifestyle lining up with God's ideal image? Am I problem-driven or solution-oriented? How can I improve myself? In what ways should I change my behavior toward my loved ones?* Remember, the best thing you can do for your family is the *best* that you can do.

No one is perfect; however, the God you serve *is*. Sometimes you may miss the mark when aiming for perfection. But that doesn't mean you should give up, cave in or quit. True success comes by recognizing the need for improvement, obtaining the wisdom and strength to begin the process, and then diligently applying what you learn. The journey to a successful family is hard work, but the rewards last for generations!

Dr. Creflo A. Dollar

Taffi L. Dollar

HOW TO USE THIS BOOK

A lthough this reference guide contains over 20 years of teaching and experience, don't feel pressured to read it in one sitting or from cover to cover. It is a manual that is designed to provide you with information that is relevant to your need or situation.

For example, let's say you're looking for information on strengthening your marriage. Perhaps you and your spouse are having issues with in-laws or money matters. You would turn to *Part II: Marriage Enhancement*, which contains chapters on everything a married couple may encounter. The information in each section has been grouped together according to the issues a family may face at various points in time. It begins with topics of interest to single people and ends with a section on abuse and other areas of concern. Remember, you do not have to read every chapter; only what applies to you.

The symbols at the end of every chapter will assist you in retaining and applying the information you read. Keep in mind the following:

Symbol	Meaning	Function
	The Master Key	The main idea of the chapter
	Now Use It!	A practical application (homework)
	Meditation Scripture	Reinforces the principles outlined in the chapter

In addition, a comprehensive list of resources has been included with this manual, located in the rear. It has been divided into six sections to correspond with the sections of the book. A word of caution: not every resource is biblically-based. However, these materials contain a wealth of information that may be useful and can be applied to your life. Be sure to carefully screen all information against the Word of God.

Your purpose should be to increase your knowledge base and apply it to your family life. The Bible says, "...*The measure [of thought and study] you give [to the truth you hear] will be the measure [of virtue and knowledge] that comes back to you—and more [besides] will be given to you who hear*" (Mark 4:24, *The Amplified Bible*).

Take what you learn and live it out. Remember, *information* plus *application* equals *manifestation*!

Before the *Ring*

1

SINGLE, UNIQUE AND WHOLE
Learning to Love the Single Life

I t seems as if everyone wants to rush it. In fact, most people think they aren't complete without it or that all of their problems will be solved when they find it. What am I talking about? Marriage.

For some reason, we've had it in our thinking that we will not be complete until we find "The One," the perfect partner with whom we can share our inner-most thoughts, dreams, fears and desires. We often feel that there are gaps in our lives or obstacles in our way that only a marriage relationship can solve.

Why do we think this way? More than likely it's because we have unknow-ingly accepted society's interpretation of what it means to be single and have not taken the time to embrace what God says about it. Everywhere you look there are television shows, movies, magazines, books and music that portray singleness as a disease or a "pit stop" on the way to a permanent relationship. The impli-cation is that if you're not *with* someone, you're incomplete, picky, frigid, or emo-tionally unstable. In addition, the continual reminders from family and friends of biological time clocks and a future as a spinster or an old bachelor only serve to place more pressure on an already stressful situation.

Unfortunately, many people get married in the hopes of easing their feelings of loneliness, frustration or worry. They usually end up separated or divorced because they did not comprehend a key principle: a poor understanding of true singleness always leads to problems in a marriage.

It's a Good Thing

Singleness, from a more positive perspective, is where everything begins. According to God, it's okay to be *single*, but not good to be *alone* (Genesis 2:18). You may be asking, "What's the difference?" Let's break these words down and discover their original meanings.

To be *single* means, "to be separate, unique and whole." Think about that. What makes you, you? Is it the way you laugh, dress or look? What about the things you say and the way in which you process information? Would you like to lose the qualities that separate you from everyone else and make you unique? Of course not!

You Are Special!

Take a moment to think about the characteristics and qualities that make you a unique person. Write them down (at least 10) on a sheet of paper and place your list in an easily accessible location where you can see it every day. On those days when you need an emotional boost, look at the qualities you have listed, and remember that you are a one-of-a-kind creation, precious in God's sight!

No one in the world will ever be just like you. In fact, even identical twins differ from one another in behavior, thought patterns, the processing of information and emotional reactions. No matter how alike two people may seem, their experiences and genetic makeup play key roles in their development.

Think of it this way. All Americans have been assigned a social security number. Each person has a *different* number. Everything is tailored to respond to that number: bank accounts, credit reports, military records and medical files, to name a few. By your number, you can be tracked down and pulled out of a crowd of millions.

The word single means, "to be separate, unique and whole."

The same is true on a spiritual level. When you stand before God, you stand as a separate and distinct individual, regardless of the fact that you may be an identical twin or married. None of these relational ties—especially marriage—change your singleness. You should therefore never have a problem with being single. In fact, it's the basis for who you are as a person!

Singleness is not a bad, negative or unhealthy state of being. And neither is it anything to be ashamed of; rather, it is something to be pursued because it highlights your individuality and uniqueness! Take, for example, your key ring. There are probably several different keys on it. Every key on that ring is unique, separate and whole in its purpose. Each one can open something another one can't. The keys did not lose their ability when they were placed on a ring with others that functioned the same way. This is how you should see yourself—a valuable part of a bigger picture.

When a person lays aside their individuality just because they are married, problems tend to arise very quickly. Why? He or she entered that marriage with the wrong mindset. They expected their spouse to make them complete or solve their problems of insecurity, inadequacy or inferiority. That's a lot of pressure to put on another person!

No one should marry until he or she is comfortable in his or her individuality. In fact, you shouldn't even think about marriage until you truly understand what it means to be separate, unique and whole. Any marriage counselor will tell you that the majority of marital problems stem from husbands or wives who have yet to see themselves as unique individuals, worthy of respect. Unfortunately, their disrespect and dislike for themselves is projected onto others, making positive, long-lasting relationships almost an impossibility.

Make a Change!

Almost everyone has something they don't like about themselves, whether it's a physical, emotional, mental or spiritual trait. But that doesn't mean you're condemned to living with those negative qualities forever. Instead of always thinking or talking about what you don't like about yourself, try this exercise. Make a list of your top five negative qualities. Create an action plan and timeline for turning those liabilities into assets. Be sure to give yourself enough time in which to do this, and perhaps recruit a partner to help you stay on track. It won't be long before you'll begin to see positive changes in your life!

The secret to enjoying life as a single person is to love yourself for who you are—the good, the bad and the ugly. Even your negative qualities set you apart from those around you. Remember, God is all for being unique! If you don't believe it, think about this. Of all the billions of people alive on the planet, no two have the same fingerprint. You have to learn to be happy with how God made you and who you are. In a comical way, that's why an ugly man can get a good-looking wife! When he presented himself to that woman, his confidence was so overwhelming in who he was as a person, she became convinced he was handsome! As actor Jack Pallance once said, "Confidence is sexy!"

Single Is Not Spelled A-L-O-N-E

The word *alone* means "isolated" or "secluded." A single person, although content in who they are, does not want to feel secluded or isolated. To get rid of those feelings, he or she may choose to surround themselves with others and establish a relationship with them. That doesn't mean they need someone else to fill a void in their lives; they simply enjoy the company of others. However, most people who feel insecure or inferior tend to swing from one extreme to the other. They either enjoy isolation and seclusion or they constantly surround themselves with people to avoid being alone with themselves. Neither extreme is healthy. A truly single person is happy with who they are and looks for companionship as a means of settling *temporary* feelings of being lonely.

I used to think that Adam was lonely in the Garden of Eden. All the animals in the Garden had another animal to be with; a bird had a bird and an elephant had another elephant, but Adam had no one. I forgot that God was Adam's companion and that they communed on a daily basis. Contrary to what I thought, Adam was so content in his singleness, he didn't even realize anything was missing in his life! Because he had been made in God's image, he didn't lack anything. God, however, didn't want Adam to be without *human* companionship, so He created Eve. That didn't mean Adam stopped communing with God once Eve was around. Rather, they spent time with Him together.

Adam didn't *need* a wife. God never said that Adam was an incomplete being, just someone who might benefit from the companionship of another single person. He didn't create a wife to complete him, but to complement him!

The same promise of intimacy that Adam knew with God is still true for us today. God tells us that we are promised to Him forever, and He will be a partner with us in righteousness, judgment, lovingkindness and mercy (Hosea 2:19). In other words, we are spoken for! If you don't have a physical companion, you already have the best Mate around! Your wholeness and uniqueness should be founded on the truth that God has *already chosen you* as His.

Just as in your relationships with others, intimacy with God is built over time. You can't get to know someone without spending time with that person. Intimacy comes through open and honest communication. The more you communicate and spend time with God and His Word, the Bible, the deeper your relationship becomes. He will commence to reveal Himself (His characteristics) to you and through you to others. He will dwell in you, walk with you daily and lead you into all truth. By enjoying God as your Companion, you position yourself to experience and enjoy true singleness.

Too many people spend their time trying to find their life partner rather than enjoying their singleness. Instead of spending so much energy on fruitless searches, concentrate on putting first things first. With God as your companion, and friends to ease the discomfort of loneliness, you can focus on enjoying your singleness and allow the gift of a spouse to be presented to you. Marriage is simply an added fringe benefit! Remember, the relationship you have with your heavenly Father is what lays the foundation for a successful marriage.

Meant As a Complement

Your life partner is meant to be just that: your partner. This is not someone who is to be controlled, manipulated or put on a pedestal. His or her function in the relationship is to *complement* you, not to complete you. God calls this being a *help meet*. This means "help that's suitable and fit," and "like him or her." In Genesis 2:18, God basically said, "I'm going to make Adam a helper who will be compatible, suitable and like him. I'm going to make another human being who will complement him and who will be complemented by him." In other words, He said, "I'm going to make another unique, whole and separate person and bring the two together for mutual companionship on the same level."

It doesn't do you any good to become involved with someone who is not content in their singleness. Why? You will have a lopsided relationship. One partner will always have to "carry" the other because he or she will not be able to contribute equally to the relationship for reasons of insecurity, inferiority, self-doubt or feelings of worthlessness. Often people battling with their singleness become the "clinging vines" in the relationship, unable to deal with the daily give-and-take in a healthy manner.

If you are having difficulty being content in your singleness, the best solution is to work on yourself and your relationship with God, then establish healthy friendships with others. Whatever you do, don't marry to avoid being or feeling alone. Many people are married but continue to battle loneliness. Why? They thought marriage was what they needed to feel complete and whole. Unfortunately, marriage is not the cure for loneliness.

A Gift to You

Contrary to popular opinion, it took a little time for Adam and Eve to get together once she was created. How do I know this? Notice a very interesting phrase in Genesis 2:22: "*And the rib, which the Lord God had taken from man, made he a woman, and brought her unto the man.*"

Eve was *presented* to Adam; God had to bring her, or introduce her, to him.

Adam liked what he saw and accepted her as a companion and friend. Eve was first a companion, then later a wife. The best relationships stem from solid friendships. If you feel alone, be a friend or companion to a few of the five billion people on the planet today. You don't need to marry any of them to solve your loneliness problem. Be a friend first—your wife or husband may come from that relationship!

I'm sure you've heard the phrase, "God chose that person just for me." That's absolutely false! God will not and cannot make that choice for you because it would violate your freedom of choice. If He only made one person for you, then He would be taking away your free will and taking on the responsibility of that relationship. And He's *not* going to do that!

The relationship you develop with another person—how you establish and maintain it—is *your* responsibility. This means you are responsible for both the successes and failures that may come of it. So when you choose, don't be overly spiritual or spooky. The common everyday events of life aren't super spiritual. You've got to use common sense and mix it with spiritual maturity if or when you choose a mate.

Forget the idea that there is only one person in the whole world for you. There are many "right" people, and God will make many presentations to you. It is His plan to give *you* the right to choose. He has purposely limited Himself to only expressing His wishes and His will for you. For example, it's not His will for anyone to live or die without knowing Jesus Christ, but He has left the choice up to every individual. If He were going to force you to do something, then everyone would get to go to heaven!

You can pray for a mate all you want, but when God makes the presentation, you must make the choice.

Some of you may be sitting back saying, "Well, this person meets all my qualifications, but I haven't heard from God yet." You'd better stop looking for a burning bush or listening for a voice from the sky because *the presentation is all* that He is going to do!

Adam *chose* to take Eve as his wife, just as you must choose someone. If he hadn't chosen her, I have no doubt that God would have made another. God illustrated our power to choose by simply *presenting* Eve to her future mate. That's a vital truth that you can't afford to miss.

Hook, Line and Sinker

I'll never forget the day that God presented Taffi to me. I was sitting in Bible study and I heard the Lord say, "Look up." There she was! God asked me, "Do you like what you see?" I said, "Yes!" I had enjoyed the presentation, but the rest was my responsibility.

Of course, I was a little slow in making the first move, so she had to help me. One day after I finished teaching, Taffi walked up to me and said, "I just wanted to let you know that I'm interested in you, so do whatever you want with that." Then she turned and walked out of the room!

I thought she would be all over me after that announcement. But then she acted like I didn't even exist. She would walk right past me without saying a word. She had given me the bait, and if I was too stupid to get it, then she was obviously through with it!

Taffi has always been a wonderful soul-winner, so true to her nature she started bringing other guys to my Bible study group. And they weren't average guys— they were good-looking gentlemen!

Can't you just picture me? I could hardly teach wondering what was up with all of that. It was becoming very clear that I had to hurry up and make a move. So after another Bible study, I caught up with her.

I said, "Don't bring anyone else to Bible study."

She said, "Doesn't the Bible tell us to do that?"

"Yes, the Bible says that," I shot back, "so let someone else bring them. You need to come to Bible study with me and let them get here in whatever way they can!"

I was determined that the Lord would help them, but Taffi was coming with me!

After that, we dated for three years. She was my friend and companion at first. We had a great time together playing tennis, going to the movies and just talking. Then one day my eyes were opened, and I realized how much I loved her. She was my choice for a wife.

Men, when God presents someone to you, act on it! A woman likes uniqueness, honesty, integrity and straightforwardness. Don't sit back trying to think of a line. Just be yourself and say something simple like, "Hello, how are you? My name is so and so. Do you think we could go out with some friends and have dinner sometime, or could I call you to talk?"

If she says no, then that's the risk you have to take. You have to know how to walk away from that rejection and remain whole. Don't feel bad about yourself or get upset and start talking about her.

You must learn to pursue what you are interested in. Sometimes a woman says no just to see if you are really interested. At times it impresses her if you try again another way. And ladies, don't be afraid to let a guy see that you are interested in him. Many guys are paralyzed by fear and insecurity. No one likes to be rejected. By giving him a smile or saying hello, you open the door for him to make his move.

It's really wise to make your first date with a group of friends. You can see a lot by doing that. If you are alone with the person, he or she will act differently than when friends are around. She might be meek and quiet when you are by yourselves but loud and rowdy with a group of friends. He might be the same way. You'll find out many things if you first "date" the person with a group of friends. If you don't like what you see, you can walk away, and no one has hurt feelings.

In the Right Light

It's important to understand that prerequisites come with God's presentations. The Bible clearly states that Christians are not to be *"unequally yoked together with unbelievers"* (2 Corinthians 6:14-18). That automatically disqualifies a lot of people. That doesn't mean that you don't have anything to do with an unsaved person; rather, it means that you stay out of the dating arena where they are concerned. You'll save yourself a lot of future heartache that way.

Remember that God has your best interests at heart. He is not going to present someone to you at a club. Nor is He going to present someone who is an unbeliever. If the person you are looking at is not a born-again Christian, then the person doesn't qualify as a suitable marriage candidate. I don't care how good they look; if you go against the principles of God and marry them, they won't look good for long. You may even end up hating the sound of their voice! Why? You cannot marry someone with the hope that they will change. Nine times out of ten, it doesn't happen, and you end up stuck in a rocky relationship.

But this principle doesn't just apply to dating the unsaved. If you've been born again for five years and the person you've chosen just became a Christian, you are still unequally yoked. There are a lot of things about God and walking in His Word that he or she doesn't know yet. You are still going to have to allow time for their relationship with God to grow and develop. That person must have time to come to the level you're at or there will be problems.

*   *   *   *   *

If you desire to be married only once, you should want to do it the right way. Your choice is going to affect the rest of your life, and perhaps the lives of your children. The way to begin is by enjoying your individuality and allowing that uniqueness to complement those with whom you establish close relationships. When you establish in your mind that being single is okay, you will avoid future heartache and instead pave the way for a successful life and marriage!

Seek to live your life as a unique, whole and separate individual by making your relationship with God and His Word your first priority.

Take a sheet of paper and write down the characteristics you desire in a mate. You may wish to divide your list into specific categories, such as "Spiritual," "Physical," "Emotional, "Intellectual," or "Optional," "Must-Haves," and so on. Once you have completed your list, look up scriptures concerning the characteristics you have written down and confess them aloud daily. In addition, use your list as a guide for selecting a helpmate after a presentation has been made. Don't settle for less than your heart's desire. God's wants you to be happy!

Matthew 6:33

"But seek ye first the kingdom of God, and his righteousness; and all these things shall be added unto you."

2

OFF THE MARKET
Saying Good-bye to the Dating Game

What does God think about dating? Does it matter to Him who we date or how often we go out with someone? Is dating even in the Bible?

I believe dating was designed as the *getting to know you* period in a couple's relationship before marriage. It is the time for learning the likes and dislikes of one another, as well as a chance to witness each other's behavior in a number of social settings.

Although "dating" isn't specifically mentioned in the Bible, there are definite guidelines throughout Proverbs and the New Testament that, if followed, will lead us into a healthy relationship and enable us to choose a life partner wisely.

Unfortunately, society depicts the dating period as the time to become romantically or sexually attached. Many people believe in the idea of "love at first sight" and blind themselves to the shortcomings of the person with whom they have gotten involved. Serious character flaws and other important issues, such as spiritual, emotional and intellectual compatibility, drug or alcohol addictions, anger management problems or a history of physical abuse are often overlooked.

Today's society doesn't make it easy to take off these "rose-colored glasses." In fact, false impressions of love are everywhere. You can hear it in the smooth ballads that speak of physical love as being the only way to express emotion or as a way to get a person through the night. Television shows and movies often use humor to desensitize us to the overt sexuality present in the dialogue. Even a 30-second commercial can be so full of innuendoes that we often focus more on what is implied than on what is actually being sold.

When you don't understand the purpose for something, abuse is inevitable. The same principle applies where dating is concerned. When you don't realize it's purpose—getting to know another person well—more than likely you'll use dating as a means to an end, either for physical gratification or for emotional code-pendency. There's no point in pushing the process or overlooking important red flags simply because you're lonely, under pressure from relatives or reaching a certain age. Dating is simply your opportunity to gather information on a person's character.

What a Character!

While "character" may not *sound* romantic, it is the foundation for a roman-tic and fulfilling relationship. Why? Character is one of the most important ele-ments to consider when you date an individual.

It is very unwise, and even dangerous, to rush into an emotional and physi-cal relationship without first getting to know an individual. You *must* know the character of a person before you *ever* become romantically involved. The charac-ter of the person you are involved with could mean the difference between expe-riencing peace or strife, prosperity or poverty, and safety or destruction in your life together.

Christians should only date someone they believe is a suitable candidate for marriage.

What attracted me most to my husband was his character. I met Creflo while we were attending West Georgia College. In the mid-dle of all the drinking, smoking, partying and good times that go on at a college campus, he was more concerned about the things of God and the weekly campus Bible study he was teaching. He was a young man who dared to be different while everyone else was doing his or her own thing. Of course I was attracted to how handsome he was, but watching him teach the Word of God with such pas-sion said a lot about who he was as a man. His character stood out above every-thing else.

Character is "the willingness to do right when you have the opportunity to do wrong." Creflo could have been a hypocrite by doing what everyone else was doing and still trying to preach the Word, but he didn't. Instead, he chose to be the exception. This enabled me to see firsthand how he would handle adversity and protect what was precious to him. I listened to how carefully he taught the Bible studies, and by his actions outside of the group, I knew that integrity was a priority in his life. Seeing these principles in Creflo helped me to decide that he was someone I wanted to know on a more personal level.

So one day after a Bible study session, I walked up to him and basically said, "Hello. My name is Taffi Bolton, and I would like to get to know you better."

Then I left without saying anything else to him. I decided that *he* would have to make the next move—it was enough that I let him know I was interested! It took a little while, but Creflo finally asked me out—*after* he saw me with the good-looking guys I had been taking to the Bible studies! We went out and had a great time, but only because the pressure to impress was not there. We were both content in our singleness and strong in character, and accepted each other as we were, without any tricks, boasts or false impressions. A lot of wasted time and disappointment could be avoided if couples would only take the time to first see what a person looks like on the inside!

Save It for Later

Worldly dating can best be described as putting the cart before the horse. It cares nothing about character. Instead, it settles for superficial traits (such as outward physical beauty) and blinds itself to obvious inward flaws. In other words, worldly dating relationships focus on appearances and fleshly pleasures. It lightly skims or entirely skips the friendship stage and immediately jumps into romance and intimacy. This is where "love at first sight," or feelings of infatuation come in. However, it's important to remember that if you put the cart before the horse, you won't go anywhere!

I have seen the classified ads in the newspaper, heard radio advertisements for matchmaking services and watched some of the dating game shows on television, and it amazes me how society views dating. For many people, it is merely an opportunity to get intimate with someone. Couples who barely know each other's name end up making out or sleeping together on the first date! Or worse, they volunteer to be "marooned" on an island with other couples to see which one will be able to remain faithful to their partners and outlast sexual temptation!

When you put the cart before the horse, you'll discover that you don't go anywhere.

The world says if you like me, then you will sleep with me. Sex is often viewed as the only real way to show someone how much you care about them, despite the fact that you've just met. Becoming intimate with someone you hardly know is foolishness. This kind of dating leads to intimacy but not necessarily to commitment. It is dangerous to open yourself up emotionally and physically without first having defined and established a level of commitment. The Lifetime cable channel is filled with far too many real-life *Fatal Attraction* stories that prove just how dangerous this is.

A Stick in a Hole

When Creflo was a young man in his teens, his father, Creflo Sr., took him outside for a practical lesson about sex. He said, "Cref, I want you to understand something about sleeping around." While he was speaking, he dug a line of several small holes in the ground with his fingers. Then he picked up a stick that was lying nearby and placed the end of it in the first hole. "Something happens when you have sex with multiple women," he stated. "As a man, you're basically taking your stick and putting it in one hole after another."

While Creflo Sr. was talking, he took the stick he was holding and began moving it from one hole to the next. Creflo noticed that as his father removed the stick from each hole, bits of debris and dirt clung to the end—not enough to discolor, damage or break the stick, but enough to notice the change. Creflo Sr., noticing that his son's eyes were riveted to the end of the stick, said, "Every time you sleep with someone, you leave a part of yourself behind and take a part of that person with you. Basically, son, you sleep with everyone they've ever slept with, and vice-versa." As they walked back inside the house, Creflo Sr. made one last statement. "Son, keep your stick out of other people's holes, and you'll be fine."

When people fornicate (have sex before marriage), they violate a spiritual law. Sex is only sanctioned within the marriage relationship because through it, a husband and wife join together physically to become one. It is an act, or law, established by God to make the relationship stronger.

God can't change a spiritual law just because you or anyone else decided not to abide by it. When you violate the purity of the sexual act by fornicating, physical changes occur because an unlawful exchange has taken place. This is demonstrated in Genesis 34. A young man named Shechem "fell in love" with one of Jacob's daughters. Rather than courting and marrying her, he raped her. Verse 3 tells us, "*And his soul clave unto Dinah....*" In other words, Dinah got up with something she didn't have before: a part of his soul (his mind, will and emotions) now clung to hers. An exchange had taken place; Shechem and Dinah now carried a piece of each other with them. I call this a "soul tie." As a result of the rape and its emotional consequences and exchange, her personality changed.

Fornication paves the way for emotional turmoil and possible heartache. You can easily lay down one way and get up another. Whereas you might have been in perfect peace before, you may now experience feelings of regret, anger, depression, suicidal thoughts or be tormented by fear and insecurity. In addition, you'll find that your focus has shifted from wanting to establish a platonic relationship with a man or woman to a desire for physical intimacy with others. You may begin to wonder why this is happening because you've never battled these things before.

These things happen because you have exchanged a piece of yourself—your peace of mind, self-confidence or emotional security—with someone who may be deficient in those areas. An "unclean spirit" has transferred from that person to you, and now it's ready to wreak havoc in your life. That's why people often change dramatically when they continue to indulge in fornication. It's not hard to figure out why God is against it.

Relationships based primarily on "great sex" very seldom last because there is no foundation for it. It's like building a house on sand rather than on stone. The house built on sand will collapse during a storm. Likewise, a relationship built solely on physical attraction will collapse under pressure.

A person's character is the most important element to consider when dating him or her.

Another consideration is the fact that you not only sleep with that individual, but everyone they have slept with as well. Regardless of how many condoms, cervical caps, diaphrams and IUDs you use, you still place yourself at a high risk for contracting a sexually transmitted disease, which can potentially damage your reproductive organs or result in contracting the HIV virus. And this is *in addition* to the emotional relationship rollercoaster you may find yourself on!

There are certain steps everyone must take to achieve happiness in a relationship. Physical pleasure before marriage only serves to cloud your judgement and hinder you from making wise choices. It is better to establish your relationship on friendship in order to avoid the problem of romantic soul ties and messy break-ups. Developing a relationship on sexual attraction only leads to disappointment and failure. You'd do better to try dating God's way!

A Better Way

As a single Christian, you can avoid the most common dating pitfalls by making the Word of God the final authority in every area of your life. This means aligning thoughts and actions with what it says. There are no specific scriptures on dating. Nowhere in the Bible does it say, "Thou shalt not hold hands with Jim-Bob," or "Thou shalt enjoy Sarah-Anne's company every Saturday afternoon." It does, however, provide practical guidelines on how unmarried believers should conduct themselves.

Physical attraction is not a bad thing. In most cases, unless you know something about the person already, it's all you have to go on. It will probably be the first thing that gets your attention. However, you can't allow a physical attraction to develop into a sinful state, and you can *never* allow it to be the foundation of the relationship. I can say from experience that you can be very attracted to someone and still remain sexually pure. But in order to do that, you must set boundaries and *keep them* at all costs!

Creflo and I dated for three years and never became sexually involved. We were determined to walk in the Spirit and not fulfill the lusts of the flesh. Yes, we were very attracted to each other. But we based our relationship on the Word of God and did not allow ourselves to get caught in compromising situations. We set boundaries, and in doing so, we respected and honored one another's body.

For example, there were ways we knew we could kiss, and ways we *couldn't*! We knew our limitations, and we worked hard to honor them because we respected and cherished one another. In doing so, it made our honeymoon even sweeter. It established a trust between us that nothing can shake.

Let me give you a vital point that will save you a lot of heartache. Because dating is the process by which a couple builds a relationship, *Christians should only date someone they believe is a suitable candidate for marriage.* This will avoid playing the dating game by beginning and ending relationships every two or three months. If you try to date someone new with the intention of having fun now and breaking it off later, this practice only prepares you for divorce. You get so used to starting over with someone new that it becomes a part of your mentality, and at the first sign of trouble in your marriage you will want to head for divorce court.

Another point to consider is that dating takes up a lot of your time—it represents an investment of time and energy. Unless you are considering that person as a possible life partner, you could be wasting valuable time that would be better spent cultivating the things of God. Being single is a gift. It is your time to develop yourself as an individual and discover your purpose in Christ. Married couples are often distracted because they have to focus their attention on overcoming daily challenges and meeting the demands of family members. Single people, however, have an opportunity to maximize their relationship with the Father and accomplish all the things they dream of.

As a result of spending time with God, you will receive direction and guidance. You will be able to recognize His voice so that you can be a blessing to the person who comes into your life. You won't bring to the relationship a lot of emotional baggage, debt, strife, unforgiveness or other negative influences. As a result, once God makes a presentation to you and you've made the choice for a mate, you will have a beautiful, healthy and whole relationship. Therefore, don't waste valuable time on something temporary or settle for second best when you're looking for a life-long commitment.

Dating Guidelines

The following guidelines are for those of you who are interested in a relationship that will lead to marriage. They are not for someone who is only interested in fun and games.

I highly recommend that before you consider dating someone, ask yourself one question: "Could I spend the rest of my life with this person?" If the answer is no, then don't become involved with that person. That doesn't mean that you should ignore him or her; only that you should have a platonic friendship.

If you answered the question with a resounding "Yes!," then follow these helpful tips and watch how God will bless you and your relationship!

1. Establish and maintain a friendship.

A healthy "romantic" relationship can only be built on the firm foundation of friendship. This allows you to communicate and enjoy one another's company without any pressure. Make it clear from the beginning that you want this time to be spent forming a friendship and that you are not looking for a deeper commitment at present.

2. Avoid any discussion of a deeper commitment or marriage.

Don't talk about your personal finances or future together, because it is much too soon to reveal that kind of information or know if you even have a future! In addition, there should not be any touching or sexual advances made toward one another. Do not place yourself in a compromising situation that may cause you to sin.

3. Don't send the wrong message!

You have a responsibility to the person you are dating. Be honest and mindful about his or her feelings. Do not send mixed messages or try to manipulate them into a relationship neither of you is ready for. Avoid flirting or dropping hints about your romantic feelings. Do not become too familiar too soon by using pet names.

4. Never isolate yourself from your family and friends.

Introduce this person to your family and friends, but make it clear that you are not a couple, only friends. There is a possibility that they may see things that you don't see. Get them involved so you can get their feedback.

5. Do not change your lifestyle.

Maintain your daily routine, including activities you find pleasurable. Look for opportunities where the two of you can do things with your family and friends and watch how everyone interacts with one another.

6. Ladies, allow the man to pursue you.

That is his job, not yours. Proverbs 18:22 says, *"[He who] findeth a wife..."* not, *"[She who] findeth a [husband]...."*

7. Set boundaries!

Avoid spending too much time alone, especially at night. Plan your dates during the day or early evening. Go to breakfast or brunch. You may also want to take in a museum or sporting event. In addition, try visiting an amusement park, attending church services or seeing a stage production.

8. Be selective when watching movies and listening to music.

Don't go to R-rated movies that have a lot of lovemaking scenes. If you have to go to G-rated movies, then do that! Creflo and I would get up and walk out of movies that planted seeds of lust. We didn't allow those things to enter in through our eyes and ears, which kept us from having to deal with those desires.

9. Be careful not to indulge in heavy kissing and petting.

These actions are forms of foreplay that lower your guard and eventually lead to sexual intercourse. Reserve passion and all intimate acts for the marriage relationship. Begin to see your abstinence as a deposit for your honeymoon. In doing so, you build excitement and anticipation.

10. Watch and wait.

Watch the individual closely for character flaws. Determine if they are serious about a future with you or just in the relationship for fun and games. Pray for direction, then wait on God to give you peace and the plan to move forward.

* * * * *

If you follow these basic guidelines and strive to date only those individuals with character and integrity, you'll establish a strong relationship and build a foundation for a marriage that will go the distance!

A healthy, long-lasting relationship must be built on the foundation of friendship.

Read through the Arts and Entertainment section of your local newspaper or surf your city's Web site for places and events you and your friend can enjoy. You may wish to make a list of the top five places to go or things to see and place them in categories, such as "Under $5," "Outdoor Concerts," "Special Occasions" or "Great Restaurants." Be creative! You can include picnics in the park, an afternoon of hiking, a visit to a botanical garden or a matinee showing of a new movie. Don't concern yourself with what you can afford—sometimes the best dates are the cheapest!

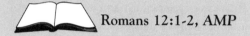 **Romans 12:1-2, AMP**

"I appeal to you therefore, brethren, and beg of you in view of [all] the mercies of God, to make a decisive dedication of your bodies [presenting all your members and faculties] as a living sacrifice, holy (devoted, consecrated) and well pleasing to God, which is your reasonable (rational, intelligent) service and spiritual worship. Do not be conformed to this world (this age), [fashioned after and adapted to its external, superficial customs], but be transformed (changed) by the [entire] renewal of your mind [by its new ideals and its new attitude], so that you may prove [for yourselves] what is the good and acceptable and perfect will of God...."

3

THE GENTLEMAN'S GENTLEMAN
How to Treat a Lady

E very man should understand the importance of being a gentleman. In fact, in addition to acquiring a basic knowledge of etiquette, courtesy and romance, you should know the basic needs of a woman and how to meet those needs. Why? If you miss the core reasons for why you should treat a lady well, then your actions will remain superficial. Not only will a woman see through those shallow actions, she won't have anything to do with you! In my opinion, life is too short to waste time performing empty or meaningless works.

Over the years I've counseled many men, both single and married, and if there's one truth I've shared with them, it's this: "A date doesn't always end in a marriage, but a marriage begins with a date." The foundation of your marriage actually begins with the principles you establish while dating. Once married, the "dating mentality" should never end. That means you should be just as romantic and considerate years later, after she's had your children, gained a few pounds, or begins covering up her gray hair.

Before we discuss the basic needs of a woman, however, there are a few preliminaries you need to know.

First Things First

You shouldn't even *consider* dating a woman unless she is a potential partner for marriage. That immediately disqualifies any woman who you wouldn't want to be the mother of your children, the keeper of your home, the person you want to grow old with and your best friend when life throws its punches.

This means that the woman who bares her bosom with a low-cut sweater or her rear end in a skirt that barely grazes her pantyline is disqualified. The woman who practices another faith and doesn't know Jesus the way you do is disqualified. The loud and rowdy women who run in packs and hang out at the clubs are also disqualified.

While it's true that those women can change, you must realize that you're *not* their Savior! I'm not being judgmental; I just remember how I was before I became born again! Here are two key principles to remember. First, whatever a woman is willing to show, she's willing to share. Second, a man will go as far as a woman will let him. You don't believe me? Think back to the days before you became born again. What did you think about 99% of the time? More than likely it was sex. A man knows an easy woman when he sees her; they're not difficult to spot. The thing is, that kind of woman will bring you pain and constant heartache, which will eventually destroy you. So hear me loud and clear—she is T-R-O-U-B-L-E!

A date doesn't always end in a marriage, but a marriage begins with a date.

As a single man—unique, whole and separate—you shouldn't look for a woman just for physical gratification or so you can fix her problems to feel masculine. You must get rid of the "knight in shining armor" mentality. If you want to feel manly, then be God's man. Have enough character to remain self-controlled while you sort through the cubic zirconias until you find your diamond.

With that said, I'm going to list the five basic needs of a woman. If you don't feel as if you are ready to meet these needs, then don't date. It's that simple. If you are married, begin practicing all five in small ways until they become second nature.

1. Affection.

Affection is the number one thing a woman needs. Deep inside the female soul is a vacuum driven by a need for love in a relationship. Women are relational creatures. Their highest goal in life is to have a relationship where they feel they are "one" with someone. How do I know that? Because God created the woman from the rib of a man; therefore, her image and values are based on achieving oneness. If a woman knows she is loved and receives affection from her man, she will work with him to overcome life's challenges.

The word *affection* means, "the state of having one's feelings and mind influenced or moved by kindness, tenderness and sensitivity." It also means "showing warmth, love and concern." Ephesians 5:25 states, *"Husbands, love your wives, even as Christ also loved the church, and gave himself for it."* This principle applies to you, even if you are single. How? Single people—especially men—should only date with the intention of getting married. Therefore, if you want to capture a lady, you need to learn early on how to show her affection!

According to this scripture, you ought to love your wife in the same way that Christ loves the Church. That means developing a servant mentality and putting her ahead of your own needs and desires. For example, if there are three candy bars in the refrigerator, don't take them all! Instead, take one and leave two for her. If there are two left, take one and leave the other. If there is one left, leave it alone and find something else to munch on!

In addition, you ought to be ready to forgive and forget. There is no record keeping of wrongs done to you in a marriage. No matter what your mood is or how badly you have messed up, God is still kind, tender and sensitive toward you. He forgives and forgets the minute you repent of your sins. That's exactly the way you should be.

Men, God told you to love your woman the same way He loves you. There's no excuse. Of course, showing affection may not be an easy thing for you to do. Like anything else in life, it takes practice to become proficient in something. By faith you may have to confess, "I'm an affectionate man," but faith is where it starts! God wants your attitude toward your partner to be influenced by kindness and moved by tenderness and sensitivity. Regardless of how trivial her concerns might seem to you, she needs you to respond with warmth, love and concern.

If you're married, you might be thinking, "It's going to take more than affection to change my wife! *Nothing* is going to move that woman!" That's where you've missed it. Affection was *designed* to move her because it fulfills her need for it. When a woman is moved, situations change for the better. If you've been waiting on her to change before you become more affectionate, forget it. *You* are designed to be the initiator. In other words, you are supposed to move *her!* Do your part and sow the seeds of love and affection. You can't wait on her to change. Be a godly man and make the first move, then keep on doing it. Allow the Holy Spirit to direct you in the area of affection. He won't let you down.

The second part of verse 25 says, *"...and gave himself for it."* There's something that rings true with all men. When they have a hobby or a sport they like, they go *all out* for it! If a man likes to restore old cars, he'll spend months searching for one little item that will set it apart from the rest. In fact, he'll even spend all of his extra cash and work into the wee hours of the morning just to tinker with that old car. It thrills him and gives him a sense of accomplishment and satisfaction.

If a man likes a particular sport, he'll give up sleep and food just to buy tickets or make a trip to see the game. Think about all those men who paint their faces and bodies and then wear silly pom-poms on their heads! It looks totally ridiculous, but they go to extremes just show how much they love and support their team!

God wants you to be the same way about your woman. Yes, you read that right. He wants you to go all out for *her*. Remember, her number one need is affection. She wants to feel close to you. That's something you need to think about if you're dating. As a married man, if you romance your wife all day, your life will be heaven on earth. Trust me!

How Do I Love Thee? Let Me Show the Ways!

You may be the type of guy who is clueless when it comes to romance and affection. You think that just because you told your woman once that you love her, that's enough! Women need to be reminded day in and day out of how you feel about them.

Here are some sure-fire ways to keep the flames of love from burning out in your relationship:

- Call her just to say, "I love you"
- Send her a card or flowers for no reason at all
- Write a love message on the steamed bathroom mirror
- Take her to an expensive, romantic restaurant and pull out her chair for her
- Arrange for a babysitter so you can take her away for the weekend
- Make her stop what she is doing so you can hug her
- Hold her hand while walking
- Clean the house or do the dishes so *she* can relax
- Open doors for her
- Help her with her coat
- Snuggle up together on the couch and watch a movie or listen to music
- Compliment her
- Take up one of her hobbies (or at least become knowledgeable about it!)

---

2. Communication.

I can just hear you moaning. I know you've been at work all day. You've been paying the bills, mowing the lawn and making sure both cars are running properly. The last thing you want to do is talk. And oh, how a woman can *talk*. They talk about this and that, what so and so said, how so and so did this, what they saw here and what they did there. But brother, that's the way God made them!

As a man, you've got to learn to meet that need within them. Communication is linked to a woman's need for a close relationship. It's joined to her trust and unlocks the door to honesty and openness—all of which women thrive on.

Men, as much as you may want her to, a woman can't read your mind! You may be well aware of why you're doing something or acting in a certain way, but if you don't *communicate* it to her, she's left in a vulnerable position. Satan loves to take advantage of those situations, and he's not slow in making a move. He'll whisper all kinds of thoughts in her mind about what you're doing and why. After battling with those doubts and insecurities all day, she has questions that need answers. And what do you do? More than likely, you get upset with her!

Instead of getting frustrated, stop for a moment and realize what is going on. Did you communicate with her? Did you tell her what you were doing and why? If you have made a commitment to her, then respect her by taking the time to share your thoughts and feelings with her. Remember that communication is directly linked to a woman's trust. By taking the time to talk with her, she won't be moved or upset by what others say or the thoughts that invade her mind.

Most men like to hear just the minimum—just the facts and none of the details. Women, on the other hand, prefer to hear it all! So take the time to indulge your woman and let her tell you *all* the details, and vice-versa. It fulfills a basic need within her and can only make life better for you both.

Realize that communication has a purpose. Seek to understand and to resolve any issues at hand. Exercise your communication skills by talking to her. If you are dating, spend evenings talking and getting to know each other. By allowing her to be your best friend, life can be very rewarding for you!

3. Honesty and Openness.

A woman loves an honest and open man. Keep in mind that your woman has put her trust in you, meaning she wants a relationship with you. Honesty is irresistible to a woman because it produces trust. If a woman doesn't trust you, she has no confidence in you or the relationship. You *never* want to vio-

You must get rid of the "knight in shining armor" mentality.

late her trust in you.

When you are wrong about something, be honest. Don't be too prideful to say, "I was wrong. I'm sorry. Please forgive me." Sometimes men think that admitting their mistakes makes them look small; on the contrary, that man will be a giant in the eyes of his woman.

Take a moment to examine yourself. If you are having trouble digesting this principle, ask yourself this question: "What is hindering me from being open and honest?" Is it pride? Fear? Insecurity? Whatever the case may be, realize that trust is an essential element in a healthy relationship. Without it, the relationship stagnates and dies. You should be able to open up to your woman if you trust her. Above everyone else on the planet, shouldn't she be the object of your trust and confidence? She's your best friend!

When she comes to you with a problem, be open and discuss all the options with her. If she wants to talk about her feelings, shift gears and be open with her as well. If you aren't used to being open because you feel too vulnerable, explain that to her, then work on it. Take it one step at a time. The more you open up to her and see how she keeps things just between the two of you, the easier it will be to continue your open and honest communication.

4. Financial Support.

Men, *never* make a woman feel that she is your meal ticket. If you do that, the first three things we've already discussed will fly right out the window!

Let your woman know that she is so valuable to you, you would do everything possible to support and take care of her. If you tell her this, make sure you do it. However, never rely solely on the world's system. Trust God to be your Source and use wisdom to assist you in your efforts to provide. All too often, hard work at the office leaves you without much time to spend with the Lord or your loved ones. Be mindful that when your spiritual life gets out of order, things in the natural tend to fall apart as well. But as you do all that is humanly and spiritually possible to financially support your family, then that woman will respect you and go to the ends of the earth on your behalf.

If you are dating, you can show godly character by your personal financial responsibility. If you want to help her financially, fill her car up with gasoline or take it to the car wash and have it detailed. Bring groceries to her house and cook dinner for the two of you. Little things like those show her the kind of provider you will be.

5. Family Commitment.

Women look for men who will be committed. Your woman *must know* that without a shadow of a doubt, you will be there for her and your family or future family. She must have the assurance that you won't run off with another woman after she has given birth to your children and invested herself in the relationship.

Although your job provides income, housing and security for the family, it takes more than that to show commitment. You can begin by showing interest in your children, or if you're dating someone with children, try taking them to their extracurricular activities, an age-appropriate movie or picking them up from school when you can. Most importantly, teach your children the Word of God. Be committed to training them in the ways of the Lord, just as Abraham did (Genesis 18:19).

A woman will see your commitment by the interest you show her and how involved you are with her life. That doesn't mean calling her 20 times a day to see what she's up to. Instead, find out what's important to her and show your support. She will also notice your level of commitment by what you value, the strength of character you display and the principles you live by. That's why you need to date someone for *at least* a year, because in that time all of these things will come to the surface.

When you invest your time, energy, effort and a part of yourself in another person, it shows you are committed to them. Choose to spend time with her on the weekends instead of running off with your buddies. As your commitment becomes obvious to the woman you love, she'll reward you for it in her own way. As a man, you can't go wrong when you do what you're supposed to do!

Final Pointers

Aside from these five basic needs, I want to give you a few more pointers. For example, be the kind of man that a woman wants to be around by *encouraging* her. Make her feel like she's the queen of the earth!

I love hanging around with people who encourage me. Don't think that you always have to say the right thing at the right time. Sometimes we encourage others just by being a good listener. Listening is an art and doing it shows how much you care for the other person.

Cleanliness Is Rewarding

Gentleman, I don't know any lady who likes to be seen in public with a dirty, smelly or ill-mannered man. If you want to make a positive, long-lasting impression on your lady, do yourself a favor: clean up your act! Here are a few pointers to help you achieve this goal:

- Take a shower before going out with your woman and be sure to clean often overlooked spots like underneath your finger nails and in your ears.
- Brush your teeth! Foul breath is not attractive.
- Dress for the occasion. Don't wear flip-flops and shorts for an evening on the town. Show some pride in how you look and avoid looking wrinkled or uncomfortable.
- Clean out your car before picking her up or taking her out. Although you and your friends may use your automobile as a trash receptacle, I can assure you your lady will not appreciate it.
- Ask her out in advance! Spontaneity has its time and place, but women need time to prepare for the date. Let her know ahead of time that you would like to spend time with her, and where you would like to take her. She will appreciate your thoughtfulness!

In addition, don't let go of who you are as a person. Your uniqueness is what attracted your woman to you in the first place! If you align your thoughts, actions and motives with the Word of God, you will always remain interesting to her, because God's wisdom and creativity will flow through you. Hold on to that and keep life *alive* around you!

On that note, stay *exciting*. Don't be an old bore! Don't be afraid to try something you've never done before. If you like to have everything planned out in advance and she is a spur-of-the-moment type (as Taffi and I are), try it her way one day. Surprise her with a spontaneous outing. Don't get nervous about it; it's not going to hurt you. Just relax and be adventurous! I guarantee that she will reciprocate by mapping out your next date—right down to a detailed itinerary!

And men, no matter how old you are or what you've been through, make sure that you remain a *giving* and *generous* individual. I'm not talking about going out and buying her a mink coat and diamonds. Just be thoughtful and kind. Buy her that CD she's been wanting. Take her to a new restaurant. Make a mental note each time she shares with you a preference or desire. Then go out and do or get exactly what she wants when she least expects it! Your circumstances should never dictate your ability to be generous or giving. You can always find ways to give, regardless of your budget.

*   *   *   *   *

God has given men tremendous responsibilities. Not only are we to be the leader and the provider, we are the ones God goes to when He wants an account of what's going on in our families. After Adam and Eve had sinned, God didn't walk through the Garden calling for Eve; instead, He called for Adam (Genesis 3:9).

Although we shoulder a great responsibility, we are also equipped to perform these mighty works and deeds. All of these areas that I've mentioned—affection, communication, honesty and openness, support and commitment—are on the inside of you. All you have to do is cultivate them and bring those abilities to the surface.

Remember, the Word of God is your blueprint for everything in life. When you transform your thinking with that Word, you are able to do anything you set your mind to!

Every man should know the basic needs of a woman and strive to meet those needs on a daily basis.

Begin thinking of ways in which you can cultivate the areas of affection, communication, honesty and openness, support and commitment in your relationship. You may wish to tackle one area before beginning work in another, or just practice all areas at once. Set small goals and work toward accomplishing each one. For example, you may say, "I will share more details about my day with my wife/girlfriend this week." Before long, your goals will have become healthy habits!

Ephesians 5:25

"Husbands, love your wives, even as Christ also loved the church, and gave himself for it."

4

ALWAYS A LADY
A Woman's Guide to Emotional, Spiritual and Physical Maturity

Being a woman in this day and age isn't easy. The voices of feminism, pro-choice, sexual harassment and discrimination, along with the challenges of daily living often make it difficult to live by biblical values and high ethical standards. From talk shows to magazines, topics regarding physical appearance, weight management, sexuality, self-perception and loneliness give us a glimpse into the pressures that women face. This also includes the area of relationships.

While men base their success on what they have achieved, women base their success on the strength of their bond with another individual. In fact, a woman's deepest longing in life is to experience fulfillment through relationships. Why? God created her from the rib of a man—hence the need for intimacy and closeness.

However, there are some snares in seeking to fulfill that need. Often women fall prey to the pursuit of those relationships. For example, if her mind is not renewed, a woman might try to secure a relationship through false impressions, manipulation or sexuality. She will try to find new relationships to erase the pain and rejection from her past. In addition, she is unable to find the balance between transparency and privacy. Because of this inner turmoil, depression, low self-esteem and other emotional issues arise.

It is important for a woman to completely understand herself and her place in a relationship. That *only* comes from a change in thinking by the renewing of the mind through the Word of God. Proverbs 31 is a passage that I read on a regular basis. From it, I've gained insight into how to function efficiently in each role I play daily—a woman, daughter, wife and mother.

The woman in Proverbs 31 could not have done everything she did without first having a personal relationship with God. From it, she was able to trust the wisdom and anointing within her to do whatever needed to be done. As a woman, you *must* spend time with God and cultivate your relationship with Him in order to mature spiritually, trust God more, and fulfill His plan for your life.

It's ridiculous to think you can operate without His efficiency, ability and might!

I encourage you to read and study Proverbs 31 so you can understand how to position yourself as a godly woman. If you are looking to establish a successful relationship, you'll first have to understand these principles about yourself.

1. You have value.

Proverbs 31:10 says, *"Who can find a virtuous woman? for her price is far above rubies."* According to this verse a true, godly woman is such a rare and precious find that she is esteemed above the treasures of the world.

Before you can establish a successful relationship with another person, you must first understand your value. As a woman, you have incredible worth. Not only are you a daughter of the Most High God, but you were created to manage a household, give birth and train children, soothe and encourage your man, listen attentively with both your natural ears and the ears of your heart, and manage your time wisely while many times holding down a full-time job!

Don't allow a relationship to determine your worth.

You have the ability to be a counselor, teacher, friend, servant, manager and accountant. You are able to sense the longings within others and help them realize their dreams. In addition, you are compassionate, giving, strong and a source of joy! You have the anointing within you, making you willing, able, capable, mighty, strong, valiant, efficient, wealthy and worthy of good things. As a woman, you are so valuable to the plan of God that creation couldn't continue to exist without you!

Through these God-given abilities and the words you and I speak, we have the power to make kings and leaders of men. If that power is abused, however, these same men can be made into weak-willed and complacent individuals, unwilling to stand in their God-given place within the family. Think about your words. They can either make or break a man!

Your mood also affects the entire household. We've all heard the saying, "If Mama is happy, everyone is happy!" Your mood will often set the tone for the atmosphere in the house. Whether you know it or not, your children and spouse can immediately sense your happiness or displeasure. When you are happy, even the blackest mood disappears! On the other hand, if you are depressed, then everyone in the house feels blue. This is simply the result of the influential position you hold in your household.

In your relationships, make sure you know your value and hold on to it. Esteem yourself the way God esteems you. Under no circumstances should you allow anyone, including yourself, to make you feel unworthy or less than your best. Never stay in a relationship just to keep from being alone. For example, if you are dating a man who refuses to work, yet sits home all day watching HBO and comes to your house to eat your food, get rid of him! That man doesn't see your value! You don't need to disregard the plan of God for your life just to have a relationship! There isn't a relationship there anyway. It's time for you to wake up!

You must renew your mind to the Word and pattern your life according to God's plan. He didn't create you to be abused or misused. When His Word is inside of you, you will know just how well a man should treat you, and you won't settle for anything less.

Think with me for a moment. In the Book of Genesis, it clearly states how Eve took a piece of fruit from the Tree of the Knowledge of Good and Evil and gave it to Adam to eat. However, Adam had received the Word of the Lord beforehand and knew what God had instructed them: stay away from that tree! If they ate the forbidden fruit, Adam and Eve would have nothing but trouble. So what did Adam do? He let Eve take the first bite to see if God's Word was true! Adam was supposed to be the guardian of the Garden of Eden *and* of the woman. Instead, he used her like a guinea pig!

Enhance Your Femininity

There's nothing wrong with making yourself appear more attractive. Just as an insect is attracted to the delicate, colorful petals of a flower, so too are men attracted to a woman who maintains her physical appearance. This doesn't mean showing your cleavage, baring your midriff or wearing tight, low-cut or skimpy outfits!

A genuine lady knows that the less she shows, the more elegant and feminine she appears. Here are a few Dos and Don'ts to help you draw positive attention to yourself and perhaps garner a few admirers in the process!

- **Do** indulge in good hygiene habits by keeping your hair, teeth, nails and ears clean.
- **Do** wear clothing that enhances your figure, such as a tailored

blazer, an A-line skirt or a conservatively cut V-neck sweater.
- **Do** apply makeup with a light hand in natural or bright light.
- **Do** allow a man to open doors for you, pull out your chair at a restaurant or help you with your coat.
- **Do** ask open-ended questions to find out more about another person.
- **Do** carry enough money in your purse for a taxi or bus ride in case your date goes sour.
- **Don't** put on so much perfume that you smell like a factory.
- **Don't** wear anything that is tight or revealing. Leave room for imagination.
- **Don't** allow your makeup to wear you. Opt for neutral shades and enhance your best feature with color, such as the eyes or mouth.
- **Don't** allow any man to make you feel as if you must "pay him back" for treating you well.
- **Don't** allow anyone to pressure you into physical intimacy, such as hand-holding, kissing, hugging or sex.
- **Don't** yell, shout, scream or speak in a loud voice when carrying on a normal conversation.

If you don't know your value, men will *still* try to use you as a guinea pig, even in today's society! They'll try to get you to have sex before you're married. They'll whisper in your ear, "We're both adults. You *know* I love you." STOP! That man doesn't value you; he's only using you. He's wasting your money, driving your car and using all of *your* gas. He's taking you through one of his experiments, wondering how long he can keep this up before you find out he has serious character flaws or other women on the side. Meanwhile, you're hoping he will marry you, but it's not in his plans. If it were, he would treat you with the courtesy and respect you deserve.

As a woman of value, you've been anointed and appointed, and that appointment doesn't lead to what Creflo likes to call "a joker." You must learn to love yourself and see your value through the Word of God. When you see who you really are, you'll begin to respect yourself and demand the same respect from others. In addition, you'll be able to recognize the man who will protect you from what's contrary to the Word. It's time to stand up for yourself and not let a smooth-talking man use you as a guinea pig! Don't let another "Adam" pull the curse over your eyes!

Hold your head high and save yourself for the sexual covenant between you and the man of God who is coming your way. If we, as women, base our success on relationships, then you should begin to value the unity, love and intimacy that will come to you in marriage. Don't miss out on that wonderful opportunity because of a compliment spoken by a godless man! Instead, seek to renew your mind and live your life as a woman of value.

2. You are a helper.

Genesis 2:18 tells us that the woman was created as a *help*—one who aids and is suitable and equipped for every task. That word doesn't imply a subservient mentality. It means that women have the ability, through God, to do whatever is necessary to get the job done! Most men are called to do *specific* things, but a woman has a pool of abilities from which she can draw and do many things.

That's why Proverbs 31:11-12 tells us, *"The heart of her husband doth safely trust in her, so that he shall have no need of spoil. She will do him good and not evil all the days of her life."* This man trusts her because the Proverbs 31 woman has learned how to tap into the anointing of the helper. It's like the old saying, "Behind every great man is a great woman!"

Whether you're married or single, you must realize that this anointing abides within you. Keep in mind, however, that being a helper doesn't mean that you fade into the shadows and make everyone else look good! Instead, you have a strong position in the process of making things work efficiently; as a result, trust is produced.

A lady should be wise enough to know what to say and when and how to say it.

As a woman of God, don't be intimidated by the man God presents to you. It doesn't matter if he's the president of a bank, the leader of a ministry or a janitor. You should never turn away from an opportunity to meet a potential mate because *you* feel inadequate. If he's a man after God, and he values you and wants to treat you right, then learn to grow into your position alongside him.

There was a time early in our marriage when I wasn't accepting the call of God on my life. Creflo sensed it and encouraged me to follow after the Lord's direction. I felt he was pushing me to be like his pastor's wife and wanted me to take a role I wasn't ready for. I didn't like it. Eventually he decided to let God deal with me about my calling. He gave me the space to learn *how* to be a helper and to grow as a minister. I didn't back away, I just took it step by step and grew in that anointing.

You must learn to grow in the anointing you've been given as a helper. In fact, every anointing has been made available to you to make your relationship successful. That means if you need to be an administrator to help the man God has sent to you, then tap into the helper anointing and administer. If you need to be a preacher, God will anoint you to preach. That's what He did for me, and now I'm pursuing new levels in my role as a helper. On top of my schedule as pastor's wife, teacher, wife and mother, I've started a record company! I want to see the musical gifts in others excel, so I've learned to tap into that helper anointing! Whatever you *need* to operate as a helper, God *will* anoint you for it.

If you are single, don't chase after a man. There's no need to. If the anointing within you doesn't attract him or keep him coming back, then he's not the right one. Let him go and believe that God will present you to another who is after His own heart. Don't waste the anointing within you on someone who will hurt you. Again, learn to value and love yourself.

Do not compromise your standards because of a person or relationship you want to keep.

On the other hand, if you are dating the man you believe is your future mate, learn how to assist him and work with him. In the dating stage, you're *not* supposed to be washing his clothes and cooking all of his meals. Those are marital privileges! Instead help him in smaller ways, like listening to and encouraging him. If he has to work late every now and then, don't put pressure on him, support him! Be thankful that he has a job and is doing his best at it. Tell him that you're proud of him. When challenges come your way, reaffirm how much you believe in and trust him. Take the time to talk about problems and don't accuse or degrade him. If he's made a mistake, then present the facts in love—the Lord does that with you! From time to time, brag on him in front of others. Every time I teach, I always try to tell something wonderful that Creflo has done as a husband or father. Each time I do that, I'm helping him to be a better man.

Once you've renewed your mind with the helper anointing and understand how to operate in it, you won't waste your time on meaningless relationships.

3. You carry yourself well.

"She maketh herself coverings of tapestry; her clothing is silk and purple. Strength

and honour are her clothing; and she shall rejoice in time to come." (vv. 22, 25).

A woman of God knows how to carry and present herself because she understands that she is a valuable and unique person. As such, she does not draw negative attention to herself by being arrogant, prideful, loud or gaudy in appearance.

You can tell when some women are going through a hard time in a relationship. Their hair is messy, they often have bags under their eyes and they don't care what they put on. Don't allow a relationship to determine how you look. It's okay to maintain your appearance—even in challenging times—by keeping your hair styled, nails and teeth clean and adding a nice aroma to your skin. Even when fasting, the Bible tells us to dress up, wash ourselves and look good! Remember, you are an awesome, single person—a woman who is whole and unique—so adorn yourself that way! Don't compare yourself to what another woman looks like or the possessions she has.

I remember watching a television show years ago where a group of women became upset when men whistled and made jeering sexual remarks to them. Then the cameras scrolled down and revealed how they were dressed: low-cut blouses and micro miniskirts just below the panty line. Yet, these foolish women were voicing their right to dress however they wanted without the threat of sexual harassment. I wondered what planet they were from! They either forgot or were never taught this basic principle: *Whatever you are willing to show, a man will think you are willing to share.* If you don't ask for trouble, you won't get any.

That's why some of you have been attracting the same kind of man over and over again. When you let go of the world's system and come up to the level that you were created to operate in, life will be much better!

4. You are not a gossip.

"She openeth her mouth with wisdom; and in her tongue is the law of kindness. She looketh well to the ways of her household, and eateth not the bread of idleness" (verse 26). Notice that when the virtuous woman said something, it was wise and kind. She didn't "eat the bread of idleness," meaning gossip, discontent and self-pity.

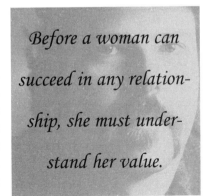

Before a woman can succeed in any relationship, she must understand her value.

You must be careful to set a barrier around yourself so idleness doesn't eat up your time. When you waste time on gossip, discontentment and self-pity, you become easily frustrated and stressed out. Women with a purpose choose to participate in productive and encouraging conversations. That's why it's so important to temper your emotions and not allow them to get out of hand. Emotions such as unchecked anger or depression can cause you to open your mouth and speak negatively about someone or something.

Do yourself a favor and watch the women and the men you associate with. Does the talk between you encourage godliness? If you're not sure who would be a good friend, then listen to the words the person speaks. Remember that whatever they say is coming from what has been stored in their hearts. What kind of influence do they have in your life? Is it one of hope, restoration and forgiveness, or division, control and ungodliness? How does this person cause you to view yourself?

Proverbs 13:20 promises us that if we fellowship with wise people, we will be wise; but if we keep close relationships with foolish people, we will be destroyed. One translation says we will "smart" from it. In other words, that friendship will come back to bite you! It's like the old saying, "Tell me who your friends are, and I'll tell you who you are." Simply put, bad company can corrupt even the most moral people, if they are not careful.

Your relationship with your man might be damaged right now because you've listened to the gossip of other women. Listening to them talk about what they would or would not put up with has caused hardship between you and your man. You might not have taken into account that some of them have been divorced three times and don't have a husband right now, or they've only ever had a string of failed relationships. Take a look at their personal lives. They may be living ungodly lifestyles, so why are you listening to their advice? They are causing problems for you and your household simply because misery loves company!

The Word says that kindness is on the tongue of the godly woman. That's a fruit of the Spirit. Be slow to speak and quick to hear. Practice temperance and self-control. When you do speak, allow those fruits to be on your tongue. A lady should be wise enough to know *what* to say and *when* and *how* to say it. The more of God that you allow to grow on the inside of you, the more He will help you to control those areas where you have been challenged in the past.

Experiencing God's Best

We spend so much time taking care of and nurturing our bodies, yet neglect the most important part of ourselves: the heart. The Bible tells us that our physical bodies will one day perish. Sure, we want to look good, and there's nothing wrong with taking care of yourself; but you must keep the proper perspective. It's the inward heart that is of great price to the Lord. As a woman, your longevity is in your reverence of God and His Word.

You can't expect to experience success in your relationships by neglecting to align your life with God's Word. More importantly, you can't compromise His Word because of some relationship you want to keep. Nothing is done in secret that won't be revealed at some point in time, whether that revealing comes openly or in the closet of your mind and conscience.

When you seek to become all that God has equipped you to be, you won't have to praise yourself—your own works will praise you (Proverbs 31:31)! You will know how to operate with sensitivity, wisdom and courtesy in any given situation and know how to carry yourself as a godly woman. You won't have to chase a compliment, because your integrity will speak for itself. By the godly life you live, your own works will pave the way for favor, adoration and the man of your dreams. And even after you've married, your husband will adore you and your children will imitate you—the highest compliment of all!

* * * * *

Change only comes when you renew your mind to the Word of God. As you immerse yourself in His presence, knowledge and understanding come, enabling you to walk confidently as a person of value, integrity and character. It is only through your relationship with God that you can mature as a woman and experience His best in your life.

It is important for a woman to completely understand herself and her place in a relationship. That *only* comes from a change in thinking by renewing the mind through the Word of God.

Examine areas in your life where you've not valued yourself. Then begin to work on those areas by changing your thoughts, the way you dress or take care of your body, protecting your conversations, and by helping others.

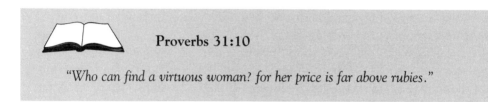

Proverbs 31:10

"Who can find a virtuous woman? for her price is far above rubies."

5

PREPARING TO TAKE THE "BIG LEAP"

Entering Into the Covenant of Marriage

W e've all heard the songs that talk of marital bliss—how when we go to the chapel to get married, the sun will shine, bells will ring and birds will chirp happily. Everyone will be on time, no one will be nervous and the reception will be absolutely perfect. We've become so consumed with preparing for the *event*, that we forget the seriousness of the commitment that event represents.

Although marriage contains elements of romance, it is a very serious thing. Many people don't realize just how serious it is. They choose a mate for financial reasons or because their biological clocks are ticking. Most have never really discovered the beauty of being content as a single person, so they try to find a mate to cure their loneliness. Others fantasize about the romantic side of two people sleeping together every night. These are the wrong motives for marriage. They stem from a lack of understanding regarding the covenant of marriage.

When a man and woman come together in marriage, they are preparing to "cut a covenant," or enter into a relationship where weaknesses are exchanged for strengths. For example, there are some areas where my wife, Taffi, is strong and I am weak. And there are other areas where I am strong and she is weak. That's why a covenant between us was a good idea. Once we married, we eliminated our weaknesses and harnessed our strengths.

You shouldn't want to marry someone just like you. Neither do you want to marry someone with whom you have absolutely nothing in common. The best person to marry is someone who complements you. In other words, you enjoy some similarities, but there is just enough difference to where you can exchange weaknesses for strengths.

If it weren't for Taffi, I would be a hard man in the area of work ethics! I believe that jobs should be done right now, quickly—work all day and night if that's what it takes to get it done. But thank goodness that Taffi's strength has tempered my weakness in that area! She comes in and gently reminds me that people are human beings; they have families and a life outside of the ministry. Her sensitivity pulls me back from working people into the ground. Life would be rough for everyone if Taffi and I were the same in that area!

That's what covenant is about. It's an exchange of strengths and weaknesses. So if you believe you've found the born-again, spirit-filled, God-chasing mate that God has brought to you, what is the next step? Talk. That's right. Like every covenant relationship that's ever been formed, the next step is to sit down and have a lengthy conversation with your potential mate.

Every Trick in the Book

It is not wise to jump into a marriage without first having lengthy conversations—and lots of them! This takes effort, openness, honesty and time. I don't believe in love at first sight. I believe in strong admiration, but love is something that has to grow. That's why after 10 years of marriage, people say they love their mates a hundred times more than when they first got married.

As with any other thing in life, love needs time to *grow* and *mature*. There's no such thing as a "Jack and the Beanstalk" way to grow love. It's impossible to know everything about a person overnight, although you may initially like what you see and hear. That's why you must allow time for a history to develop and that comes through communication and time spent with one another.

Love is something that must be allowed to grow and mature.

During the dating process, the two of you should have plenty to talk about. If you are a Christian, the first thing you need to know *before* you make a lifetime commitment is if the person is hungry for God. Find out if the person is truly born again.

I can't tell you how many times Taffi and I have heard this statement: "Well, he/she *told* me he/she was saved!"

Of course the person you're interested in is going to say they are born again. Most people will say whatever you want to hear if it means they'll be able to be with you. That's the oldest trick in the book! If he or she is interested in establishing a relationship with you, they will say they're saved, filled with the Holy Spirit and have an international ministry—but it can only be seen from somewhere like Siberia! Here's an important point to remember: About 99% of Americans will tell you that they're saved, especially if they're from the Southern half of the United States!

Jesus never said that a person's geographical location or religious background saved them. Their words mean little if their actions don't correspond. Jesus said to judge a tree by its *fruit* (Matthew 12:33). In other words, don't take someone's word for it. Remember, even the fig tree He cursed had *leaves* on it, but no fruit (Matthew 21:19).

Take the time to find out the following:

- Does he/she read the Word? How often?
- Do they pray? When and how?
- Do they pray in the Holy Spirit (in other tongues)?
- How do they talk? Do they curse? Speak negatively?
- What do they think about?
- How often do they go to church?
- Do they go to church because *you* want them to or because they are in love with God?
- Do you have to motivate him/her to seek after God?

The driving force behind these questions is to find out where the other person is spiritually. The key trait to look for is whether or not they have a *personal* and *intimate* relationship with God. Don't brush over obvious indicators or make excuses for the person. Be careful about that, *especially* if you're thinking about getting married. Avoid trying to rush the process just because you're feeling old or lonely. You'd better back up and establish yourself in the Word, or you are in for big trouble.

If the other person has just become a born-again Christian, you must allow them time to mature in their faith. By not doing so, you could seriously damage their walk with God. It would be like an adult marrying a child—completely out of order. Date the person for a year or two and see how their fruit develops. If they can hold out that long, they're for real. And be sure to maintain a proper perspective. Don't put down or avoid unbelievers; simply make up your mind to abide by the Word and not be joined with them in marriage (2 Corinthians 6:14). I don't care how nice they are or how good they look. You *don't* have to date an unbeliever to witness to him or her.

True Colors

I can't stress enough how important it is to know *whom* you are marrying. Just because you are dating with the intent of marriage or are already engaged doesn't mean that it's okay to let your guard down and stop observing the other person. On the contrary, the engagement period is *the most critical period* in your relationship, because it not only allows you to see how your partner responds to the stresses of wedding planning, it also gives you the opportunity to become closely involved with your future in-laws.

There are several things you should watch out for during this period. For example, how does your man or woman treat the members of his or her family? Do they put the needs of their parents and siblings ahead of their own? Their relationship to their family—how they talk to and treat one another—will give you a good indication of how he or she will relate to you once you are married. In addition, consider the following:

- How do they respond to challenging situations?
- Do they express their anger or frustration in positive ways, or do they shout, throw items, make snide comments or give others the silent treatment?
- Are they quick to resolve problems, or do they allow those negative situations to fester?
- Is their sense of humor at the expense of others? Are they able to laugh at themselves?

Be sure to discuss "hot" topics as well, such as political affiliation and your stance on controversial issues such as abortion, euthanasia, affirmative action and the death penalty—you'd be surprised at how much strife these issues can stir up in a household! Remember, you may not see eye to eye on every issue; therefore, be sure to discuss how you will handle your differences so that you can maintain a happy and peaceful atmosphere at home.

When the Bible talks about not being "*unequally yoked*," it does not refer to a person's *race*, but to *spiritual compatibility*. God doesn't care if you are black, white, red, yellow, brown or a mixture of them all. He only speaks of the distinction between light and darkness—good and evil, righteous or unrighteous, saved or unsaved. Those are the only kinds of pairings God warns against. Of course if the person you want to marry is of a different race, there are other things to consider, such as cultural distinctions, that may produce challenges. But that doesn't mean He is against interracial marriages! His only command in that area is for us to be joined together in marriage with another *believer.*

More Than Kisses

If you've determined that the two of you are born-again, spirit-filled believers hungry for more of God, congratulations! You're off to a great start. However, you are still going to have to sit down and talk before you can decide whether or not marriage is an option.

A great way to do this is to ask questions. Find out what he or she would do in a hypothetical situation. What would they be willing to do? How far would they be willing to go? When Taffi and I discussed marriage, I was already in the ministry, and she was preparing herself to enter into that area. But there were other things I wanted to know. So I asked, "What if, for some reason, I had to go to war and I accidentally stepped on a mine that blew off both my legs and I couldn't walk or perform any of my marital duties anymore. What would you do with me?"

She said, "I'd take care of you."

It was a good answer, but I wanted to dig deeper to see what she was made of and if she was being honest. So I asked, "But how would you *feel* about it?"

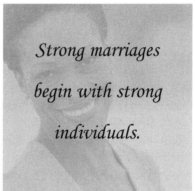

Strong marriages begin with strong individuals.

She replied, "It would be an inconvenience, but I love you, and I would take care of you."

Her honest response satisfied me.

But she had questions for me, such as: what was my work ethic? Did I plan on working all the days of my life? Would I be able to take care of her and buy more than electricity and water? Would I like to have children? How many? When did I plan on having children? What about birth control? What involvement would our families have in our lives? Would I allow her to have animals? What kind of cars did I like?

We talked about *everything!* And we didn't get married right away, either. Instead, we waited for three and a half years, carefully watching how the other person handled the challenges life threw their way. We learned how to be friends and argue without destroying each other. We realized that eventually we were going to make a lifetime commitment, so we were serious in how we handled our relationship.

During this time of conversation, make sure that you cover one another's basic needs as a male and female, and also as unique individuals. In a marriage, a man needs sexual fulfillment, recreational companionship, an attractive spouse, domestic support and admiration. Find out what he's looking for in those areas and make sure you are willing and able to meet those needs. Notice that I said, *in a marriage*. Don't engage in activities that are marital privileges, like washing one another's clothes.

In addition, don't become sexually involved with your man or woman *before* making that lifetime commitment before God and witnesses. You need a license to practice that! There's no such thing as "trying it out." Avoid placing yourself in temptation's way. Instead, *run* from it! There were certain ways of kissing that Taffi and I could not indulge in before we were married. We set boundaries and stuck to them. That's why our honeymoon was so sweet!

Men, your woman has needs in a marriage also. She needs affection, open and honest dialogue, financial support and a strong sense of commitment to her and your future family. Discuss those things with her. As a man, you must strive to fulfill those needs for the rest of her life.

Details, Details

During or right after those lengthy conversations, you should sit down with your partner and discuss the details of the marriage.

Taffi and I sat down and discussed our preferences and what we would and would not allow in our marriage. Question after question arose from our discussion: Would I be the main breadwinner? Would we always work to stay attractive? What about sex? What were the boundaries with the opposite sex? Would we start in an apartment and work our way up? What was her view on submission and mine on being the head of the family? How would we work together to raise our children? How would we balance family and ministry? What were our priorities? Would I always take care of her and our children?

Once an agreement has been reached concerning those things, the man is then ready to ask the woman to marry him. If she says yes, then she has just committed herself to him for life. At that time it is appropriate for them to inform their families of the commitment they have made. Afterward, you are ready to plan the wedding!

Here Comes the Bride

The wedding ceremony is a holy thing, created for a man and a woman to voice the terms of their marriage in the sight of God. A minister or justice of the peace has the bride and groom recite vows outlining the responsibilities of each person. During this time, the Holy Spirit takes two people and joins them together as one.

Think about what the preacher is asking you to promise your fiancée. Are you going to protect, love and cling to one another as long as you live? Will you stick together in the good and challenging times? Are you going to encourage one another in the Lord? Will you be willing to communicate and show concern and affection at all times? You can't say, "I do" until you realize what you are committing to!

This means you had better be ready to leave mom and dad and cleave to your spouse. Your parents are no longer your first priority—your spouse is. Your husband or wife should be the first person you run to when you need a listening ear, a shoulder to cry on or advice regarding a certain situation. Those vows mean that what is said between you and your spouse stays between the two of you— you should not be sharing your business with your folks anymore!

Mr. Fix-It

When Taffi and I were first married, her car developed a serious condition and broke down. I was excited about it, because it presented me with an opportunity to provide for my wife. My plan was simple—fix her car and look like a hero in the process. But Taffi had a plan of her own—she called her father! When I told her what I was going to do, she replied, "That's okay. I called my dad, and he said he would take care of it."

I recoiled in shock. How could she do that to me? I was her husband! So I told her, "You'd better call him back and tell him to forget it because I'm going to take care of the situation. I'm your husband and I can handle it."

After Taffi got off the phone with her father, I said, "Please don't ever do that again." To this day, I'm the first person she comes to with a problem, and vice-versa.

Women, when the minister or justice of the peace asks if you will take so and so as your husband, he is asking if you are willing to *submit* yourself to that man. To *submit* means to *comply* and *obey*. Your husband may not be right all the time, but your commitment to being his wife means you support and encourage him daily. In other words, you place yourself in his hands, trusting that he will act out on your best interests. That's a huge commitment on your part and why it's so important that you *know* the man you are marrying.

On the other hand, as a man, are you going to turn your eyes away from other women and only look at her? Are you going to protect, provide and care for her when she's old? Are you willing to be a father to your children? If you say, "I will," then you *must*!

The Changing of the Guard

Once the vows are over, an important thing happens: what was yours now belongs to the other person, and vice versa. Your material possessions are now theirs, and their material possessions are now yours. Family members and ties are "transferred" to each of you. That's where we get the term, "in-law." By law, you both have a right to those family members.

When Taffi and I married, she immediately applied this principle to her life. While on her way to run an errand, she said, "I'm taking the car. I'll be back." I figured she was talking about her car; but when I looked out the window, I saw her driving off in my BMW!

There is an exchange of authority that takes place during the marriage ceremony. When the father of the bride presents his daughter to the bridegroom, he relinquishes his right to protect and provide for her. At that moment, the bridegroom begins to assume that responsibility. The same is true of the bride. Once she has let go of her father's hand and taken hold of the groom's, she is taking on the responsibility of caring for that man as she would for herself. The bride and groom are no longer under the authority of their parents or themselves, but each other's. Rings are exchanged between the couple to seal this "changing of the guard."

In addition, the wife now takes on her new husband's surname. In doing so, she positions herself to carry his authority. In other words, when she speaks, it's as if he were speaking. Everything that was once his is now hers. That's not a bad deal!

Eat, Drink and Be Married

The reception is the final piece of the wedding ceremony, although we now separate the two. Centuries ago, this was the time when food and drink was exchanged between the bride and groom to symbolize the exchange they had just made. The husband and wife fed bread and wine to one another, pledging, "I swear that I'll never break the vows I've made to you. If I ever break our agreement, you have the right to kill me." Even family members participated in this confirmation of wedding vows by blessing the union (what we now call a toast) and stating what they would do if either party violated those vows!

What would happen if wedding receptions today had these elements in them? I think many more people would stop to consider whether or not they were ready for marriage. They'd get cold feet just thinking, "Wait a minute. If I violate this marriage agreement, I'm dead!" The divorce rate would drop drastically!

You should make it a point to enjoy your wedding reception. Make it as lavish or as simple and elegant as you want, just don't get into debt over it. Be practical with your finances and remember that the reception only lasts a few hours, but the marriage will last for years! There will be many more special occasions to share with family and friends.

* * * * *

Marriage is serious business. It was never intended as a solution for beating biological time clocks or loneliness. Entering into it lightly only paves the way for eventual disappointment, disillusionment and heartache not just in your life, but in the lives of those who care for you, such as friends and family members. There isn't much that hurts an individual more than the pain of divorce.

Strong marriages begin with strong individuals. By taking the time to know yourself and your future mate, you establish a firm foundation for your future together. Allow time for your relationship to grow and develop. Don't rush the process. In addition, stop and consider the seriousness of the vows you wish to make to one another. By taking a moment to really think before you leap, you'll avoid learning from the school of hard knocks and guarantee success!

Marriage is a lifelong commitment that requires forethought, planning and continual maintenance and should not be taken lightly or entered into casually.

Begin thinking of questions that you would like to ask your partner. Jot them down on a sheet of paper and place in your wallet or by the telephone as a reminder for your next conversation. You may wish to present a hypothetical situation, discuss a controversial issue or traumatic experience, or ask about his or her relationship with their parents. Be sure to listen carefully to their answers and reciprocate by sharing information about yourself. The more you know, the better off your marriage will be!

Numbers 30:2

"If a man vow a vow unto the Lord, or swear an oath to bind his soul with a bond; he shall not break his word, he shall do according to all that proceedeth out of his mouth."

Part II

Marriage
Enhancement

6

FOLLOW THE LEADER
The True Meaning of Submission

D on't think this chapter isn't for *you!*
When most people hear the term *submission*, they automatically think it refers to a woman's place in a marriage and the way she must relate to her husband. That's only *one* aspect of it.
The reality is that this principle of submission is one by which we must all abide, whether male or female, married or single. By this I mean it is *already* a part of our everyday lives. For example, we submit ourselves daily to our employers, civil authorities and spiritual leaders, not to mention those with whom we have established relationships. Many people have divorced over the issue of submission because neither party wants to give in to the other. However, you're going to submit to someone, somewhere, sometime—so it's better to get a clear understanding of it to avoid future misunderstandings and heartache.

You may be surprised to discover that in marriage, submission not only involves the wife, but her husband as well. Ephesians 5 contains a powerful key for a successful marriage: *"Submitting yourselves one to another in the fear of God"* (verse 21). Submission is a mutual action. Both parties in a relationship must submit to one another.

You've got it all wrong if you're equating submission with a subservient, "maid-servant" mentality. Instead, submission means to put all of yourself—your knowledge, opinions, feelings and energies—at the disposal of another. In simple terms, it means putting yourself under the mission of another—hence the prefix "sub," meaning under. That doesn't mean you can treat your spouse like a doormat or abuse them in any way. That's not submission; that's stupidity!

Sadly, many people think that submission *is* stupidity. They say that in submitting to your spouse, you cease to exist as an individual and that it produces weak, dependent people who cannot think for themselves. Only those who understand *why* they must submit are the ones who walk in God's wholeness and power. In true submission, you find out who you *really* are!

The Chain of Command

The Bible lists a chain of authority. First we are supposed to submit to God (James 4:7), then to the laws of our government and all governing officials (1 Peter 5:5). This chain of command continues even into the family. Genesis 2 tells us that God created man, then woman from man, and children from the woman. The wife submits to her husband *and* the husband submits to his wife. It's like the old argument, "Which comes first: the chicken or the egg?" Although woman came from man, she is an essential part of him and he of her. Then children submit to their parents.

Submission finds its strength in two areas: the will and the ability to adapt.

Submission is the plan God designed to work for our benefit. But those benefits—protection, safety and strength—can never come into play as long as we try to share equal authority. Although men and women are equal in spirituality, there are definite distinctions when it comes to the mental, emotional and physical arenas. This includes the areas of leadership and headship. This is not to say that one gender is better than the other—not at all! It's just that men and women were made with different purposes in mind; therefore, their abilities to process information, deal with emotional issues and handle physical challenges differ from one another. We must be very cautious with the issue of equality or it will lead us into error, deception and disobedience and out of the will of God.

When Creflo and I were first married, I had a problem with submission—especially with the word "obey." I didn't see how he could ask me to do something that I didn't want to do. I wanted to be an independent and career-focused woman. I didn't want to be accountable to him for every little thing I wanted to do.

At the time, I didn't understand God's design for submission, and I certainly didn't know anything about its benefits. Only after I aligned my thinking with the Word of God and learned to submit to the Lord did I become a mighty woman of God. Once I gained understanding and began to change my responses, I saw miracle after miracle take place in our lives and marriage.

Over the years, I've discovered that for submission to work, you must be willing and able to adapt. That means changing your thinking *and* your corresponding actions just as I did. Submission is *not* for the weak. Anyone can be proud, haughty and independent. It doesn't take strength, ingenuity or courage to act that way. But it *does* take courage to submit yourself to God and to those in authority over you. This kind of mental determination is what separates the women from the girls, the men from the boys and the wise from the foolish.

It's Up to You

James 4:7 tells us to *"Submit yourselves therefore to God. Resist the devil, and he will flee from you."* Submission, as with anything else in life, is an act of the will. You must make up your mind to do it and then stick to that commitment, no matter what. Before you can ever submit to anyone or anything else, you must first learn how to submit to God.

If you're honest with yourself, you'll admit that you have a tendency to get haughty when those in authority try to tell you something. At that time you may think, "Who the heck are *you* to tell me what to do? You're not the boss of *me*!" Often your back stiffens and you may utter a few snide comments or negative remarks. Or, you may sit back and do nothing in a passive-aggressive attempt to get back at the person with whom you carry a grudge. Both of these responses are wrong. To receive the blessings of God, you must put yourself in remembrance of His Word and be subject to earthly authority just as you submit to His authority. It's absolutely an act of the will.

Do you submit to what God tells you to do, or do you argue with Him? I can always tell if a woman obeys God by observing the way in which she submits to her husband and to those in authority over her. The same principle is true for a man. I can tell how he obeys God by the way he leads his family and submits to the will of God.

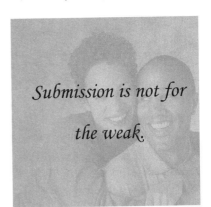

Submission is not for the weak.

Submitting to God is the foundation for submission to others. In doing so, you avoid having to deal with contrary thoughts and bitterness, not to mention unforgiveness and other critical spirits. Your mind will be at peace because you are abiding by the mandates of God's Word.

To *submit* means to *"retire, withdraw, yield and obey."* When you retire your plans—how *you* think something should be done—you become adaptable. When you are adaptable, you comply. That's when the power of God begins working on your behalf. Submission enables Him to do things that will benefit you.

Women, even if your husband is wrong about something, God can cover the situation and make it turn out all right *if* you let go of your own resolutions and turn the problem over to Him. If your trust and submission isn't to the Lord *first*, you'll fall apart every time your husband makes a mistake. You'll walk around in fear, thinking you have to control *all* of the decisions and actions of your man. As a result, your marriage will be filled with strife. You don't have to worry about your husband if he's wrong. Put your trust in God. He will hold your man accountable for his decisions. And believe me, God will take care of him!

Even as godly as Creflo is, I'm not always ready to shout, "Yahoo!" when he asks me to do something. There are times when he has to bring certain things to my attention so I can be better in fulfilling my obligations and responsibilities. To be honest, at first the hair on the back of my neck stands up, and I want to bristle with indignation! But I know the power in submission, so I retreat to the Word that I've hidden in my heart. I have determined to be slow to speak and quick to listen. I immediately begin to judge myself and look at those areas needing change. That's an act of my will.

When I do that, God works on my behalf. If my husband is wrong, the power that is on my life convicts him, and he is quick to make things right. Because of my submission, we are *both* able to witness the power and peace of God working in that situation, and we are *both* all the better for it. But if I had threatened, cried, screamed or sulked, nothing would be resolved. Instead we would be still be "duking" it out, only to walk away later hurt and scarred.

The Ultimate Example

Philippians 2:6-7 states that although Jesus was the human form of God and equal to Him, He took on the role of a servant. Jesus could have done or said anything He wanted to, but He *chose* to do the will of God.

Throughout the Book of John we read that Jesus willfully submitted to God's plan of salvation for mankind. Before the crucifixion, He prayed, "*...not my will, but thine, be done*" (Luke 22:42). Jesus was totally submitted despite how bleak the circumstances looked or how hard it was to follow through. It was His submission to God that enabled Him to be an effective minister—one who healed the sick, delivered the captive and rescued the lost!

Just as with Jesus, everything revolves around our will. God created it that way. We have the freedom to choose peace or strife, life or death. Submission works the same way. It enables you to choose obedience and its blessings, or disobedience and its consequences.

Submission continually offers you the opportunity to enter higher levels in your character and faith. In addition, it may lead you to something new, or offer some other anointing that is required for a particular task that you have been given. But unless you are willing to think beyond your ability, you'll never truly be able to fulfill the will of God.

Man, oh Man!

There is a difference between *equality* and *equal authority*. Men and women are equals in spirituality—their born-again status—but have different roles and responsibilities in marriage.

Once I was talking to Creflo about a play I had seen. I said, "You know, I believe Adam and Eve were probably equal in the Garden before they fell."

He disagreed. "The reason they weren't equal is because she came out of the man. Anything that comes out of something else is submitted to what it came out of. It establishes rank."

That's why children submit to their parents and employees submit to employers. We submit to pastors because they "rule" over us, giving an account to God for our souls (Hebrews 13:17).

The beautiful thing about submission in a marriage is that the husband, although he may pull rank, must also submit *"in the fear of God"* (Ephesians 5:21). His submission is a little different from the wife's. He submits by reverencing the Word of God and not doing his own thing. That means laying aside his plans and aligning himself with God's will for his life. He can't rip the doors from their

Submitting to God is the foundation for submission to others.

hinges and shout, "I'm the head of this house. You do what I say!" Instead he submits to his wife *and* the Word of God by communicating God's plan for their lives clearly. In this way, he provides her with the necessary leadership and direction she needs and desires. In addition, he strives to immediately resolve problems or clear up any misunderstandings that may arise.

A husband also submits by controlling his anger when upset and valuing his wife just as he would a precious possession. He spends time with his children, grooming them in the ways of the Lord and being a father to them. He understands his responsibilities as a godly leader in his home and ensures that his family grows and matures in the Lord. He not only submits by accepting his God-given rank and authority, but also in laying down his life for his family to ensure their well-being, protection and financial security.

You can see that husbands carry the burden of responsibility regarding submission in a marriage. Why? They are directly accountable to God. This is not a task that should be taken lightly. Only a shallow and insecure man would point his finger at his wife and yell, "Submit!" just because he is the head of the house!

A Tender Reed

Wives also have their own accountability in regard to the submission issue. In Genesis 2:18, God said that He was going to make Adam a *help meet*, or someone who was proper, suitable and fit for him. *God* was the One who said that man *needed* help, and a woman was His solution to the problem!

A helper can tap into any anointing that is needed to get the job done.

Women are not alone in the category of helper. Many scriptures refer to God as our Helper (Psalm 46:1; Isaiah 41:10). In addition, the Holy Spirit is also referred to as a helper (John 14:26). What awesome company! You should never think badly of yourself or take on a slave mentality because you are a woman and have been labeled by God as a suitable helper for your mate. No one loses value in humbly assuming the role of a helper because it implies function, not worth. When a married woman walks away from her God-given responsibility to help her man, she is actually walking away from her calling!

It's important to remember that as helpers, you and I shoulder some of the responsibility as to who our spouses become. But don't be alarmed! If women were created to be proper, suitable and fit for their men, then they are also able to adapt. In fact, women assume a variety of roles in their lives, making it necessary for them to adapt! For example, you begin life as someone's daughter, then evolve into someone's wife, mother and grandmother. Adaptability provides strength, direction and a sense of purpose for you and those around you.

One of the reasons many marriages fail is because the helper—the woman— is not willing to be adaptable. This could be for a variety of reasons, from obstinacy to a spouse's abuse of headship. But no matter what situation you face, there is a way of escape if *you* will just tap into the power of adaptability. It is a power designed by God to keep His plan operating and flowing through your life.

For example, men have a great responsibility to provide and be the leader, so they always have something on their minds. If they aren't hearing from God, they're hearing from tyrannical bosses or thinking about some other pressure that's coming against them. As a result, they can become moody and withdrawn. How can his wife help him? She must be willing to adapt. That may mean giving him some space to think and unwind when he comes home instead of attacking him with bills, questions or other issues. She waits for the best time to approach him.

As a wife, your job is to help him be all God has called him to be. There is a pool of anointings available to you to help you accomplish this task. A helper can tap into any anointing (power and ability) that is needed to get the job done, whatever it may be. When you remain adaptable, you tap into God's power and ability to support your husband.

Keep in mind, however, that adaptability doesn't mean that you accommodate sin or abuse! Those are never good enough reasons to adapt. Submission and adaptability are not about being someone's doormat. Instead, it is about supporting—encouraging, uplifting and positively challenging—your spouse. It is the power to *fit* God's ways into a dark situation.

Beware of Man-Eaters

In 1938, the movie *Jezebel* was released in theatres across the country. It starred Bette Davis as Julie, a hardheaded southern belle, and Henry Fonda as Preston, her softhearted fiancé. Because of her selfish and prideful ways, Julie lost her fiancé to another woman. In trying to recapture him and rekindle their love, she managed to lose many of her friends, damage her reputation and instigate a duel that resulted in a fatality. The only way to redeem herself was by caring for the man she loved as he lay sick with yellow fever. The movie ends with the two of them being shipped to a quarantined area near New Orleans, Louisiana.

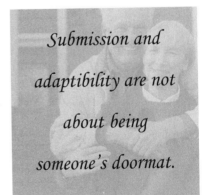

Submission and adaptibility are not about being someone's doormat.

Although Julie was a beautiful woman, she neglected to cultivate that beauty within her. No one dared oppose her, which only served to fuel her obstinacy and pride. Even her fiancé, Preston, refused to deal firmly with her. It was because of those out-of-hand emotions that she lost everything dear to her, including the love of her life. Julie's refusal to humble herself and refrain from outrageous behavior pushed away everyone who loved her.

Although *Jezebel* was just a movie, it did a fairly good job in portraying the struggle many couples have regarding submission. In fact, many couples end up divorced over this very thing. What they fail to remember is that the antithesis to submission is rebellion. There is no in-between. With rebellion comes pride, hatred, bitterness, anger and the desire to manipulate and control others. This is what is known as the "Jezebel spirit."

This spirit got its name from the wicked Queen Jezebel (1 Kings 21) because she portrayed so many of its attributes. In an effort to rule Israel and exalt her gods and her ways, Jezebel tried to kill as many priests of God as she could. Although she was not a direct heir to the throne of Israel, she inherited her power though marriage to King Ahab, an Israelite. Like Julie's fiancé, Preston, he refused to subdue his wife. Instead, Ahab allowed Jezebel to rule the kingdom in his place, even killing others in his name.

The Jezebel spirit fights against submission, humility, reverence and holiness—everything that produces a powerful Christian. Contrary to popular belief, "Jezebel" is not the term for a loose woman; rather it describes a wife who is out of control and a husband who is weak and indulgent. While the Jezebel spirit does have elements of sexual impurity (as in using sex as a weapon or to get your way), it relies more on self-indulgence and weakness of the flesh to produce strife and cause division.

There are different levels of its operation; but even the most immature level is subtle and crafty. Just as submission is an act of the will, the Jezebel spirit also operates from a strong self-will that is motivated by hatred and the desire to control.

Women's Lib: Good or Bad?

I am all for women's liberation when it comes to my rights as a female. Women should not be discriminated against because of their gender. I believe in equal pay for equal work, equal employment opportunities and the like. Women are equal to men in intelligence, spirituality and emotional capacity.

However, you must realize that God has a purpose and an established order for everything in life—from your walk as a Christian to your role as a family member. Men and women were created to fulfill different roles. As the stronger and first-made, the man has a responsibility to protect, provide for and lead his family in a way that is pleasing to God and sets an example for others to follow. A woman is responsible for nurturing, supporting and encouraging those in her home.

Problems arise when women try to usurp the chain of command God has established by assuming a role of headship. Although many single-parent women have been able to adapt and be both father and mother to their children, they still experience the frustration and regret that comes from living outside of God's established authority.

The next time you are confronted by someone who says women are equal, or even better than men, remember that you are special and have been made with a purpose. Although "girls can do anything boys can do," it's not always in your best interests to do so!

Several types of personalities are more vulnerable to this spirit than others, such as those with prophetic gifts, dominant personalities, or those who have been wounded or rejected by parents or people in authority. Because of unresolved past hurts, these types of people can develop the tendencies to control others, manipulate to get their way or rebel against any level of authority.

Through irresponsibility, Ahab gave up his headship, and Jezebel took advantage of it. She assumed a position she wasn't originally designed to do (head of the family), and through manipulation and deceit, took control of things. If a woman "wears the pants" in a marriage, it's because the husband has a weak-willed Ahab spirit. If the man will step up and take his rightful position as the leader, then order can be established. The Jezebel spirit cannot operate efficiently unless an Ahab spirit precedes it.

The Jezebel spirit is fiercely independent and intensely ambitious. It will use every means available to achieve its goals. Even the word *Jezebel* means "without cohabitation." Like the *Highlander* movies, its motto is "There can be only one!" A person with this spirit will not live peacefully with anyone. It wants to be the number one authority and in complete control. If it seems submissive, it is only for the sake of gaining some important, strategic advantage. In addition, because this spirit is anti-God, it hates repentance and humility and fights hard to keep them from happening. It works to conquer and divide. I would watch out for a person or a ministry that refuses to be accountable to other ministries or leadership.

The weak-willed spirit of Ahab and the controlling, rebellious spirit of Jezebel will cause trouble in your relationship with your spouse, eventually damaging or killing the marriage altogether. That's why it's so important to aggressively attack any Jezebel or Ahab tendencies you may see. This spirit will stop resurfacing once you get rid of it and use what God has placed within you to set others free from it!

*   *   *   *   *

Men and women have the ability to influence others one way or another. The way in which you tackle your God-given responsibilities and respond to your spouse often makes a huge impact on your marital and family relationships. Remember, if there is no change from the top down, a revolution from the bottom up will inevitably follow.

Make a quality decision today to submit to the will of God instead of your own. Submit to those in authority over you. As you release the seeds of submission in your family, watch the power of God begin to operate on your behalf as never before!

The power of God operates through those who are submitted first to Him and then to others.

Take a moment to reflect on your character. Is there any place where the seeds of rebellion, pride, unforgiveness or bitterness have taken root? Take a sheet of paper and list the instances where those seeds were sown. It may be as long ago as a childhood incident or as recent as five minutes ago. When you have finished, lay your hands on the sheet of paper and make this confession out loud: "I make a quality decision to forgive [list people by name]. I release [him/her] right now. I will no longer allow anger, bitterness, unforgiveness or pride to take up residence in my head or heart. From now on, as much as it is possible, I will strive to live at peace with everyone I know and love."

 James 4:7, 10

"*Submit yourselves therefore to God. Resist the devil, and he will flee...Humble yourselves in the sight of the Lord, and he shall lift you up.*"

7

WHAT DID YOU SAY?
Discovering the Principles of Successful Communication

U sually couples wanting to reconcile their differences and save their marriages from the brink of destruction visit marriage counselors. Quite often the root cause of their differences is never discovered and dealt with effectively. Consequently, divorce is inevitable in most cases.

Root causes of problems in marital relationships can be likened to a tree's root system. If left alone for a long enough period, they grow deep and branch out. As the tree grows, so do its roots, which absorb water and minerals from the soil, enabling it to live and grow.

Hurt, anger, bitterness and resentment are tree-like emotions that thrive in many relationships. Over time, they are allowed to grow out of control as their roots continue to feed on and grow in polluted soil. Many things can pollute the "soil" of a marriage and perpetuate the life span of these emotional trees, such as misunderstandings, upbringing, unresolved childhood issues and poor advice from friends and relatives.

Dig Out the Roots

In order to get rid of a tree, you cannot simply trim its leaves and cut off its branches. As long the tree has its roots dug deep into the soil, it is still able to survive and regenerate. You must destroy it from top to bottom, including its entire root system. The same principle is true where marital problems are concerned. Every branch must be cut off and every root dug up and destroyed if true reconciliation is to occur. If you only deal with surface issues, you may find *temporary* relief from your problems. Later, however, you are going to find yourself arguing over things that are related to past issues.

Think back to the tree metaphor. Just as a tree has many branches, so do hurt and pain in relationships. For example, one spouse may speak harsh words and hurt the other. That hurt gives birth to the "branch" of low self-esteem, which then gives birth to other branches of anger and distrust. In order to eliminate these offshoots, each person must dig out and destroy the root cause so harmony can be restored in the home. Without uprooting the cause, true reconciliation is impossible.

Digging out the root cause of problems isn't an easy task. Past hurts are resurrected and one or both spouses are forced to come to grips with the truth. Often the truth reveals that *both* parties played key roles in the issues they face.

Effective communication is the ultimate tool needed to uproot the causes of broken relationships. When used properly, the result is a successful marriage. Every Christian couple should strive for this. Remember this simple, yet powerful concept:

> ### Successful Communication = A Successful Marriage

Bridging the Communication Gap

Communication is not limited to an exchange of words. A husband and wife may talk to each other, but it's possible that neither one is *listening* to the other. If you speak to your spouse in a language that he or she doesn't understand, then you've not communicated effectively. That would be like me trying to speak French to a person who speaks Chinese. It just doesn't work! You may have spoken words, but your communication is unfruitful. Your spouse didn't receive any information from what you said.

Merriam-Webster's Dictionary defines *communication* as "a process by which information is exchanged between individuals." For example, when you purchase items from a grocery store, you *exchange* money with a cashier in order to take those items home with you. When both you and the cashier receive something from the transaction, you've communicated with one another.

The same is true concerning effective communication between spouses. There must be an exchange where a husband and wife receive and understand the information that is given by the other. Think of this exchange as an impartation, or sharing, of thoughts and opinions. *Miscommunication* occurs when both parties fail to exchange information clearly and effectively.

A good example of effective communication is the mail system. When someone sends you a package by mail, they expect you to receive it on time. They've done their part to make sure they had your correct address and that the postage was paid. When you actually receive, open and confirm the package's content, both of you have achieved successful communication; the objective was accomplished.

The Missing Link

Try this experiment. Take a sheet of paper and write down the following sentence without showing it to anyone:
"You have the most unbelievable eyes I have ever seen."
Strike through every other word. Now, read the sentence out loud to your spouse. Did he or she understand what you were trying to say? Probably not. Take turns performing this exercise, keeping in mind the importance of communication!

Have you and your spouse ever disagreed on something because one of you failed to understand the point the other was trying to make? In this case, you didn't receive the "package" of information as intended. You heard something entirely different than what was said.

Wives, let's say you purchase a new dress and show it to your husband. You ask, "Honey, do you like my new dress?" He says, "Not really. The color doesn't suit you." But your reaction is, "So what you're *really* saying is that it makes me look fat!" He didn't say anything about your weight; however, that's how you *interpreted* what he said.

Husbands, let's say you come home from a long day at work. As soon as you come through the door, your wife greets you with a kiss and a hug. After you settle in she says, "By the way, the electric bill came today." You say, "Stop nagging me about the bills! Don't you know that I'm doing my best to pay them on time? You probably think that I'm not a good provider, don't you?" Wait a minute! She didn't say a word about you not being a good provider!

In both cases, we have a problem—a communication breakdown. Neither of you heard the message that the other was trying to communicate. Instead, the information that was transmitted was filtered incorrectly. The outcomes of situations like these are hurt feelings and strife, and that's what you should avoid. What's the solution?

> *Communication is "an exchange of information," not just an exchange of words.*

Stop Talking and Start Listening

Someone observed that God purposefully created humans with two ears and one mouth. Perhaps it's a clue that we should listen twice as much as we speak. It's usually the reverse in our everyday conversations with others. Some of us dominate a conversation by speaking more than listening. We would rather get *our* point across than allow others to express their point of view.

If you think about it, we also tend to do this in our time with God. We're so busy petitioning Him that we rarely stop speaking to hear what He has to say. If God were to speak to us in plain terms about our communication with others, He would probably tell us that we should learn to keep our mouths shut and start listening. That's when we'll learn something!

No behavior is more self-centered than when we demand to speak and refuse to listen.

No behavior is more self-centered than when you demand to speak and refuse to listen. This is the root cause of most conflicts between spouses. In fact, it is a violation of a biblical principle: "...*Let every man* [or woman] *be swift to hear, slow to speak, slow to wrath...*" (James 1:19). *The Amplified Bible* says that we should be "ready listeners."

In some counseling sessions, each spouse is given the opportunity to express his or her feelings about a particular situation without interruptions. One spouse usually says, "I never knew you felt that way." Often, the response is, "I've been trying to tell you all these years" or "You never gave me a chance to tell you."

When you take the time to listen, you learn what habits or behaviors irritate your spouse. You learn what words or actions trigger certain unwanted responses. And you allow the opportunity for past unresolved issues to surface so you can deal with them once and for all.

Most importantly, you learn what truly makes your spouse happy. There is a saying that bears repeating: "Happy wife, happy life!" This also proves true with a happy husband. Ladies, when your husband is confident that he can openly express his hurts and most intimate thoughts to you without ridicule and rebuke, he'll be a happy man.

Listening is an act of love. It tells your husband or wife that you are really interested in hearing what he or she has to say. I've found that being a good listener makes you a good friend. Listening with compassion quenches the fire of anger and indifference because it brings understanding and love. Love conquers all. It is a fortified shelter that can withstand the greatest storms that often destroy many marriages.

Demonstrating love for your spouse by being quick to listen and slow to speak will work miracles in your relationship. Yes, sometimes you may want to put your "two cents in," but consider the possible consequences. It's not worth the separation and resentment, regardless of who is right or wrong.

The Apostle Paul said, "…*let us then definitely aim for and eagerly pursue what makes for harmony and for mutual upbuilding (edification and development) of one another*" (Romans 14:19, AMP). You can apply this scripture to your marital relationship. Your pursuit should not be to have your say. Rather, you should pursue peace and harmony with your spouse at all costs. Sometimes that may mean not having your way simply to preserve peace in your home.

By seeking to establish peace by listening to your spouse instead of looking for an argument, you create an opportunity to build him or her up. Remember, listening helps you to learn more about your spouse—and yourself. However, you must apply what you learn in order to strengthen your relationship.

Build Up, Don't Tear Down

Train yourself to build up your spouse daily. Develop a list of 30 positive things you can say to encourage him or her. Every day for the next 30 days, speak something from that list. After 30 days have passed, begin again until it becomes a lifestyle. By "overloading" your mate with encouraging words and supportive actions, he or she will become convinced that you are genuinely concerned about their well-being and will more than likely return the favor!

Both husband and wife have the responsibility to preserve their relationship; however, as head of the household, *he* should always be the one to seek peace first. God holds the man responsible for what happens in the home. It's his duty to make sure his house is in order. He is the leader and should be the one to choose the "high road" when it looks like his marriage is heading in the wrong direction. It stands to reason that he should be the one who is quick to listen before an argument ensues.

Right vs. Wrong Listening

Is there such a thing as right and wrong listening? Yes. Right listening occurs when you maintain a positive attitude while listening to your spouse. Wrong listening occurs when you remain quiet, yet are formulating a response to "get back at" him or her. Sometimes, you can listen with the motive of looking for something to use against someone. That's very childish.

There are four basic principles for proper listening: (1) listening *intentionally*; (2) listening *attentively*; (3) listening *understandingly* and (4) listening *actively*.

1. Listening intentionally.

This is a conscious act of your will, because you're not *forced* to listen as you would be in a counseling session. Think of it as *purposeful* listening.

Set a specific time when you and your spouse can talk. Make that time sacred and don't allow anything to disturb it. It's part of your covenant together! This should not be a time to only deal with problems. If you do that, communication will be viewed as a negative experience instead of a positive one.

Use your talking times to share your hopes and dreams for the future. You can also talk about things you've done during the day, what you've been thinking about and how you feel about certain issues. Bedtime is usually good for most couples, especially those with children. Breakfast and dinnertime are other excellent opportunities. The point is to *purposefully* take the time to listen to your spouse and enjoy this element of your marriage. It'll be much easier to discuss any problems that arise.

2. Listening attentively.

This type of listening is done by eliminating distractions. There's nothing worse than sharing your feelings and intimate desires with your spouse only to be interrupted by the telephone, children, visiting friends and relatives or the television.

Giving each other your undivided attention is critical to effective communication. Therefore, maintain eye contact by sitting face to face. Attention says, "I love you more than anything else. Nothing is worth more than my time with you."

3. Listening understandingly.

Being an understanding listener involves having an open heart. To have an open heart means taking into consideration what you hear *and* making whatever adjustments are necessary to strengthen your relationship in that area.

When your spouse shares something with you that you may or may not agree with, let them know that you will seriously consider their point of view. Assure him or her that you understand what they are feeling and that you want to change in order to honor them.

Husbands, if your wife says, "Honey, I'd like some flowers and a card once in a while." Don't be quick to say, "But I gave you flowers last month! What more do you want?" The issue isn't the last time you gave her flowers. Instead, she's probably trying to communicate her need to receive tokens of love on a regular basis. Don't try to defend the fact that what you're doing is enough. Obviously this is an area that is very important to her. Your wife's language of love may be to receive gifts. Your job is to fulfill her desires. That's the bottom line!

Listening is an act of love.

Wives, the same is true for your husband's needs. Whatever he expresses to you, make it a point to satisfy that need. Let him know that you take him seriously and will do whatever it takes to make him happy.

Skillful listening involves a determined effort to perceive what your spouse is attempting to convey. When you don't understand what your spouse is saying, ask him or her to explain it to you further. An understanding listener will always take the facts into consideration and make the necessary changes.

4. Listening actively.

This last principle involves quickly acting upon what your husband or wife shares with you. Don't quickly forget the simple things your spouse has shared, such as helping with the chores or speaking words of encouragement. If you act on what you hear, it shows your spouse that you understood them.

Establish the following agreement between you and your mate: Never allow any need to go unmet when you know it exists. Regardless of the request, make it your mission to fulfill it. The fact that the request was made indicates that you have some work to do anyway. Simply demonstrate that you honor your spouse enough not only to consider what he or she has expressed, but that you're going to do something constructive about it.

Forgive and Forget

The greatest thing that you can do to establish effective communication is to forgive your mate of any wrong done or said to you. God took the time to forgive you of your sins and cleanse you of all unrighteousness. How much more should you be willing to forgive your mate? Based on what Jesus did for you on the cross, you should be willing to forgive him or her, regardless of what was said or done.

Unforgiveness will not only hinder God from forgiving you, but it will clog up the flow of His blessings into your life (Mark 11:25-26). Your mountain of circumstances won't budge when unforgiveness stands in the way. Unforgiveness is a major roadblock against true reconciliation in a marriage. Therefore, do yourself a favor and learn from the Apostle Paul's example: forget what is behind, and strive for what is ahead (Philippians 3:13).

It may not be easy to forgive, let alone forget; however, it's a necessity for success in marriage. Forget those things that hurt you; they're not worth holding on to! There's nothing worse than going through life overloaded with emotional baggage. It's time to experience the wholeness and peace that you have a right to in your marriage!

I've listed several communication dos and don'ts to help maximize communication in your relationship. Although this chapter has focused primarily on marital communication, keep in mind that these principles can be applied to any relationship.

Communication Do's and Don'ts

- **Do** make the Word of God your final authority.
- **Do** speak words of encouragement.
- **Do** communicate exactly what you feel, truthfully and with love.
- **Do** respect your spouse's opinions and thoughts and carefully consider his or her responses.
- **Do** your part to establish peace in the home.
- **Do** listen intentionally, attentively, understandingly and actively.
- **Do** forgive and forget.
- **Don't** go to bed angry.
- **Don't** allow anger or unforgiveness to fester.
- **Don't** walk away from your spouse in the middle of your discussion.

- **Don't** ignore your spouse.
- **Don't** interrupt.
- **Don't** yell or use sarcasm.
- **Don't** belittle your spouse's opinion.
- **Don't** discuss "your side of the story" with outsiders, such as relatives and friends.
- **Don't** make absolute statements, like "You never" and "You always." Instead, say, "I feel."
- **Don't** forget to pray and seek God's guidance.
- **Don't** give up, cave in or quit.

Successful communication between spouses produces a successful marriage.

Set aside 15 minutes to an hour of uninterrupted time with your spouse each day. Be sure to ask open-ended questions and give him or her your full attention. In addition, share an anecdote, story, joke or incident that occurred during the day to foster intimacy.

Proverbs 25:11

"A word fitly spoken is like apples of gold in pictures of silver."

8

No Rabbit Punches!
How to Fight Fair

friend of mine once said, "If you don't have personality conflicts, it's because you don't have a personality!" Personality conflicts are often the key reason for strife developing in a marriage. In the meshing together of two (sometimes) opposite personalities, arguments arise. However, it's not the arguments that destroy the marriage, but rather how the conflicts are handled and resolved.

In my pastoral counseling sessions over the years, I've discovered that many married couples either never received instruction in conflict resolution, or they ignored everything that was imparted into them. As a result, they resort to "fighting" in the only way they know how, and often with disastrous results.

If you don't know the proper way to resolve issues, chances are you'll probably act out in one of these four ways:

1. The Eskimo Style.

You freeze up and ignore the situation, hoping time will take care of it. You don't speak to your spouse directly, but instead withdraw emotionally and nurse a grudge because he or she couldn't read your mind. This is more commonly known as "the silent treatment."

2. The Cowboy Style.

You shoot 'em up and leave 'em for dead. By this I mean saying things in the heat of passion that you don't mean. It hurts your spouse and leaves a lot of damage. Usually there's a great deal of shouting.

3. The Houdini Style.

You are an escape artist! You don't like conflict and avoid it as much as possible. Rather than facing an issue head-on, you always say, "I'll just leave," then turn to drinking, shopping, television watching or excessive eating—*anything* to keep from dealing with the situation.

4. The World Boxing Association Style.

You handle conflict with your fists. You may begin to deal with an issue rationally, but your anger always gets the better of you. Before you know it, you've hit someone. If that's you, get help *now*. Under no circumstances should you resort to physical abuse!

Before I got married, I envisioned marriage to be a constant nest of love, complete with a picture-perfect house where Taffi and I would cuddle up in front of the fireplace listening to Lou Rawls in the background, and never have a disagreement of any kind. It didn't take long to find out that that wasn't real life! That's Hollywood!

Real-life marriages consist of two people coming together and being made one in the spirit and body—but not quite one in the soul! It is a relationship where there are two people with differing opinions, outlooks and backgrounds; however, all the while they trust God to help them face the storms and pleasures of life together. Having said that, you can see that marriages *will* have conflicts. So you had better train yourself on how to resolve them!

Say a Little Prayer

When a conflict arises, you need answers right away; and in the middle of a heated discussion, you know that you probably won't get them from your spouse! The first step toward resolution is *prayer*. Not the two-second kind you used to recite before bedtime when you were a child, but heartfelt, earnest, Word-based prayer. It's important to step away from the situation to hear from God. Often, couples are too angry to call a temporary truce in order to seek God, but it's still the best thing to do.

To begin, step away from the situation, gather your emotions and focus on God. If you must leave the room or go for a walk, do it! Then start praying, "Father, show me what's wrong." You'll be amazed at how He will cut the problem down to size. Human nature tends to cast blame on others and deny any personal guilt. But the Holy Spirit has an amazing way to bring balance and perspective to your situation.

Jesus spoke about this in Matthew 7:3-5. He asked, "...*why beholdest thou the mote in thy brother's eye, but considerest not the beam that is in thine own eye? Or how wilt thou say to thy brother, Let me pull out the mote out of thine eye; and, behold, a beam is in thine own eye? Thou hypocrite, first cast out the beam out of thine own eye; and then shalt thou see clearly....*"

God wants you to judge yourself in order to see clearly. No one wants to be told something is her fault or that he's wrong. It's human nature to respond in a negative way when accused. But when you back up and pray before allowing your emotions to get in the way, you are able to judge yourself so that you can clearly see the role you played in the situation.

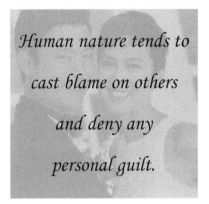

Human nature tends to cast blame on others and deny any personal guilt.

The best thing to do is to ask God, "Am I the problem? Am I being unreasonable? Am I being selfish?" As a pastor, I do that all the time. I ask, "God, where am I to take responsibility? Show me. Am I the problem?"

Your personal walk with the Lord determines the receptivity of your heart. When you are striving to put Him first in all things, you aren't able to tolerate being at odds with someone—especially your spouse. As a result, you'll do whatever it takes to be reconciled to others.

You know you are growing in the Lord and as a person when you can accurately judge yourself and take responsibility for the things you've done. That's how an individual matures. Once you see clearly and have judged yourself, you can take the next step.

Give Peace a Chance

Plan a formal peace conference in a quiet setting where you and your spouse can face your issue head on. Don't try to deal with anything when you are tired, stressed out or when the kids are around. *Schedule* time for your peace talks.

It's all right to put certain problems on the shelf until the time is right to deal with them. You may not be mature enough or have the right attitude the moment something happens. In that case, wait. Taffi and I often wait until the kids are in bed, and then go out for a quiet dinner or for a long walk so we can discuss the problem without interference.

After you've prayed and come together for the peace conference, there are some principles you must remember.

1. Maintain a positive outlook.

Dissolve all fear by reinforcing the positive. Begin by saying, "I love you with all of my heart, and I'm committed to our marriage. I want you to know that first and foremost." Don't start off your peace conference by saying, "When are you ever going to change?" Or, "You're just like your mama, and I don't know what to do with either of you." That's a declaration of war! Right away your spouse feels threatened, and now the two of you are fighting about an unrelated issue!

2. Be willing to take the blame.

Bring to your meeting whatever it is that you received from God in prayer. Acknowledge your role in the creation of the problem at hand and take responsibility for it. You can say something like, "Honey, the Lord told me to judge myself. I discovered I have a tendency to blame you for things because I want to protect my own feelings, and I don't want to take responsibility."

To resolve a conflict, you *must* take responsibility for your actions. Your spouse probably already knows what you've done, so go ahead and confess it to heal the situation.

3. Apologize.

Don't *ever* underestimate the power of an apology! A sincere apology produces great results. It heals, soothes, restores and brings back joy. Only a prideful person would have a hard time with it.

In case you don't know how to apologize, let me help you. Begin by saying, "I should have never said what I said. I'm sorry I was so selfish. My ego got in the way. Forgive me for blowing up in front of the kids. It's unfair for me to think that you can read my mind, and I apologize for misleading you." An apology is nothing more than admitting your wrongdoing and asking forgiveness for it. Once the apology is out, the two of you can make clear-cut rules to see that it never happens again.

4. Express hurt instead of hostility.

Hurt is a legitimate response to disappointment or offense. A lot of men like to hide the fact that they feel hurt. If you don't express those feelings, they will stay locked inside until they mature into anger, resentment and bitterness.

Anger is a secondary emotion. Whenever you feel angry, ask yourself why. People don't feel angry without a reason. Something started those feelings, and it is usually an unresolved hurt.

Your words reveal the hurt you have accumulated. You'll begin making snide or sarcastic comments or saying mean things, trying to make the other person feel as badly as you do. Deal with hurts as they arise. Ephesians 4:26 cautions us to avoid going to bed without resolving the issues that led to that hurt. Even if you have to say, "We'll talk about it tomorrow, but for now, please forgive me," that's better than sleeping on the couch or passing messages to your spouse through your children.

I'll never forget the time I went to bed mad at Taffi. Here I was lying on one side of the bed pretending to be asleep, while she was on the other side, doing the same thing. I was folding that pillow up and turning it all around, ready to spit out fire! But neither of us was talking. The only thing you could hear was my body tossing and turning on the mattress!

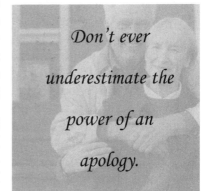

Don't ever underestimate the power of an apology.

The next morning I got up to pray, and the Lord wanted to know what I thought I was doing. He let me know that I had nothing to pray about until I apologized to her! I couldn't believe that! After all, the entire argument had been *her* fault! Instead, I knelt down in my place of prayer and tried to ignore Him. Wasn't that silly? Each time I tried to pray about something, God would respond, "Apologize to Taffi."

Finally, I couldn't stand to hear Him say the same thing over and over again. Some people say that in moments like that one, it feels as if their prayers are only hitting the roof; however, my prayers weren't even getting that high. So I got up and went in the bedroom to wake Taffi up and apologize to her. Once I started speaking, the words came very easy for me, and something in me broke. I had revealed my hurt and it felt good. In telling her that I was hurt, it destroyed the wall that our argument had built.

Unresolved hurts build walls. If you keep building that wall, it may take years to break it down. So knock it down and destroy it before it becomes fortified.

There is nothing weak about revealing what hurt you! Simply say, "What you did hurt me." You'll be surprised at what it will do for you. Once that hurt is dealt with, you won't have that weight hanging in your heart and mind.

5.   Make direct statements.

One definition of *integrity* is "straightforwardness." Hints and off-hand remarks accomplish very little. Say what you mean: "You hurt me when you decided to spend all night watching the Super Bowl." Don't hint and say something like, "Well, maybe I was a *little* disappointed when you spent all your time watching the game, but it's no big deal." And you know full well that you were ready to spit fire!

Say what you mean and mean what you say. That's the only way to resolve the conflict so your spouse will know to *never* do that again!

6.   Avoid absolute statements such as "always" and "never."

Peace talks are quickly sabotaged when you make accusatory statements like, "*You always* do this!" or "*You never* help me around the house!"

Using the words "you," "always" and "never" will immediately put your mate on the defensive. Instead, tell your spouse how you feel. "I *feel* left out of your life because of your work. I *feel* frustrated about our money situation. I *feel* overwhelmed by the household activities." This is a softer way to make your point and opens the door for further communication.

7.   Be solution-centered.

Have you ever met someone who was problem-centered? All the person wanted to do was talk about the problem rather than the solution. Instead of talking about what you *can't* do, focus on what you can do! Although the problem is real, it is the perfect opportunity to be a team player and put your problem-solving skills to work.

8.   Seek godly counsel.

Advice and guidance doesn't always have to come from church leaders; it can also come from mature believers. Although secular counseling is available, it is not always a good idea. It is best to seek counsel from someone that can give you good, seasoned and sound biblical advice.

A key point to remember is to seek counsel for yourself, not your mate. When people come to me and point the finger at their spouse, I shift my focus back to them. Why? Because "it takes two to tango." Problems in a marriage don't surface just because of one person. You're living in a fool's paradise if you think you can sit back and lay the blame on someone else without having to accept responsibility for your own actions.

You can also seek counseling from Christian professionals. Sometimes it takes a professional mediator to help destroy the walls you've built between each other. If you stick with it, you'll see results.

In addition, there is one key principle that will remain the same regardless of how many counseling sessions you go through. *Until you get the life of God inside of you and your spirit in line with God's Word, you will always be susceptible to the schemes of the devil.* Don't expect a lasting change in your marriage until you put the Word of God first in your life and make it your final authority. Only then will a lasting change take place in your heart, which will positively impact the future.

Guard Your Heart

The condition of your heart, or spirit, has a lot to do with the condition of your marriage (Malachi 2:14-15). When you accepted Jesus as your Lord and Savior, your spirit was made new, but that doesn't mean you automatically became a walking, talking Bible. It's your responsibility to put the Word in your heart so when trouble comes, that Word will spring up from within you and help you overcome that adversity. The Word is a lamp that will illuminate your steps (Psalm 119:105). It will instruct you on how to stand against the schemes of the devil.

The words you speak show the hurts you have accumulated.

When I was a young Christian and new to the Word, I was just as susceptible to temptation as I had been *before* I was saved. Just as a baby is unaware of how to protect itself, so too is a baby Christian unable to mount a defense against every attack of the devil. It takes time to develop discernment and the ability to battle through Word-based prayer.

This same thing is true of someone who does not actively spend time with

God studying His Word. For example, you're more susceptible to participating in gossip when you're not in the Word. But if your spirit is full, you turn away from it. You won't want to watch x-rated movies, look at pornographic magazines or have a desire to commit adultery. You won't even be tempted to drink, smoke, fornicate or take illegal drugs. The outside forces aren't the problem. The problem in your marriage comes from the inside out! You must guard your spirit by watching what you listen to, watch and speak!

Don't allow negative words to destroy the potential of your spirit. If "divorce" has been a regular part of your vocabulary, wipe it out. That word wounds your spirit and sets your course for future action. When you're not abiding by the principles outlined in God's Word, you'll eventually throw your hands up and say, "I'm fed up. I can't take it anymore."

Human nature tends to look for instant answers and quick fixes. Guarding your heart takes time and effort. The Word on the inside of you is what rises to the surface when strife and division try to separate you from your spouse! In the midst of doubt and confusion, in the midst of an argument, the spirit of faith will stand up and shout, "Not here!"

Filling your spirit with the Word of God makes the difference between your family staying intact or becoming another casualty of divorce. The devil is out to destroy married couples because marriage carries the image and imprint of God in it.

You are the very key to the outpouring of God's power in the earth. It's for this reason that you must do whatever is necessary to maintain a healthy and loving marriage.

* * * * *

Matthew 19:6 states that what God has joined together should not be separated. It is up to both the husband and wife to work together to develop a successful relationship and a harmonious home. I believe that as you put these principles to practice an anointing for success will arise in your household. As you fight the good fight for what is yours, your marriage will be a witness for the generations to come.

Conflicts arise even in the best of marriages. By resolving them quickly, hurt, anger, disappointment and division are obliterated.

Take a moment to think back to the last disagreement you had with your spouse. In which of the four ways did you act out: *Eskimo, Cowboy, Houdini* or *World Boxing Association?* Once you have identified your "style" for handling conflict, write down a few ways in which you can improve your skills. Share them with your spouse and post them in a place where you can see them. The next time you find yourself in a heated discussion, take a moment to review the items on your list and put them into practice.

Proverbs 15:1

"A soft answer turneth away wrath: but grievous words stir up anger."

9

WHAT EVERY MAN NEEDS
Fulfilling a Man's Needs in Marriage

Men and women have different needs. Although figuring out what they are can be a source of frustration to some, it's not as difficult as it appears to be. While it seems that men come from Mars and women from Venus, that doesn't mean you will *never* be able to figure out a man!

The Word of God tells you *everything* you need to know about the opposite sex. In fact, Genesis 3:17 says that because of Adam's failure to obey God's Word, the ground would be cursed and his labor would be hard. As a result, a man's greatest need is for *significance*. Men are task-oriented and measure success by what they achieve.

On the other hand, a woman's primary concern is to *nurture*; this usually occurs as she manages the home, imparts wisdom to her children and encourages her family. A man's way of nurturing is to provide. His main concern is money—does he make enough to keep the family secure? Is it enough to take care of the family's needs? The money he makes and the way he provides for those he loves is how he measures success and failure. If he's not a good provider, he often feels like a failure.

A man's greatest enemy is the pressure to perform. Most men are terrified of not being able to do their part, which has a direct impact on their self-worth. Many wives do not understand this fear and often react the wrong way. Men skillfully hide these feelings until they blow up; but if the wives can gain understanding, they can work together to build a healthier and more satisfying life.

Here are some basic principles that, when diligently applied, will show your husband that you love him and desire for him to be the best individual he can be.

Show Some R-E-S-P-E-C-T!

Everything a man *is* and *does* is tied to respect. He needs you to respect him because his self-worth hangs on it. To disrespect a man goes right to the heart of his being and drastically changes him because it wounds him and zaps his energy and desire to do things right.

I'm not talking about a husband who is a lazy, selfish and self-centered person. I'm referring to a man who has done his best to provide for and protect his wife and family. Although your husband will make mistakes along the way, that is no excuse for a condescending attitude or a complete disregard for his thoughts, feelings or opinions. When you respect his God-given position as the leader of your family, you are respecting God's order of authority.

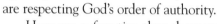

Men are task-oriented and measure success by what they achieve.

Here are a few tips that show your man respect:

1. Be his best friend.

If a man is feeling that "pressure," it's difficult for him to talk about it. When he does open up, be a non-judgmental listener while expressing love and concern for him. Help him to see that God has always brought the two of you through hard times, and He won't stop now. Show him through the Word that he is God's son and God is with him. Remind him that wisdom is the principle strength in his life; then pray together to receive the wisdom you need for the situation at hand.

Remember, you are his confidant. By confiding in you, he's putting his heart into your hands; therefore, treat it with honor and hold it carefully. He needs to know that you will not betray him by telling his business to an outsider such as a friend or other family member.

In addition, if your husband tells you that he needs something from you, respect what he tells you, whether you agree with him or not. Make the adjustments and do your best to meet that need.

2. Tell him he's significant.

A man needs to know that he matters and is very important to his family. If he thinks he is worthless, his significance as a man is depleted. He'll walk around feeling insecure, inferior and inadequate. *You* can change that by telling him how much you love him and need him in your life. You can also remind him that he matters greatly to you and your family.

3. Have a meek and quiet spirit.

First Peter 3:4 states that a meek and quiet spirit is of value to God. That doesn't mean you sit in a corner and never speak, but that you remain teachable, knowing when to allow your husband to take the lead!

Have you ever been in a place where the husband was asked a question but the wife answered it for him? That is embarrassing and detrimental to a marriage. I don't allow it to happen in my presence. If I ask a man a question and the woman steps up to answer it, I wait until she's finished, then I look at the man and ask the question again. If a woman is making all the decisions, then her husband cannot build his confidence and leadership in the Lord.

You may know more than your husband or have been a Christian longer; if that's the case, show your spiritual maturity and build your husband up. Give him the time to speak and let him lead.

4. Praise him publicly.

There's nothing as degrading as seeing a woman disrespect her husband in front of other people. It is absolutely wrong. The only thing that woman is showing is the hellish attitude inside of her.

Never criticize your husband in front of others or allow anyone else to do it either. A great deal of damage is done to a man when you put him down or disrespect him in front of others. Instead, stand up for your man and let him see you doing it. What you say about your spouse in the presence of others should always be positive. Brag about all of the wonderful things he's done for you and what he means to you.

Light His Fire

It's no secret that physical love is a primary need for men. But that doesn't mean he always wants to be the initiator. In fact, he wants *you* to be the aggressor too!

You can surprise him by pouncing on him at unexpected moments, such as when he's stepping out of the shower, walking in the front door or vacuuming the den. Men love that! Your husband needs you to communicate that you are just as interested in sexual activity with him as he is with you! By whispering in his ear, sneaking up and hugging him from behind, or kissing him passionately before he leaves for work, you let him know that you think he's just as attractive to you now as he was when you married him.

Make him feel like he's the best thing that ever came into your life! Stop being shy and proposition him. Meet him one day at the door and grab him!

Never criticize your husband in front of others or allow anyone else to do it either.

Don't be put off if he tries to brush you off by saying, "No, don't play with me. I'm tired." Just tell him to hush up, then take him and throw him down on the bed! You'll be amazed at how energetic he'll become. All that pressure and exhaustion he thought he was feeling will fly right out the window!

Taffi can still make me blush! There are times when I'll be standing at the pulpit making closing remarks and she'll wink at me! That's when I start blushing and stuttering like a schoolboy, and she'll smile and wink again. I have to turn around sometimes just to get myself together. Men love that!

In addition, don't be afraid to admire your husband and share that admiration with him. I love it when Taffi tells me how handsome she thinks I am. She'll stand back and say, "Oooh! Look at my fine husband!" I smile and say, "Ah, hush girl." But the truth is I hang on her every word. I walk to the car with my head a little higher because my woman thinks I'm handsome. Ladies, do that for your husband!

Even if you may not feel like initiating or participating in sex, be *willing* to get in the mood. God invented sex not just for procreation, but for fun and to strengthen the bond between a husband and wife. The Holy Spirit can help you get in the mood. A quick, two-second prayer for help to meet your husband's needs will ensure that he will reciprocate by meeting yours.

Indulge in Hugs and Kisses

Don't think that a man doesn't need hugs and kisses from a woman. This kind of non-sexual touching is reassuring and makes him feel that everything he's done that day was worth it. When he comes home, throw your arms around him and just kiss awhile. Make him drop his briefcase at the door!

When I get home from a meeting after I've been gone all week, I look forward to my family's homecoming celebration. Deep down I want them to stop what they are doing and line up at the door to greet me. Hug me, kiss me, laugh with me, spoil me and shower me with attention! It doesn't matter what problems might be going on, when a man's family shows love to him, those problems stay outside the door!

Initiate the hugging and the kissing. If your husband wasn't raised to show affection that way, he may remain stiff at first. Just tell him to loosen up because you *know* that he likes it! As you continue to show him love, over time those walls of not knowing how to receive affection will come crashing down. Be the tool of love in your household and break down barriers with it. Not only does your man need it, it's just plain fun!

Understand Him

Your man needs you to understand *why* he does what he does and feels the way he feels about things. Listen to him when he talks. Watch what he does. Take notice of the ways in which he is trying to show you love.

Try to understand what he deals with on a daily basis. Is there a quota he has to meet? Are there clients he has to impress? Is his boss demanding or unfair? What is involved in the work he does? What are the challenges? Once you understand these things, you've gained insight into his world and he will want you to be a part of it.

An Eye-Opening Experience

Some people think that all I do as a pastor is pray and preach. At the beginning of my ministry, Taffi couldn't understand why I was so tired when I got home. Even *she* thought all we did was write Bible studies! After coming on staff, however, she saw that ministry work involved everything from negotiating business contracts and buying office supplies to banking, counseling and even refereeing.

Now when we hear people saying how wonderful and easy it is to work in a ministry, we just smile and say "God has equipped us for every good work!"

So take the time to see what's happening in your husband's life. Only then can you develop the sensitivity that comes with understanding.

Care for His Castle

I'm sure you've heard the expression, "A man's home is his castle." This is actually a true statement. A man needs a clean and orderly home. Ladies, you are the ones with the "nesting" ability—the ability to create a warm, relaxing and nurturing environment—so make your nest beautiful. If you have the luxury of not having to work outside the home, don't sit around eating candy and watching Oprah all day! Clean the house and make it attractive! If both of you work, you can make a list to share the responsibilities. But if not, the job is yours.

A messy house clutters the mind. It can make a tired person even more so. The atmosphere you create in your home can soothe a person's mind, body and spirit. Take pride in how clean and orderly your house is. As a woman, that is your domain. It shows what you value. Make your house an inviting place that your husband can't wait to return to.

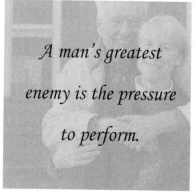

A man's greatest enemy is the pressure to perform.

Make Him Laugh

Never forget to laugh and have fun. There's a boy in every man and he still likes to have fun. Don't let financial circumstances, children or other issues wear you out. A great sense of humor often diffuses a stressful situation. Rather than allowing your situation to depress you, do something out of the ordinary instead.

For example, jump into a pile of autumn leaves, tickle each other, tell a joke or talk about funny things that have happened. You'll feel much better when you laugh every day. Your man needs that humor to add balance to his life. In addition, humor makes you appealing to your husband. He wants a partner he can laugh with.

Trust Your Man

If a woman tells her husband that she trusts him, there's nothing he won't do for her. Trust is directly tied to a man's ability to achieve. It's the fuel that gets him to the same old job every day, trying to put his family ahead.

Maybe he's done something in the past that damaged or destroyed your trust in him. If he's making the effort to regain your trust, then honor his effort. While it's true that trust cannot be rebuilt overnight, you must strive to put it back together brick by brick. Let him know that you forgive him, and are willing to make a fresh start. Trust is vital to him, and he must know that his woman believes in him no matter what and is willing to follow him as he follows the Lord.

After God, your first priority is your husband—not your job, children or church commitments.

A woman who trusts her husband believes he will never betray her, and she is free to be her best for him and love him unconditionally. Do you trust God? Then apply that same trust with your husband and let him know it.

Stay Attractive

Time takes its toll on everyone. When you are 50, you don't look like a 20 year-old anymore. It may take a little bit more work to get there, but the principles of staying attractive should never change.

A man needs his wife to look good. Remember how you were when he was dating you? You made sure every hair was in place. This behavior shouldn't change just because you're married to the man. For example, if he saw you dressed in a nightshirt and curlers before he left for work, don't let him come home seeing you the same way. That's why some secretaries start looking good to their bosses—at least they put on make-up!

Take care of yourself, no matter what your age might be. If you have put on a few pounds because of your children or bad eating habits, lose them. If you need to cover your gray, do it. If make-up makes you look irresistible, wear it. Buy perfume or scented bath beads and perfume your skin. A man is attracted to how good you smell, and your husband needs that stimulation. He needs you to look your best for him. He wants to be the envy of other men when he's walking down the street, holding your hand. Yes, he's already proud of you and loves you—but it doesn't hurt to give him an extra bonus and look good too!

It's hypocritical to try to be meek and godly *outside* of your home without first developing the same attitude *in* your home with your husband. You shouldn't try to help others without knowing what your own husband needs and doing your best to fulfill those needs. God is looking for genuine people willing to work on the real issues of life. After Him, your first priority is your husband—not your job, children or even church commitments!

* * * * *

Remember, the degree of harmony in your marriage will be in direct proportion to how your husband's needs are met. You can solve 95% of the conflicts in your home by identifying his needs and fulfilling them. Stop waiting to stumble into a "heaven on earth" and instead work to make it a reality in your marriage!

A man's greatest need is for significance. He measures success by what he has achieved and his ability to provide; as a result, he is driven by the pressure to perform.

For the next week, make an effort to carefully observe your husband, making mental notes as to his preferences, habits and particular behavior patterns. At the same time, think about the needs listed in this chapter and how you have or have not met them in the past. Use the knowledge you have gained through this chapter and your observations and put together a plan of action. Cut out funny comics, write out the lyrics to "your" song, purchase a few items of sexy lingerie or obtain your husband's favorite recipe and surprise him with what you have collected. Be sure to continue what you've started by making him and his needs a priority in your life.

Proverbs 11:25

"The liberal soul shall be made fat: and he that watereth shall be watered also himself."

10

HER NEEDS
Fulfilling a Woman's Needs In Marriage

P
roverbs 18:22 states, *"Whoso findeth a wife findeth a good thing, and obtaineth favour of the Lord."* Traditionally, many of us have interpreted this scripture to mean that the *good thing* is a wife. In the *King James Version* of the Bible, however, the word "thing" is italicized, meaning it was *added* to the original text. The scripture actually reads, *"Whoso findeth a wife findeth a good and obtaineth favor of the Lord."* The "thing" that is referred to here is marriage. If you're in a marriage, then you've found something good and have obtained favor of the Lord.

That misinterpretation has caused some men to treat their wives like a "thing" by *lording over* them—putting on airs—instead of being the lord *of* them. By rank, the man *is* the head of the family, but he's not the lord. Even God doesn't mistreat us in that way!

Walking down the aisle and saying, "I do" doesn't automatically impart the knowledge of *how* to be a good husband. That comes with time and with a great deal of communication between you and your wife. Contrary to what you may have heard, it *is* possible for a man to understand a woman.

What a Girl Wants

Genesis 3:16 gives us the reason why women think and act the way they do. *"Unto the woman he said, I will greatly multiply thy sorrow and thy conception; in sorrow thou shalt bring forth children; and thy desire shall be to thy husband, and he shall rule over thee."*

A wife has two primary concerns: the family and security. Because the woman was created from the rib of the man, her needs are met through close, meaningful relationships. Family is important to her. Her "desire to her husband" means that she longs for an intimate friendship and relationship with him. The "sorrow" in rearing her children means that their safety, education and well-being is of great concern.

With those things in mind, it's easy to see why a sense of security is so important to a woman. Although she may marry a man who gets paid on commission, she'd feel more comfortable with a steady paycheck. By the same token, she may settle for an apartment, but what she'd prefer is a home big enough for the family. As long as it belongs to them, she's happy.

A wife has two areas of concern: the family and security.

If you don't understand how your wife is made, it will be easy to dishonor and abuse her. If you demean her in her role of nurturer by saying she is "babying" the children, or criticize her concern for the security of the family as frivolous worry, you will only drive a wedge between the two of you.

God has given you special insight on how to treat your wife. He knew that a man's nature prefers to hear "just the facts." That's why He gave them to you in one scripture. *"Husbands, love your wives, even as Christ also loved the church, and gave himself for it"* (Ephesians 5:25). The key to a better relationship lies in two words: *even as.* Think of how powerful that is! In what ways does God show His love to you?

You may be thinking, "Yeah, but that's God! I'm just a man!" While that may be true, God still requires that you love your wife *even as* He loves the body of Christ. Let me share with you how He wants it done.

Apply the "Even As" Principle

Most people think that love is based on *feelings.* Think back to the first time you saw your wife and how you felt while you were courting her. Didn't it feel good just to be with her? You couldn't wait until the next time you saw or spoke to her. You did everything you could to make yourself more attractive to her because you wanted her to feel about you the same way you felt about her. Even in the early years of your marriage you couldn't seem to get enough of her.

Over the years, however, the intensity of your *feelings* may have dwindled, or in some cases, disappeared completely. But that doesn't mean you don't still love your wife! Love is *more* than feelings—it's a commitment. In order for us to truly love our wives, we have to understand the love Jesus has for the Church.

The Greek word for *love* is *agape.* It describes the love of God as a giving, serving type of love. Think of what Jesus did for you and me. He saw us in our sinful state and said, "I'm going to take care of these people by cleansing them and not only giving them eternal life with Me, but also everything they need to enjoy life." He didn't care where we came from and He never gets tired of being with us. He showed us what real love was and what a real man does for those he cares about.

Verse 28 says, "*So ought men to love their wives as their own bodies. He that loveth his wife loveth himself.*" How do you take care of yourself? By establishing and sticking to a regular exercise regimen, eating nutritional meals and getting the proper amount of sleep. You don't wear yourself out deliberately or try to make yourself sick. Neither do you give yourself a black-eye or belittle yourself. That's exactly how you ought to treat your wife. The scripture says that men should love their wives "*...as their own bodies.*"

Your actions should match the words you speak. If you tell your wife that you love her, you should back it up with action. The more you learn how Jesus loved the Church, the more capable you will be to love your wife. When you repeatedly give and show love, nothing can stop you from enjoying the peace and happiness your actions bring!

I want you to think about the principles I've just mentioned. Then I want you to work on fulfilling the following needs.

Spend Time With Her

Hasn't God always been there when you needed to talk with Him? When your wife wants to talk, she wants and needs you to listen and be there for her. Don't ignore her because there's a game on television or a good article in the newspaper. Remember, her basic needs are for closeness and security. Your wife wants to feel that she has a best friend in you. Maybe she just wants to hear your perspective on an issue she's dealing with. Perhaps she wants to discuss one of the children or tell you a funny story. Although it may not seem like a big deal to you, being able to discuss and share even the little things with you fosters a sense of intimacy and trust within her. Honor her in this.

If you don't understand how your wife is made, it will be easy to dishonor or abuse her.

In addition, keep in mind that women love to relate, and it could be that's what she's trying to do when she asks you to explain a football game to her. She knows you love football. Instead of getting upset, appreciate the fact that she's trying to understand something you like. Don't be irritated when she asks about a term or a move in the middle of the game! Don't say, "Can't you see that I'm watching this? Ask me at halftime and I'll tell you."

That is no way to treat your wife! She's the one that cleans your clothes, trains your children and cooks your meals. Be wise enough to realize that she is trying to relate to you! Take the time to listen and talk with her. She notices how you treat other women; therefore, you'd better take more time with the one you chose to be with forever! She deserves respect, reverence and kindness!

If you're in a job where people ask for your advice or seek direction all day, be careful to not shut your wife out when you get home. She'll want to discuss things also, but don't isolate her because you're too exhausted from talking all day. Remember, *she* is your first priority. I've seen some men who use the ministry as an excuse for not having time for their wives. If you put the ministry or your job above your wife, you are committing adultery and are out of God's order for the family.

Communication is very meaningful to your wife and indulging her fulfills her need for oneness. If your wife is being fulfilled, then everyone else is going to be happy too!

Women do not equate love with sex.

Be Her Soul Mate

You should endeavor to be so close to your wife that the two of you are thinking the same things at the same time. It is possible to be so unified in your spirit that when you open your mouth to say something, she is able to finish the sentence. There have been times when I've started humming a song, and when I go upstairs, Taffi is singing the same one! That kind of oneness comes from the time you've spent with your spouse, becoming her best friend and enjoying your lives together.

Play Romeo to Her Juliet

Your wife is not a sex machine, although that's how many men tend to treat their spouses. All he wants her to do is cook, clean and have sex. He may not speak to her all evening, but once the lights go out, he turns into some cooing, coaxing animal!

To a woman, romance doesn't mean sex. For example, she still likes all the corny things you used to do before you were married, like holding hands or hugging. She still likes the romantic cards, the phone calls to say, "I love you," or watching the sunset. Those things don't go out of style just because you got married!

If your wife asks, "Why don't we do that anymore?," it's a good sign that Romeo needs to make an appearance. Of course, this may not be the easiest thing to do when you have a mountain of bills to pay, children to care for and a high-pressure job. But if you cut romance out of your relationship, you're missing one of the greatest pleasures in life!

A woman desires non-sexual touching in order to make her feel special. A hug doesn't always have to lead to sex! Control your libido and kiss her gently without expecting anything in return. Run your fingers through her hair. You don't have to say anything; just show love to her with a soft caress. Or stop what you are doing and gaze at her for a minute, then tell her how beautiful she is.

When a wife "wears the pants" in the house, it means her husband isn't doing his job.

Don't allow yourself to become so busy that you don't kiss her like you used to! Call her during the day just to hear her voice. Walk in while she's cooking dinner or dressing the children, and say to her, "Have I told you today how much I love you and how blessed I am to be your husband?" Talk about a melt-down! Women love those things!

Foreplay doesn't begin in the bed; it begins early in the morning and lasts all day. You must first make love to a woman's mind and emotions with words, affection and tokens of love. Then when you get to the bedroom, you can enjoy the physical manifestation of your effort.

Years ago I experimented with this principle with Taffi by romancing her all day long with phone calls, flowers and notes. On my way home I gave her a courtesy call. She shocked me by saying, "Bring it on home, Reverend." I gasped, "Sista' Dollar!" She answered, "Sista' Dollar, nothing. Hurry up and bring yourself on home. I'll meet you with a headlock at the door!" I'm telling you, this thing works!

As men, we've made the mistake of trying to get what we want from our wives without planting the seed for it. As believers, we plant seeds for the things we desire. Everything in life—especially marriage—functions by this principle of seedtime and harvest. If you desire a better relationship with your spouse, you must plant the right seeds!

Put on the Apron

The day you got married, you formed a partnership with your wife that affects every area of your life—even housework!

Whatever she asks you to do around the house, do it. Don't pout or sulk while you are helping, either. Many men tend to agree to perform a certain task, but they often ensure that everyone is just as miserable as they are while they're performing it! Take the initiative to do something *before* she asks you, like taking out the garbage, loading and unloading the dishwasher, vacuuming, folding clothes or even cooking a simple meal. It may seem like a petty thing to you, but your initiative will impress her and stay in her mind for months.

Send Her Packing!

You may not realize how much your wife actually does around the house. To give you a greater understanding of how much she does for you, send her packing for a weekend. Surprise her on a Friday morning with a map, the keys to a rental car and a hotel confirmation number. Depending on where you are sending her, be creative with your presentation. For example, place these items in a beach pail or ski boot. Reassure her that you will be in charge, and the one who will take care of everything (including the children!) while she is away.

In addition, be sure to clean up before she returns from her mini vacation. Dust, vacuum and have dinner ready when she arrives. You may wish to greet her at the door with a kiss and a hug to let her know how much you missed her, or have the kids make a "Welcome Home" banner and string it across the doorway where she will be sure to see it.

You'll not only quickly realize how much work she does around the house, you'll also discover how much you need and miss her—and vice-versa!

Some of you have wives who work a full-time job outside the home, only to return in the evening to work another eight hours cooking, doing laundry, taking care of the kids and paying some of the bills. The irony is that you'll be upset with her for falling asleep as soon as her head hits the pillow!

If you want more attention from your wife, help her help you. Take on some of the responsibility. Don't work your eight hours and then come home and watch television the rest of the night! Let her know you appreciate her by taking your share of the chores. This also means helping her with the children. If you've just had a new baby, don't expect her to give birth and then get up at all hours of the night to feed and change it! If she asks you for help, don't look at her like she's crazy and say something silly like, "I don't know how." The school is open, brother! Believe me, she is more than willing to show you how. A good father does more than just donate his sperm.

In addition, take your rightful position as the head of the house. That means taking an active role in the lives of your family members—especially your children. Know who their friends are, how they're doing in school and what activities they like to take part in. Reassure your wife that the two of you are a team. Pray the prayer of agreement with her regarding the children, and stand firm with it. If there's a situation that needs your guidance and discipline, quickly step in.

There are demonic spirits that are specifically assigned to households and marriages with the intention of hindering or harassing them. I remember when our eldest daughter, Jordan, kept getting up during the night because she couldn't sleep. One particular evening after Taffi had put Jordan back to bed again, she commented to me, "I don't know why she keeps getting up." All of a sudden I realized what was happening. I quickly got out of bed and went into my daughter's room. I took authority over the evil spirits that had been assigned to my household and commanded them to go. Jordan slept like a baby after that and was never bothered again.

Men, you have a role to fulfill in your household. Your home is more than a place for you to rest and sleep. It is your "Garden of Eden," and just like Adam, God desires you to care for it by taking dominion over any evil that comes against it.

Understand Her

Tradition says that the wife is supposed to adapt herself to the man, while he just goes along his merry way in life. That's wrong. My marriage was revolutionized after I began to understand Taffi's needs as a woman.

There are two scriptural reasons why you must understand her needs. First, you can't love your wife as God requires unless you understand what she wants and needs; and second, you can't submit "...one to another in the fear of God" unless those needs are met (Ephesians 5:21).

You now know that a woman is primarily concerned with security and family. In addition, she needs intimacy within that family. This adds up to one principal need—being cherished.

Fear and insecurity come when her sense of security, intimacy and her need to be cherished are threatened or unmet. If your wife is fearful, evaluate the situation. Ask yourself these questions:

- What need is not being met?
- Are you being transparent with her, telling her everything, or is she hearing it from someone else?
- Are you telling her how you feel or what you're thinking?
- Are you cherishing her?
- Does she feel financially secure? Do you have a steady income?
- Are you taking care of your home?
- Are you taking better care of her or your car?

Once you've understood her basic needs, don't belittle them! Accept your wife the way she is. Husbands who demean their wives for worrying would do well to remind themselves that the pressures they feel are in reality their own fears.

Help her to grow in her trust with God. Listen to her concerns, and then confidently point her to the Word. Make her feel like you are privileged to know the information she's confiding to you. It's a great blessing to your wife to feel understood by you.

Don't get caught up in thinking you are "the man of the house" and that she needs to get over whatever she's feeling and "just submit." Do you know what it means when your wife submits to you? It means that your relationship with her is established and developed, and she knows without a shadow of a doubt that you'll come through for her. She trusts you.

If a wife "wears the pants" in the house, the man isn't doing his job. I've noticed that most women *want* to submit. A wife *wants* to look up to her husband and say, "That's my man. That's my lover. That's the father of my children." Don't make it hard for her to do so!

* * * * *

Your wife is a treasure waiting to be discovered. If you treat her like a queen, she'll make you feel like a king. But that won't happen until you get in the Word and begin loving your wife as Christ loves the Church. There's nothing more priceless than a successful and prosperous relationship between a husband and wife!

A woman's needs are met through close, meaningful relationships and by providing her with a sense of stability and security.

Think of the ways in which you can show your wife that you love her. Make a list of seven different things you can do, and use one a day for the next week. It can be something as simple as cooking a meal, taking care of the children for a day to give her a break, giving her a massage or leaving a love note in her purse. In addition, you may want to set aside time during the day or evening to allow her the opportunity to blow off steam. Listen attentively, ask open-ended questions and avoid trying to offer your opinion or solving the problem. Practice being a shoulder she can cry on to foster trust and intimacy between the two of you.

Ephesians 5:25, 28

"Husbands, love your wives, even as Christ also loved the church, and gave him-self for it...So ought men to love their wives as their own bodies. He that loveth his wife loveth himself."

11

LET'S GET PHYSICAL
Strategies for Passionate Lovemaking

G od invented sex as a blessing to you. And just like all of His other gifts, it is something that should be enjoyed and improve with time.

I am going to be very explicit in this chapter, because if you don't learn about sex from God's perspective, you *will* learn about it from the world's view. In fact, there is a high probability that many of you learned about intercourse in a variety of ways, such as watching television or movies, indulging in pornography, hearing stories and jokes from other people or attending mandatory health classes in school.

Regardless of the method of education, the objective remains the same: God not only established sex for the purpose of creating children, He also meant it as an act of physical pleasure to be enjoyed within the framework of marriage.

It's a shame that the Church has not taught on sex more thoroughly. As a result of this lack of training, many believers are left to follow the advice of sex therapists, talk show hosts, friends and magazine columnists. A born-again Christian should not use secular methods to figure out something that God created for him or her, because they are no longer equipped to operate in that way! You wouldn't go to a chef and ask him the ins and outs of coaching football, would you? Of course not!

There is a better way to learn about sex. In fact, everything you need to know about the subject is in the Bible, and it is very specific (Hebrews 13:4; Genesis 4:1; Proverbs 5:15-20; Song of Solomon; 1 Corinthians 7:1-7).

Learn the Basics

Sex is designed to first take place between you and your spouse on your honeymoon, *after* you have been joined together by marriage before God and your friends and families. It seals your vows to one another and joins you together as one person in spirit, soul and body.

One of the first things God commanded Adam and Eve to do was to be fruitful and multiply (Genesis 1:28). He desired for them to enjoy one another physically and in the process, have babies. This means that because sex is good in God's sight, it is also good within the framework of your marriage. The physical intimacy that takes place between husband and wife reinforces the commitment between them while providing pleasure and satisfaction.

When sex takes place *outside* of the marriage covenant, God's original plan is perverted, or twisted, and is no longer a good thing. An act that was originally intended for the mutual gratification of two spouses now becomes adultery, fornication (premarital sex) and in some cases, rape. This violation of a spiritual law ends with a gradual change in personality, including the way you dress and what you desire. In addition, your relationship with God suffers as your focus shifts from Him to your next encounter. And the threat of disease or pregnancy causes added stress and a change in lifestyle.

Forget what you've learned about sex from locker rooms or associations with friends and relatives.

Most people forget the emotional aspect of sex because they are so focused on the physical pleasure it brings. They think that "safe sex" involves the use of a variety of birth control methods, such as the Pill or a condom. The truth is, there is *no such thing* as safe sex. No prophylactic or other method of birth control has proven to be 100% effective on its own. Even condoms offer an individual some risk of contracting a venereal disease, as they do not completely cover a man's genitals (his scrotum) and they can rupture! And they certainly cannot protect you from emotional entanglements. The only truly safe sex is abstinence.

Make Love, Not War

Every couple should know how to make love in a way that is honorable and brings satisfaction for both the husband and wife. A reinforcement of the love they share should be the focal point in sexual fulfillment. Without it, sex will be unsatisfying.

This God-kind of love is centered around giving. It says, "I want to please *you* more than myself." It is not concerned with its own selfish interests, motives or agenda. Love is more concerned with meeting your spouse's needs than your own.

Great sex is not something that just *happens*, and it certainly is not a skill that comes naturally. It's erroneous to think you can just hop into bed with your spouse and have an earth-shattering experience right away. As with most things in life, pleasurable lovemaking takes practice. In addition, it must be properly understood through detailed explanation, effective communication *and* experimentation.

Talk It Out

How well do you know your spouse—sexually, that is? Marriage relationships should free you and your mate of inhibitions where making love is concerned. The key to passionate lovemaking is *effective communication*. Rid yourselves of sexual fears and myths by talking about sex as often as the subject arises. Spend enough time discussing your likes and dislikes. Feel free to express your most intimate sexual desires.

When it's time to make love, put into practice what you've discussed. Remember that each preference you act out on will benefit your relationship and bring you closer together as you foster trust and arouse passion. And be sure to take your time! Don't rush—you have a lifetime to experiment and enjoy one another!

Couples need to understand and discuss what arouses and gratifies them. Ignorance regarding the purpose and passion behind lovemaking often causes some to view sex as a "dirty" act or something to dread. This negative mindset closes the individual off from his or her spouse, causing them to be labeled as "frigid." Making love should be enjoyable for all, not drudgery.

Sexual fulfillment starts by understanding that men and women differ in their basic sexual and emotional needs. For a man, making love generally means five specific things:

1. **Satisfaction of his sexual drive.**
2. **Fulfillment of his manhood.**
3. **Enhancement of his love for his wife.**
4. **Reduction of friction in the home.**
5. **Provides life's most exciting experience.**

For a woman, it provides:

1. **Fulfillment of her womanhood.**
2. **Reassurance of her husband's love.**
3. **Enhancement of her love for her husband.**

With these facts in mind, the following questions can be answered: How should intercourse begin? What should you do or never do? What can guarantee satisfaction? What happens when intercourse is completed?

You have God's permission to enjoy sex with your mate. So let's review the process of lovemaking and study each phase carefully.

Enforce the Privacy Act

Before lovemaking can begin, there must be privacy. That's something that is very important to a woman. Her mind has to be clear and able to concentrate on what's going on.

Get rid of any distractions. Take the phone off the hook and make sure the children are gone, in bed or being entertained. Ensure that your bedroom door has a lock on it. If it doesn't, then train your children to knock before they enter. Let them know that if your door is closed, they must knock and wait for a response before entering.

Don't allow distractions to disrupt you. Treat this time with honor and plan ahead to optimize privacy. Create the setting for a rapturous encounter with your spouse.

Rev Up Your Engines

Arousal takes place during the period called "foreplay," or sexual stimulation. What happens during this phase determines the level of satisfaction during penetration. This is the time to communicate your preferences, because men and women think, respond and act differently. Here's what I mean.

It's common knowledge that men can become easily aroused because they are *visually* stimulated. They are just like a rodeo. The minute the gate lifts up, the horse comes charging out! But that's how a man is. The minute he sees his wife, he's ready. Just the sight of her is all the stimulation he needs.

A woman is totally different. She may love and desire her man and think he's attractive, but it still takes her more time to become aroused. A woman is stimulated by *touch* and *emotion*. She likes to be romanced and seduced during this time. She is not in a rush. It's important for her spouse to be gentle and patient, not forceful or rushed. His tenderness is what prepares his wife for the sexual act itself.

Men, you must control your desires during the arousal stage and not jump ahead. You might be saying, "But Dr. Dollar, you don't understand!" Believe me, I *do* understand! But it's the love and concern you have for your wife's pleasure that will make you contain yourself.

The only reason a man would be in a hurry is out of selfishness or lust. You cannot experience the fullness of lovemaking when selfishness is involved. God wants you to have passionate, enjoyable sex because He created it to be that way. It isn't the time to be crude, abusive or mechanical. It's a time to patiently experiment. If she requests for you to touch certain areas, do it. Pay attention to her responses. A sigh or moan lets you know you're on the right track. Wherever she needs your touch, do it tenderly. Play with each other by kissing, embracing, petting and fondling.

Also, stimulating the clitoris, which is a part of the vagina, arouses a woman. Scientists have discovered that this is the "sexual seat" for the woman's orgasm, or sexual peak. The man's orgasm is not enough for both to have true fulfillment. This is one area of your wife's body that must be stimulated for her to have an orgasm as well. Keep in mind that it may take a while for her to have one, as women take longer to peak than men; however, they are capable of multiple orgasms and they usually last much longer. A lack of an orgasm, however, should not be perceived as failure, either. Lovemaking can be just as pleasurable without one.

During foreplay, the man's penis is usually erect. But just because it's erect doesn't mean that it's the time for penetration into the vagina. Remember, the wife must be aroused as well. As the husband, make sure your hand or your penis stimulates the clitoris of your wife so she can come to the place of excitement.

Pornography: A Trap For Men Only?

When most people think of pornography, they think of men, masturbation and the action in XXX movies and magazines. While it's true that many men indulge in these practices, even after they have tied the knot, it is not true that they are the only ones who do it.

Women also indulge in pornography and masturbation; however, these take the form of romance novels, soap operas and vibrating machinery designed to stimulate the clitoris and bring a woman to orgasm. Both indulging in pornography and masturbation are practices that go against the Word of God. In addition, they rob your spouse of his or her right to stimulate and arouse you. Whether you are male or female, as a Christian, you are to control your fleshly desires and conduct yourself in a manner that is pleasing to God. It's difficult to do this when you are continually filling your mind with sexually explicit material.

The next time you are tempted to watch or read pornography or masturbate, reach for the Word of God, instead. Concentrate on scriptures that talk about self-control, power over temptation and your body being the temple of the Holy Spirit. In addition, put away sexually explicit material and avoid conversations, areas or associations that may cause you to cave in.

By watching what you listen to, read and watch or the words you speak, you gain control over your mind, the control center of your life!

Enjoy the Plateau

This is the time when excitement is heightened, the nipples are firm and blood begins to flow into different areas of the body, particularly the genitals. In a man, the penis become fully erect; in a woman, her clitoris begins to swell and the vagina secretes a clear, natural lubricant in preparation for penile penetration. Gentle caressing of these areas will greatly increase sexual excitement.

The Big "O"

The orgasm is the explosive stage where all things work and come together in their fullness.

For a man, the orgasm comes when he ejaculates semen. For a woman, it is an explosive feeling that has reached its peak through clitoral stimulation. Once orgasm has reached its height, it is a place of no return. Its earth-shattering feeling doesn't end until the ejaculation has taken place for the man and runs its course for the woman.

If the husband is experiencing an orgasm too quickly, ejaculation can be delayed by gently squeezing the head of the penis *before* penetration. Otherwise, orgasm can be controlled only by position: missionary (man on top), side-by-side, seated or standing (with the wife slightly elevated).

For a woman, the position that offers her the greatest control over orgasm is when she is on top of the man. This allows the husband to relax and control himself while permitting the wife to initiate the movement necessary to give her the most stimulation by forcing her clitoris over the penis. The friction of the penis rubbing her clitoris ignites the orgasm within her.

It's usually easy for a man to have an orgasm. If he is having trouble, he should add more zinc to his diet and get the vitamins, minerals and rest his body needs. In addition, talking about daily challenges or issues helps in relieving stress. If that doesn't work and the problem persists, he may wish to seek medical attention or counseling. God intended for the husband to be fulfilled in a sexual relationship with his wife, and he should do all that is necessary to experience that. As a side note, keep in mind that what works for one person may not work for everyone. Therefore, be sure to consult your physician before making any dietary changes.

The most important part of intercourse is not the act itself—it's what happens before and after that matters.

If a woman is not experiencing an orgasm on a regular basis, there may be several reasons for it: ignorance regarding her right to enjoy sex, unawareness of what stimulates her to the point of excitement, or even a husband who is rushing her through their sexual experience. He may be satisfied after a few minutes, but she's left without a climax.

Another reason for a lack of orgasms could stem from the woman's need for affection not being met. As a result, she may be dealing with anger, resentment and unforgiveness. In addition, mistrust (due to abuse, neglect or adultery) or fear of letting go may be other root causes.

Sometimes passivity causes wives not to experience orgasms, because they've not communicated to their husbands what they need for stimulation. Even the best of husbands can't read your mind. An orgasm is not going to just fall out of the sky. Wives, tell your husbands what you need, and if you have to, show him how.

Fatigue is a factor for many wives. Often the demands of motherhood, work or marriage can exhaust even the most energetic individual. That's why proper rest is so important. If a nap is needed in order to be ready to make love, then do it! Being overweight also hinders a woman from feeling comfortable enough to enjoy sex. If your sexual relationship is suffering because you feel overweight, then begin exercising, eating healthy and drinking plenty of water. Don't make excuses. Be willing to change so nothing hinders your sexual fulfillment.

Cuddle Up

The "afterglow" period is a time for *bonding*, not *sleeping!* The most important part of sex is not the act itself, but what happens *before* and *after* that matters.

Every couple should know how to make love in a way that is honorable and brings satisfaction for both the husband and wife.

Men, after you make love to your wife, do whatever it takes to keep from immediately falling asleep. Hold each other. If the husband just rolls over, it makes the wife feel like a "thing." She'll feel used. Don't allow her to feel that way under any circumstances! She's a special treasure to you. Run your fingers through her hair and hold her. Say how much you love her. Don't have her telling you how much she loves you only to be answered by a snore.

Take time to appreciate what you have with and in one another. Enjoy the moment of ecstasy. When you fall asleep, do it while holding your spouse. Make this time just as important as the arousal stage.

In addition, there are other areas that a husband and wife can explore to enhance their sexual experience.

Invite the Holy Spirit

If you don't think the Holy Spirit can be invited into your lovemaking experience, then you've missed the point. Remember that sex in marriage is God's idea. He wants to be part of every area in your life.

We highly recommend that before you make love, invite the Holy Spirit into your bedroom. This may sound a bit weird, but the Bible says that the Holy Spirit will "guide you into *all* truth" (John 16:13). I believe that includes the truth concerning lovemaking. He wants to reveal God's will concerning this area of your relationship. At your request, He will help you to do and say the rights things to propel your sexual experience to greater heights. Although you may not hear Him audibly, pay attention to the "feeling" or "nudge" in the pit of your stomach.

Invite the Holy Spirit in by holding hands with your spouse and offering a quick prayer. Thank God for joining you as one flesh in order to fulfill His will for your lives, as well as for His wisdom and guidance. Ask the Holy Spirit to overshadow you both as you make love. Don't be afraid to involve Him every time you come together.

God gets great joy when you take part in His blessings. He wants you to be prosperous in every area of your life, and He desires for your sexual relationship to be successful.

Look on the Bright Side

It's very important for the two of you to show affection to one another. In fact, affection is what opens the door for a wife to have sex. Women are responders, so your wife responds to the ways in which you show affection. She is stimulated through kind acts and words. Romance her all day long. Call her when she's not expecting it just to say, "I love you." Study her to see what she likes and buy her special gifts.

God not only established sex for the purpose of creating children, He also meant it as an act of physical pleasure to be enjoyed within marriage.

Gentlemen, having a positive attitude also means forgetting what you've learned from the locker room and from associations with your friends and relatives.

For example, pain doesn't mean that sex is good! Pain is not a sign of masculinity; it's a sign of cruelty. Don't hurt your wife. Renew your mind regarding the way in which God wants you to treat her, and make sure it is done gently and tenderly.

Women, when your husbands show affection, don't reject it or else he might not do it again. When he does something special for you, don't look at him like he's crazy. Don't tell him that you're too tired when he has a special dinner planned for you. Remember that if he shows you affection, he has put effort into it. Respect him and receive it. Show affection for him as well through your encouraging words. Tell him how handsome he is, and how proud of him you are. Affection opens the door to fulfilling relationships.

Stay Attractive

A thoughtful lover will prepare for lovemaking by bathing. And be sure to wash your feet and genitals! Smelly genitals and grimy feet will make anyone not want to have sex. Also, don't forget such simple things as cleaning your ears, trimming your nails, brushing your teeth and having fresh breath. Body odor can be a turn-off and is sure to ruin the mood.

Wives, wear your husband's favorite perfume or lotion. Invest in a sexy nightgown or other eye-catching piece of lingerie. As an added bonus, do something as minor as painting your toenails fire engine red! Husbands, wear your wife's favorite cologne or aftershave lotion and trim any long ear or nose hair.

It is especially important that wives observe daily feminine hygiene. After sexual intercourse, it's important for women to bathe and freshen up. The fluids exchanged during lovemaking must be cleansed from the body. Many times, just taking a shower won't do the job effectively. You may want to douche in order to cleanse the vaginal canal; however, be sure not to indulge too frequently (no more than once a month), as douching can upset the acidic balance that protects you from infection.

*   *   *   *   *

Sex is an outward physical expression of the love, affection, appreciation, care and concern that a husband and wife have for one another. It's all tied up into one act that is orchestrated and conducted by the Holy Spirit.

Lovemaking should be pleasurable for both people. Each time you make love, you should want to shout, "It can't get any better than this!" It should be so good that it brings tears to your eyes just thinking about it.

By diligently applying the principles in this chapter, you will discover a world of ecstasy that is just too good for words!

God not only established sex for the purpose of creating children, He also meant it as an act of physical pleasure to be enjoyed within the framework of marriage.

Take a few moments to honestly evaluate your sex life. Is it stagnant or vibrant? Are you and your spouse receiving the fulfillment and satisfaction you crave, or has lovemaking become routine? Discuss your thoughts with your spouse and share several ways in which you can enhance your sexual pleasure. Don't be afraid to be spontaneous and creative—enjoy one another!

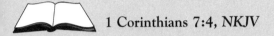 **1 Corinthians 7:4, NKJV**

"The wife does not have authority over her own body, but the husband does. And likewise the husband does not have authority over his own body, but the wife does."

12

DIVIDE AND CONQUER
The Division of Labor and Management of the Home

A happy, successful marriage does not automatically happen. It must first be constructed in the same way as a house—first a strong foundation, then the walls and finally the roof and other little decorative amenities. Only after it is complete can the owners enjoy their home. Likewise, once the foundation of a marriage is established by the Word of God and the structure of daily obligations has been set up, the husband and wife can then freely enjoy their relationship.

After the wedding and honeymoon are over, married life begins, and with it comes a barrage of questions: "How are we going to divide the workload? Who is going to cook? Who does the laundry? Who will take care of the yard? Who pays the bills? Do we both need jobs? What is right?" Although you and your spouse may have already discussed these issues during your courtship, nothing blows a plan to pieces like reality.

For example, you may have had excess energy while you were dating because of the excitement of being around someone you love. However, the truth is that once you're married, you'll be exhausted when you come home from work each evening, and the last thing you'll want to do is cook, clean or review the children's homework. In addition, arguments may arise over who will balance the checkbook or handle the finances now that you share accounts and discuss expenditures. Therefore the division of labor and management of the home are *definitely* topics worth revisiting once you have said "I do!"

God has a perfect plan for the structure of your marriage, and it is found in His Word. Even though times have changed and our society is vastly different from the Greek, Roman and Hebrew cultures illustrated in the Bible, His plan for the division of labor is still the same today as it was then. It can be divided into four categories that include two for the husband and two for the wife. Keep in mind, however, that this plan only works in marriages where both partners are willing to submit themselves to it. Let's begin with the husbands.

Lead On

When it comes to the role a man plays in ministry, the term "bishop" is often used to describe it. The qualities he must possess are outlined in 1 Timothy 3:1-5:

> *This is a true saying, If a man desire the office of a bishop, he desireth a good work. A bishop then must be blameless, the husband of one wife, vigilant, sober, of good behavior, given to hospitality, apt to teach; Not given to wine, no striker, not greedy of filthy lucre; but patient, not a brawler, not covetous; One that ruleth well his own house, having his children in subjection with all gravity; (For if a man know not how to rule his own house, how shall he take care of the church of God?)....*

It is interesting to note that when the five-fold ministry gifts are listed in Ephesians 4:11, the term "bishop" is never mentioned. Those ministry gifts only include apostles, prophets, evangelists, pastors and teachers.

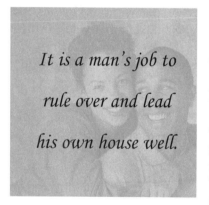

It is a man's job to rule over and lead his own house well.

A bishop actually refers to *anyone* who operates as an overseer. The same characteristics that apply to a bishop also apply to *every* Christian husband. As the head of his house, the man is the bishop, or leader, of his household. According to 1 Timothy 3:4, he is "*one that ruleth well his own house....*" The word *rule* means "to stand before" or "to stand in front of and lead." In other words, a man's job is to rule over and lead his own house well. This does *not* mean that you dominate your family. Responsibility and accountability come with headship. In fact, it is the husband who is responsible and accountable for what his wife and children learn and do—including the sins they may commit.

Think about this. When Eve partook of the forbidden fruit in the Garden of Eden, it wasn't called sin until after *Adam* ate it. Why? God gave the command to Adam, *not* Eve. It was his job to enforce that command and ensure they remained obedient to God. The eyes of their understanding didn't open until Adam ate of the fruit: "*So when the woman saw that the tree was good for food, that it was pleasant to the eyes, and a tree desirable to make one wise, she took of its fruit and ate. She also gave to her husband with her, and he ate. Then the eyes of both of them were opened...*" (Genesis 3:6-7, NKJV, emphasis added).

Later on, when God later entered the Garden, He called out to Adam—not

Eve. He even gave Adam an opportunity to take responsibility for the wrongdoing he and Eve had committed. God asked, *"Who told thee that thou wast naked? Hast thou eaten of the tree, whereof I commanded thee that thou shouldest not eat?"* (verse 11). As is human nature, Adam pointed the finger at his wife. As a result of his refusal to take responsibility for their actions, sin invaded the earth.

God holds leaders accountable for the actions of those who follow them. In the same way, if a child breaks the law, the parents are held accountable. If a dog gets loose and bites someone, the owners of the dog may end up in court. That's the same accountability and responsibility that the man has with his family. God will look to you when things go wrong.

Men, it's time to stand in your position as head of the household and discontinue the practice of delegating your responsibility to your wife. Remember, your family dynamic is simply a reflection of your leadership.

Provide for Them

Men, in your wedding vows you promised to provide for your wife. First Timothy 5:8 says, *"… if any provide not for his own, and **specially for those of his own house**, he hath denied the faith, and is worse than an infidel"* (emphasis added). In God's division of labor, it's the man who should provide for his household. If your wife looks bad, that's a reflection on you.

This responsibility to provide includes taking care of her. This means supplying her with the funds needed to dress well—such as making sure her stockings don't have runs in them! You are the one who ensures she has the money to get her hair and nails done and buy the make-up and perfume she needs to make herself beautiful for you. When she walks into your office, she should be a reflection of God's goodness that you are proud to show off! You should be shouting, "Look here! This is *my* wife!"

Taffi has three styles of dress: moderately dressy, really dressy and just plain sharp. I want her to always look dressy or sharp, so I buy her the things she needs to look that way. Why? When Taffi looks sharp, I look sharp. Even when I don't look good, if she is dressed to the nines, it makes me look better.

Husbands, when it comes to doing something nice for your wife, don't let the cost stop you. It doesn't take much to win her heart—remember, you already have it. You don't have to buy her designer labels to make her happy; just provide for her.

In addition, don't think that just because she eats and uses electricity she needs to work. Actually, it's not the wife's responsibility to work at all! I don't say that so any woman who reads this book will quit her job tomorrow. Let's continue to gain understanding about God's division of labor and discuss the two main areas for which women are responsible.

Queen of the Castle

Titus 2:4-5 says that a woman's function is to *"...teach the young women to be sober, to love their husbands, to love their children, To be discreet, chaste, keepers at home, good, obedient to their own husbands, that the word of God be not blasphemed."*
The Greek translation for *keepers at home* literally means "housekeeper." Don't get mad at me, wives. God desires for the man to provide for and protect his family while the woman maintains the home by keeping it clean and orderly. She is the one who cooks, vacuums, washes the dishes, irons the clothes and polishes the furniture.

Ensure that your wife has the money she needs to make herself beautiful for you.

Ladies, do your part to run your household efficiently. Don't sit around all day eating candy and watching television. A messy house is not something anyone wants to come home to. Take pride in your home and do your best to turn it into a warm, inviting sanctuary.

On the other hand, if the lifestyle you desire requires a joint income, you must make the necessary adjustments to accommodate your choice. That means the husband needs to understand that because his wife is now *helping him* to fulfill his responsibility to provide, he must now help her to fulfill her job to care for the home. For example, if you are both working, your spouse shouldn't come home, kick off his or her shoes and sit down in front of the television to ask, "What's for dinner?" or "Why is this house so messy?" One of you should be vacuuming while the other cooks!

God's set order for the division of labor is a principle that doesn't change. If you agree to make some adjustments because of the lifestyle you want, then you have to share the responsibilities that go with it. If a husband wants his wife to stay at home, then scale down the lifestyle. There are cheaper homes and cheaper cars. Do you *need* two luxury vehicles? On the same note, the husband can't be so prideful that he won't *allow* his wife to work, yet they're starving because there is not enough money to buy groceries!

Use your common sense and honestly discuss what you want and need. Whatever the two of you decide is fine, as long as you agree on it.

A Competent, Creative Manager

The second responsibility that women have is to guide, or manage, household affairs (1 Timothy 5:14). You are the one who ensures that the household runs smoothly and efficiently by making sure every bill gets paid, that the pantry is stocked and the children are properly trained—in addition to taking care of whatever else needs to be done. It may help to think of yourself as the manager of a small, yet powerful corporation. With your guidance and inspiration, your family flourishes.

Muster the Troops!

It's been said that a woman's job is never done. I think it's safe to say that that statement rings true in almost every household across the nation and around the world.

Ladies (or gentlemen, if you are a single parent), do yourself a favor and stop trying to do everything yourself. Instead, call a family meeting to discuss and assign chores that are age-appropriate. For example, a five-year old may not be able to unload the dishwasher, but he or she can help to set the table. A 12-year-old can take out the garbage and water the plants, while your teenager or spouse can wash the car, put away groceries or vacuum the house.

By giving everyone a job to do that is suitable to their age and ability, you bolster their confidence and sense of responsibility and accomplishment while ensuring peace of mind for you and the opportunity to complete other tasks!

A large portion of responsibility lies in the training of the children. Taffi and I discussed this before having Jordan, Alex and Lauren (and adopting Gregory and Jeremy). She had graduated from college and wanted to use her degree; however, we agreed that when we began having children, she would leave her job. When the children were younger, Taffi took the responsibility to train them in the Lord. We wanted to make sure they were well educated. The last thing we wanted to do was depend on a nursery school to teach them.

Guiding the household means you also discipline the children. Don't tell them, "Wait until your daddy gets home. You're gonna get it then!" It's not wise to instill fear in your children—especially when it comes to another parent. You are well able to discipline them. In fact, whichever parent happens to be around when discipline is needed is the one who should follow through.

In addition, be sure to manage your money wisely. If you are the one who makes sure the bills get paid, don't spend money on things you can't afford. Make every effort to be a wise steward. Work together with your spouse to properly manage household funds. One way of doing this is to have one checking account. In this way, both parties are forced to take responsibility for management. Neither you nor your spouse will be able to spend money foolishly. Here's a rule of thumb to follow: Don't ever spend money without consulting your partner!

That doesn't mean that whoever writes the checks for the bills gets to handle the money. Not at all! That decision should be based on which person is the better money manager. In other words, if you have trouble balancing a checkbook, you shouldn't be the one doing it! This is not a gender thing, either. There's no need for the man to insist on handling the money because he's the "man of the house." The partner who is the most anointed in this area should take the lead while the other assists.

A messy house is not something anyone wants to come home to.

In addition, don't take yourself out of the loop just because you're not great with numbers. Although your partner may be the better money manager, take a proactive role in financial affairs. Sit down together to pay the bills and balance the checkbook. Knowledge is power. The more you know about your finances, the better off you will be when it comes to future decision-making.

What a Team!

The key to the *successful* division of labor is both spouses' willingness to support one another when needed. This can be summed up in two words: submission and honor.

Submission is not an action that applies only to one gender, but to both male and female. Ephesians 5:21 commands us to submit to one another in the fear of, or reverence for, God. A submitted wife is not a slave, and a submitted husband is not weak-willed. In fact, submitted spouses are spouses that love, honor and respect God and one another.

In submitting to your spouse, you support one another. When one needs help, the other is there to provide it. For example, the wife may rake the lawn while her husband mows it, or the husband may chop vegetables while the wife prepares the omelet. No one in your house is responsible accomplishing the mission alone!

The foundation of submission is honor. The husband must honor the wife in what she does, and she must honor her husband in what he does. If one of you belittles the other, then you dishonor your spouse, which sets the stage for future problems.

Wives, remember that you are to submit to your husbands *as unto the Lord* (Ephesians 5:22). Just as you submit yourself to God's plan for your life out of trust and confidence in Him, so should you submit to your husband, knowing that he loves you and has your best interests at heart.

Husbands, you are the head of your wives *even as* Christ is the head of the Church (verse 23). That doesn't mean putting on airs and bossing her around. What it means is that you assume complete responsibility for her well-being and happiness, caring for her as God cares for you. You may have to set aside your wants and desires in order to provide for and protect your family.

As with all things in life, submission and honor take practice because they are in opposition to your human nature. When you make a concerted effort to assist your spouse in whatever way they need you to help them, you pave the way for a happier, more fulfilling relationship.

* * * * *

Teamwork is essential to running a peaceful and efficient home. In fact, Ecclesiastes 4:9-10 says, *"Two are better than one, Because they have a good reward for their labor. For if they fall, one will lift up his companion..."* (NKJV).

It's not easy having to do everything by yourself. Although you have God's power and ability residing on the inside of you, it doesn't mean you're equipped to be a superman or superwoman. Keep the Golden Rule in the forefront of your thinking at all times: "Do unto others as you would have them do unto you." By taking others into consideration, you sow seeds of generosity that will be reciprocated by those you love the most!

Work together with your spouse to properly manage household funds.

God has a perfect plan for the structure of your marriage, and it is found in His Word. However, it only works when both partners are willing to submit themselves to it.

Set time aside to talk with your spouse about the division of labor in your home. Lovingly point out areas that need improvement and offer suggestions as to how he or she can help you accomplish your daily tasks and God-given assignments. Put them into practice immediately, and be sure to encourage and thank your partner when he or she has assisted you in some way.

Ecclesiastes 4:9-10, NKJV

"Two are better than one, Because they have a good reward for their labor. For if they fall, one will lift up his companion...."

13

MONEY MATTERS
Managing Household Finances

Money problems can place more stress on a marriage than any other outside threat. Most marital arguments and frustrations stem from money. A person's economic status doesn't make money less of an issue. Both the rich and the poor fight over how to spend, save and invest money; they just do so out of differing motives and perspectives.

Often, people—especially Christians—are quick to blame two parties for their financial problems: the devil, or the country's economy. In reality, they had nothing to do with it. It was a management problem on their part, because they didn't live within their budget or they misheard God. Now they're in a financial hole.

Some people strive to obtain money for power. They esteem the wealthy while ignoring the hard-working middle and lower classes. These people often feel that their worth lies in the amount of their annual income. They strive to replace spiritual things with money. The Bible says that this *love* of money is the root of all evil. When people seek after money more than they seek the Lord they end up with many problems (1 Timothy 6:10).

If you don't think money management is important, think again. People become suicidal and abusive due to financial difficulties. In fact, they even resort to extortion, sabotage or situation ethics and shady deals for the power that money brings.

What does God say about money? Is it supposed to own you? Is your worth measured by the money and the possessions you have? How are you supposed to manage your finances? What do you do when you can't afford something you need? What are your financial priorities?

Manage Your Corporation

God wants you to be wise and use common sense where your money is concerned. Unfortunately, if you weren't wise in financial planning *before* you married, more than likely that same trait will follow you into marriage. The good news is that it is never too late to start. I have found that most couples spend more time planning the details of their wedding ceremony than they do their financial future. The fact is, it's vital that you and your spouse develop a solid plan for your monetary survival and the well-being of your family.

Money problems can place more stress on a marriage than any other outside threat.

You can begin by setting aside time each week, or each day, if possible, for you and your spouse to take care of financial matters. Set up this time as though it was a business meeting and you are the CEO of a corporation. Have an agenda and any items on hand that you may need, such as scrap paper, pencils and pens, a calculator and your checkbook and bills. You may wish to create an Excel spreadsheet to help you see the big picture.

Afterward, follow through with the plan of action you have discussed. You may wish to set up a "task list" to keep track of who is doing what and when it should be done. After all, this is a family business, and your financial management is at the center of how your household operates efficiently or shuts down.

Don't use this time to argue or point blame. If there is a problem, offer your solutions and stay positive. Once your financial plan is established, you have set the course for how you will save, spend and invest your money. This leaves little room for argument over purchases.

Here are some of the principles you and your spouse should discuss and implement in your weekly business meeting.

Create a Budget

Luke 14:28 tells us, *"For which of you, intending to build a tower, sitteth not down first, and counteth the cost, whether he have sufficient to finish it?"*

A budget helps you "count the cost" to see whether or not you can afford to buy the things you want. It has nothing to do with *how much* money you make. It simply shows what you have to work with and tells you where the money is going by listing your expenses for each month. It shows what money remains after the bills are paid or if you need to scale back your lifestyle to accommodate your salary. In other words, a budget will keep you from coming up short. It helps you see problem areas *before* they arise.

The first step in establishing a budget is to prioritize your obligations.

1. Put God first.

Your first obligation is to tithe. We are instructed in Malachi 3:10 to *"Bring ye all the tithes into the storehouse...."* Some people act like that's such a big thing! God is only asking for 10 percent of your *gross* income. He's leaving you the other 90 percent!

This makes me think of the time when I was growing up, and my mother had baked one of her delicious apple pies. I had been waiting all day for it. When the pie came out of the oven, my sister wanted a piece! I thought, "No way! She's not getting *any* of my pie!" Although I would have been left with the biggest part, I still refused her one little piece of it. That was selfish of me.

A budget shows what you have to work with and tells you where the money is going by listing your expenses for each month.

But that is exactly the attitude many people have about tithing. God is the one who gives you the power to get wealth. The job you have and the money you bring home are blessings from above. He only requires a tenth of what you earn, and He doesn't ask for the tenth without giving you something in return. He promises to rebuke the devourer and to throw open the floodgates of heaven so He can pour out so much blessing on you that you won't be able to keep track of it (vv. 10-11).

Some people think they will come up short each month if they tithe. But when you honor God and put Him first in your finances by giving Him what is owed, you'll actually come out ahead.

2. Add in the mortgage.

The second item listed on your budget should be the rent or mortgage. Don't pay the car note before you pay the house note! Would you rather live in your car? Pay the rent first! At least you'll have a roof over your head, even if you have to rely on public transportation to get around!

3. Make sure you eat.

Next should be the food budget. You and your children have to eat. Put the food expenses in your budget *before* the utility bills. If the electricity gets shut off, you may have to eat by candlelight, but at least you are eating! If nutritious food is not provided for the children, they won't feel well or do well in school. You can't perform on your job like you're supposed to if you are starving. Ensure that the nutrition needs of your family are being met.

Ask the Lord to give you wisdom when you walk the grocery aisles. Never shop when you are hungry—you'll buy twice as much as you need. Don't be afraid to clip coupons, and go ahead and buy those "3 for a dollar" cans of vegetables. That kind of food savvy will go a long way!

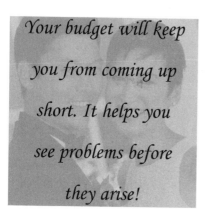

Your budget will keep you from coming up short. It helps you see problems before they arise!

4. Include the cost of transportation.

This is where your car note or public transportation is listed. It's slated *above* the utilities because you must have a way to get to work and run errands. If you don't allot money for transportation, what difference does it make if the electricity is on? You won't be able to get to pay the bill if you can't get to work to earn the funds to do so! If you do use public transportation regularly, check with the transit authority to save money on weekly or monthly passes.

5. List your utilities.

Determine what your electricity, gas, waste disposal and water costs are monthly, but estimate a slightly higher figure when adding them to your budget. That way if your bill is smaller than what you've budgeted for, you'll have some extra money; if it's more than usual, you can rest assured that the expense is covered. This is also where you figure in the telephone, cable and Internet services. However, those things are luxuries. You may have to temporarily eliminate them from your budget if necessary.

Consider These Areas Also

After these necessities, give yourself a clothing budget. I'm not talking about a designer wardrobe! Some people wear the same clothes all the time and that's okay. If you only have three dresses, make sure they are always clean and ironed. Look the best you can on the budget you have. You don't have to have something new each week. There are many accessories you can add that can make any outfit look new or different. Experiment, and have fun doing it!

In addition, don't forget to consider your credit cards. They are designed to keep you eternally in debt if you only pay the minimum balance due every month. Whenever possible, pay *more* than the minimum, even if it's $20. Also keep in mind that banks charge a hefty fee if your payment does not arrive on time, if you pay less than the minimum amount due, or if you exceed your limit. Your credit card should only be used in cases of emergencies or with the thought that you will pay the entire balance off each month.

Debt Reduction Strategies

There are several ways to reduce credit card debt. For example, begin with the credit card that has the lowest balance on it. When you have any extra money, put it toward that card. After you have paid off one credit card, tackle the next lowest card. Then take the money that you were paying on the first card and add it to the minimum payment of the second credit card. Keep doing this until all of your credit cards are paid in full.

If you feel as though you don't have any extra money, look at the little things you can cut out of your budget. How much money do you spend each week at the vending machines in your office? Instead of soda, drink water; it's much better for you anyway. If you *have* to have an afternoon snack, buy snacks at discount stores like Wal-Mart or Sam's Club and keep them in your desk. Instead of eating out every day, brown-bag your lunch.

Once you have made a plan to reduce your credit card debt, stick to it. If you don't, the monthly finance charge is added to your total, increasing the amount you owe. At that rate, it will be years before the card is paid off.

The key to debt reduction is not using a credit card, but dealing on a cash-only basis. Another alternative is a debit card. It offers the same convenience as a credit card; however, since the funds are taken directly from your checking account, you will know your balance and exactly how much you can "charge."

Your budget should always include luxury items such as movie rentals, dinner out or other activities. It's okay to treat yourself every now and then—just stay within your budget! It's foolish to spend all of your grocery money on dinner in a fancy restaurant! It might be fun at the moment, but you and your children will get hungry as the week progresses. You'll wish you had thought about that when your stomachs start growling.

It's also healthy for each of you to have some "no questions asked" money. That means giving yourself an allowance for your personal enjoyment. If someone asks you to lunch, you can use that money without having to account for it with your mate, because it's already been approved.

For the couples that have been previously married, you may have to add child support into your budget. This is an important item, and you'll need to list it high in the priorities. Make sure that you and your spouse have discussed the responsibility of paying child support before getting married or remarried. If something happens to the job of the paying spouse, the other must realize that the payment still has to be met. Openly communicate with one another in this area, and meet the obligation as a team.

Save and Invest

It's important to have a savings account. Doing so plans ahead for life's little surprises such as a new baby, unemployment or a medical emergency. Discipline yourself to put something into your savings account each pay period. If you don't have any extra money right now, set a goal to get there. The ideal amount for a sufficient savings account would sustain your family for three to six months.

If your wife is working and it's not really necessary for the family budget, use her paycheck to start a savings account. The bank gives you interest on those accounts, so it's always worth your while to do it. The discipline may seem hard at first, but when you need that extra money, you'll be glad you have it.

The stock market varies from day to day, so don't invest in something you haven't taken the time to investigate. If you're interested in a particular stock, request a copy of the company's annual report. Search the Internet to find as much information as you can about the company. As your portfolio increases, seek the advice of a good investment counselor.

Another way of investing is giving to a ministry or another Christian's life. A word of caution, however: Be led by the Holy Spirit. He will show you who to "invest" in. Here are some practical guidelines to follow:

- **Does this person tithe?** If not, you are throwing your money away because it can't produce a harvest. No one plants a flower bulb in a desert and expects a garden. Look for someone who exhibits Christ-like character traits.

- **Does this person minister to others?** They don't have to have a pulpit ministry; there are many opportunities to minister to those around you on a one-on-one basis. That person is fertile ground to give to, and you will receive a blessing for doing so.

You can also give to those in need. Proverbs 19:17 says that in giving to the poor, you are giving to God and He will repay you for your generosity.

To Borrow or Not to Borrow

Contrary to what you may think, God never said it was wrong to borrow money. However, you must be wise when borrowing because it can get you into trouble.

Many people are completely governed by credit. They borrow money to buy furniture, automobiles, clothes and appliances. They even get one credit card to pay off other credit cards. Then, when their first child graduates from high school, they make the mistake of going out and helping him get his first loan! Now he's a slave to debt in the same way his parents are. What would happen to this family if one or both spouses suddenly became unemployed? They would be in serious trouble. With no way to pay off their debts, they could be ruined.

Contrary to what you may think, God never said it was wrong to borrow money.

Don't operate that way. Borrowing money becomes wrong when it stops your cash flow. It's wrong when you are up to your ears in debt and have little with which to pay it.

As long as you are easily paying off what you have borrowed, there's no problem with it. If you borrow, then pay it off. That's the *only* way it can be done successfully without putting your family in a bind.

When do you believe God instead of borrowing? That's a timing question. It all depends on God's timing in the situation, and you must be able to hear from

Him on the subject. If He tells you to wait and believe Him for a certain amount of money, then you'll know when it's coming because you'll sense the timing. If you've diligently sought God and He tells you to go ahead and borrow, then He'll help you cancel the debt you owe. It just depends upon the situation and the people involved.

Work It Out Together

The foundation for successful money management comes through communication. You must talk about why you are doing something, what you are spending and when you want it done.

Men, don't keep your wives in the dark. If she wonders where all the money is going, don't put on a macho attitude and spout back, "You don't need to know where the money is going. Just let me handle it." You dishonor her when you make comments like that, and I can assure you, problems will result from it.

Your wife has a right to know every cent you make. Taffi knows every dime I make, where it came from, when I received it and where it's going. She's my partner! She has a right to know everything I'm doing and to voice her opinion. I'm obligated to hear and respect it.

One of the most common areas of miscommunication is in the area of the checkbook. I don't believe in having several checking accounts for the family. That tends to stimulate dishonesty, insecurity and suspicion. If you have a business, however, you will need two separate accounts: one for the business and one for the family. Don't create unnecessary suspicion by having multiple accounts for the family.

When the monthly statement comes in, one or the both of you needs to balance it against the check register in your checkbook. It doesn't matter who does it. It's not a gender thing. The person who is best with numbers is the one who should take on the responsibility. Men, don't become prideful and think that you have to be the one who balances the checkbook—especially if you have trouble counting! Let your wife do it. That way, there will be no miscalculations and no bounced checks.

When talking about money, avoid pointing the finger at your spouse. If someone is overspending, discuss it and find out why. Talk about how your parents handled money and the financial principles they taught you. Obliterate any fears you may have, such as the fear of investing. Don't ever do anything without your mate's consent. Even if you don't agree on every point, just the willingness to communicate goes a long way in building a solid financial present and future.

Healthy finances require wisdom, time and effort. Organization and teamwork are key factors. God is willing and able to do a miracle for you, but you can't live a lifestyle of miracles. Accountability must take its place as well. Remember, the quality of your stewardship will determine your profit.

*   *   *   *   *

If your finances could use a little work, don't panic! Simply see the picture as it is; don't deny that a problem exists. Focus on what the Word of God has to say regarding money management, as only His Word can turn your situation around for the better.

Believe for the wisdom to change your condition and apply the steps necessary to remedy it. God will bring you from a place of struggle to long-lasting success!

Sound financial planning is vital for the success and well-being of your family.

Plan a financial meeting for this week. Set aside at least one hour to establish a budget based on your incomes, and prioritize it according to the steps in this chapter. During this meeting, set the budget for the week, and stick to it! Be sure to keep track of what you spend by placing your receipts and check stubs in one location. At the end of the week, review your budget and the totals of your receipts. If you didn't overspend, congratulations! If you did, bring that information to your next meeting along with solutions to remedy the situation. Learning from your mistakes puts you on the path to wisdom!

1 Corinthians 4:2, NKJV

"Moreover, it is required in stewards [managers] *that one be found faithful."*

14

DEALING WITH IN-LAWS
Guidelines for New Families

I n-laws have been the brunt of jokes for years. No doubt you've heard humorous anecdotes and snide comments about them on television, radio, magazines, talk shows and among your circle of friends. The irony is that most times, those making up the jokes and sharing the stories are the in-laws themselves!

Although you and I laugh about it, it's a well-known fact that in-law trouble is the second largest cause of strife in marriages. This stems from two reasons. First, the husband and wife have neither learned nor applied the "leave and cleave" principle, or second, they haven't learned how to work with differing personalities.

Everything that God instituted for marriage has its foundation in Genesis, the book of beginnings. In the second chapter, God presented the woman to Adam, and he liked what he saw. In verse 23, Adam chose her to be his wife: *And Adam said, This is now bone of my bones, and flesh of my flesh: she shall be called Woman, because she was taken out of Man."*

You can't be any more united than to make someone "bone of [your] bones" and "flesh of [your] flesh." That is total "oneness." That meant everything Adam had, Eve now had. Everything he represented, she represented. Because of that oneness, verse 24 came into existence. *"Therefore shall a man leave his father and his mother, and shall cleave unto his wife: and they shall be one flesh."*

God instituted this principle for the generations to come, since Adam himself did not have an earthly father or mother. This "leave and cleave" principle is not gender-oriented; both male and female must leave their fathers and mothers and cling to his or her spouse.

Let's review each part of this principle to give you a better understanding of why it is important to apply it in your marriage.

Say Good-bye

When I say that husbands and wives are supposed to leave their parents, I'm not saying they must now disown or ignore them. Your parents raised, loved, trained, cried over and nurtured you to the place where you could mature and eventually live on your own.

In Genesis 2:23-24, the Hebrew word for *leave* means to "relinquish or refuse." Once you are married, you are to relinquish your parents of their parental responsibilities toward you. That means you don't run to mom and dad every time a problem arises so they can solve it for you. They've already done their job, and now it's time for you to learn to deal with life according to the Word of God. If you can't leave, don't get married.

God's plan is for you and your spouse to come into the marriage as single people—unique, whole and separate individuals. That meant you both were mature, accountable and complete in God. But the ones who never allowed the wholeness of God to come into their lives are filled with insecurities, jealousy, inferiority and other emotional problems. Because of this, they are unable to bring wholeness into the union, and consequently have the most trouble leaving their parents.

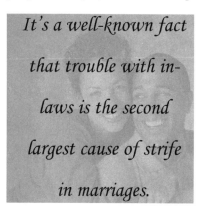

It's a well-known fact that trouble with in-laws is the second largest cause of strife in marriages.

To *leave* means recognizing that you now have a wife or a husband, and that your mate is not your parent. Husbands, don't compare your wife's cooking to your mother's. Avoid making statements like, "Mom didn't make cornbread like this. She doesn't cook okra like that. Why don't you trying cooking like my mom?" Your wife is going to get fed up with being compared to your mother, and she'll let you know about it too. When you're ready to make love, you'll tap her on the shoulder only to hear her respond, "Ask your mother!"

No matter how much you love each other, the application of this principle is not easy, and it certainly doesn't happen overnight. If you've been with your parents for over 20 years, and they've provided for you and always been there when a need arose, it's difficult to relinquish them of that responsibility all at once. This is especially true for women. It takes time and discipline to learn how to turn to your mate instead of your parents. In addition, those individuals who have lived independently from their parents for some time may find it difficult to rely on another person.

It's very easy to turn to your parents because they have the wisdom that comes from experience while you and your mate are just starting out. However, you've got to build up to what they have and where they are. It takes time to do that, and you've got to work at it.

From time to time your parents will want to help you or give you things. That's fine. The Bible says that a good man will leave an inheritance for his family (Proverbs 13:22). But if you become completely dependent on them, there's a problem. Marriage is much more than two people sleeping together while their parents take care of them. Remember, it's just as hard on them to relinquish their responsibility as it is on you. So work together, learn to *leave* and come into God's perfect plan for your lives.

Stick to Your Mate

Although I'm going to discuss the challenges of cleaving from a woman's point of view, the examples I'll use can fit any gender. As you read, apply these principles to your own life. In order to have a successful marriage, the woman *and* the man must learn how to cleave, or cling to one another.

When Creflo and I got married, I had to learn that marriage was more than cooking, housekeeping and sharing his bed. I had to learn how to stick by him through thick and thin, in good times and difficult ones. I had made a commitment before God to be one with him, and I had to learn how to prove my commitment throughout the trials of life.

The Hebrew definition of the word *cleave* means "to follow close and hard after; to stick fast together." Not only are husbands and wives to relinquish their parents of responsibility for their well being, but they are also to *stick together as one*.

Successful marriages are built on the "leave and cleave" principle.

One of the easiest ways to hurt a relationship is through gossip, or allowing the negative words of another to influence you. When two personalities join together as husband and wife, there *will* be differences, and those differences aren't always bad. A difference of opinion can cause the relationship to be balanced. When you don't understand something your husband says or does and you haven't taken the time to talk with him about it, it's easy to talk to others. But you had better watch who you talk to!

It's tempting to call your parents when you're distressed. You must be careful of that because no matter how much they may like your husband, you are still their child. In the beginning they have difficulty accepting the idea that he is good enough for you. After all, you are dear to them, and they may believe that no one can treat you as good as they.

If you and your spouse have an argument, you must resist the temptation to call your mother or father and vent your frustrations. Long after the two of you have resolved the issues and forgiven one another, you may find your parents are still holding a grudge against your spouse—over a fight the two of you can't even remember! You must use wisdom in determining how much of your marital business you share with your parents.

You and your husband are building a family that is different from theirs. The principles might be the same, but the circumstances will differ. Perhaps your husband accepted a job that your mother disagreed with. So, the first time something goes wrong, you mistakenly call her to complain about it. She will be tempted to say something like, "I *knew* he shouldn't have taken that job! You are going to starve! He can't take care of you! What is he thinking?"

You can't change anyone else, only yourself.

Although they may seem harmless, those words can take root in your heart, provoking suspicion and doubt. You then become unsupportive, and you've sabotaged the principle of oneness. When your husband comes home, he can't figure out what's wrong with you. Before long you're arguing. That's when the seeds of those words pop out of your mouth: "It's just like mom said. You *are* crazy!" Of course this only serves to escalate the conflict, and one or both of you wind up feeling frustrated, hurt and betrayed. If you had only clung to your husband by talking to *him* instead of your family, there wouldn't be a problem in this area of your marriage.

Or perhaps your spouse has to work late at night. Instead of communicating your concerns to him, you pour your heart out to a friend. She may say, "I wouldn't put up with that! Do you think he's having an affair? I don't know anyone who stays away from home like that without another woman waiting for him."

Now you've set yourself up for turmoil. Your girlfriend isn't the one who is married to your husband! She doesn't know his heart like you do; she may be speaking out of unresolved anger and bitterness from past hurts or even jealousy. Regardless of the motives, your husband's character is now damaged. Instead of following hard after your husband, you're chasing lies and suspicion. Rest assured that nothing but trouble will come as a result.

When he comes home, you're waiting to pounce on him. You instantly spout, "Where have you been? There's no way you've been working all this time! Are you having an affair?" Your husband just stands in the doorway in amazement, wondering what world you've come from. When he lays that paycheck down on the table, you feel like a fool. Now you've got to comfort him and try to heal the damage your words have caused.

The devil plays with minds that are open to suspicion. He'll magnify that doubt and fear through friends or family, and before you know it, you've plotted out what was wrong, what you're going to do about it, how you're going to say it, and where you can go when you leave. The irony is that nothing has happened!

Here's an outstanding principle to live by: *Believe the best about your spouse.* After all, he or she makes *good* decisions—they chose *you* for a lifelong mate! First Corinthians 13:7 says that love is ready to believe the *best* of every person.

Following hard after your mate requires effort. Don't sabotage your efforts by spreading ugly thoughts about your spouse to others. They may surprise you by adding even more negativity to an already sticky situation. Although you readily forgive your mate of any wrongdoings, outsiders tend to nurse grudges for long periods of time. Remember, you are one with your mate, and when they talk about him or her, they are also talking about *you.*

Simply the Best

I believe the best of Creflo. I always have. In fact, I have a confession that I make all the time. I look at him and say, "Boy, nobody wants you but me. Another woman won't take the time to look at you because I've seasoned you with prayer and intercession."

When you believe the best in your mate and cleave to him or her, you don't listen to your in-laws or anyone else criticize, ridicule or belittle them. Sometimes in-laws think they have a right to comment on your mate, but they don't. When you married, they relinquished their responsibility over you—including their right to openly voice their opinions concerning who you married and what you do together as a couple.

If and when they begin criticizing, stop them immediately! Tell them that although you love them dearly, you don't allow that kind of disrespect in your presence. Don't allow them to belittle your mate, because if you do, it will produce a poison within your relationship that will bring forth a harvest of trouble in the days to come.

Don't allow the opinions of others to wedge you apart. As you learn to make your own way in life, stick by your spouse. Believe in your marriage, stand for your oneness and fight off any words that would seek to damage your relationship. If you cleave, there's no room for strife.

Treat Them Well

Another area of conflict arises when you dishonor your in-laws. I'm not talking about in-laws who are trying to disrespect your marriage. Don't allow anyone to do that. Instead, I'm referring to an individual not liking an in-law because of their personality, or jealousy of the love his or her spouse has for them.

There's no room for jealousy in the life of a believer. Jealousy stems from insecurity. If this is a problem for you, renew your mind with the Word of God, build trust in your mate and become confident in the role God has given you.

Conflicts that arise from personality differences are entirely another area, so here are some principles that Creflo and I have learned over the years.

1. Realize that your in-laws come from a different background.

Chances are, there are radical differences in the way they were raised, how their marriage operates and how yours will operate. Be at peace with that. Respect them for what they've been through and for the wisdom they have. Open yourself up to learning from them. Act as if you have just met someone that you wanted as a friend. When you do that, your behavior will be much different. In addition, remember that you're not married to them, so relax.

2. Deal with reality.

Often we get upset when our in-laws don't turn out to be all that we had hoped for. Many people tend to create an image of the ideal family, imagining the wonderful friendship they'll have with their in-laws. Your in-laws are also fostering the same thoughts about *you*. They had their own ideas of how you'd be, what you would be doing career-wise and how you'd treat them. However, what they got was *you*, and you may not have been what they were expecting.

Don't be unrealistic. Forget your expectations! You can't change anyone else, only yourself. If you're adding to the conflict with your unrealistic expectations, recognize it and change it. Every time you see them, try to find one good thing to comment on, and do it.

3. Your in-laws aren't your parents.

Don't be horrified when your in-laws don't abide by the same rules as your parents. If you think they'll be just like your parents, you're wrong. While they may do things you don't like or agree with, remember that they *did* raise the wonderful man or woman you are married to. That in itself is a great deed, so respect them for it.

Never dishonor them, because that will hurt your mate. Learn to compromise on the differences that are the least important, and negotiate on the ones that violate your principles. If you haven't discussed everything that's bothering you with your in-laws, don't talk about it to others. Set your boundaries, maintain a positive attitude and *then* discuss it with your in-laws.

> *If there's trouble with in-law interference, it usually means you and your mate need to build a stronger family unit.*

Keep in mind that if your spouse came from a single-parent home, they may have a difficult time relating to their father or mother-in-law. He or she may not be sure of what to expect from them, so give your mate time to adjust. Sometimes spouses hold back from fostering a relationship with their in-laws for fear it might betray their relationship with their parents. However, a loving in-law may offer extra guidance in an area in which the natural mother and father are unable.

4. Set boundaries.

Dealing with the personality traits of in-laws can be exhausting. That's why you must establish boundaries within your marriage. Priority-wise, your mate and your children *always* come before your in-laws. If you have an in-law that is constantly violating this priority, take a stand. Let them know you love them, but they are draining your emotional energy, and your family is being neglected because of it. Above all, don't ever be the "middle person" and speak for your mate or your in-law. Remember, if there's trouble with in-law interference, it usually means you and your mate need to build a stronger family unit.

*   *   *   *   *

In-laws can be a blessing if you know how to handle the relationship. Before that can happen, however, a level of privacy must be established and in operation within your marriage in order for it to grow and develop without outside interference.

There are times when you will need to go to your parents for help in enhancing your marriage. Tap into their wisdom and obtain assistance and guidance when needed. Above all, apply the "leave and cleave" principle to ensure a stable and peaceful marriage relationship.

Interference from outsiders can be kept to a minimum when you apply the "leave and cleave" principle to your marriage.

Take a moment to ask yourself the following questions: Have I left any doors open that would cause a wedge between my spouse and me? Have I dishonored my spouse by speaking negatively about him or her to my parents, in-laws or friends? How do I behave toward my in-laws? Once you have answered these questions, create a plan of action that will allow you to improve or enhance your relationship with your spouse and in-laws. In addition, study the Book of Ruth to gain a better understanding of in-law relations. By keeping your expectations within reasonable limits and making an effort to honor others by your words and actions, you set the stage for success!

Ruth 1:14, NKJV

"Then they lifted up their voices and wept again; and Orpah kissed her mother-in-law, but Ruth clung to her."

15

LOVE 'EM OR LEAVE 'EM?
Relating to an Unsaved Spouse

I t's time to change your thinking.
The idea that you can divorce your husband or wife because they are not born again is totally unscriptural (1 Corinthians 7:10-16). You would be amazed at some of the outrageous things people tell others to do. For example, I have heard of people telling husbands and wives that their unsaved spouses are against the "calling" of God on their lives, they should divorce them and "go on with Jesus." That is ridiculous! Unless domestic violence, repeated immorality or verbal abuse are issues in the home, you have no reason to separate from your mate.

Your spouse is not your enemy. If that's your mentality, then you need to change your thinking. He or she was not created to be your puppet or slave. They are also not to be controlled or manipulated so you can get your way in your marriage and in life. If you want to see your husband or wife saved just so *you* can be happier, that's selfish. You should be more concerned about their spiritual condition and eternal destination than you are about the temporary feeling of happiness. Ask yourself, *"What is my motive?"*

God loves your spouse and wants them to be saved more than you do. He's invested much more in him or her than you have. It's not your job to save your spouse. That's God's job and He's equipped to handle it. Trying to force the issue on your own is foolish and can not only damage your relationship with them, but also push them further away from God. There is a saying that goes, "You can lead a horse to water but you can't make him drink." That is so true. The horse will buck if you try to force him to do something he doesn't want to do!

Know Your Real Enemy

No matter how ugly the actions of your unsaved spouse may be, it's not your spouse that you're fighting against; it's actually the devil.

The Bible says we don't fight *"...against flesh and blood, but against principalities, against powers, against the rulers of the darkness of this world, against spiritual wickedness in high places"* (Ephesians 6:12). In other words, your battle takes place in the spirit, or invisible, realm. Since Satan is the *real* enemy, your job is to attack him and his forces because they are the ones keeping your mate from seeing the true condition of his or her soul. In fact, they have been literally blinded to the truth of God's Word (2 Corinthians 4:4)

> *The more honorably you live in front of your mate, the more the presence of God will infuse and change your marriage.*

When I say attack the enemy spiritually, I'm not suggesting you tie your spouse to a chair and start quoting scriptures over him or her. He or she probably wouldn't understand what you're doing, and they definitely wouldn't like it. They will just think you've lost your mind!

Here is how you fight the devil and evict him from your home: win your spouse over to Christ by your "conversation." The Greek interpretation of *conversation* is "a lifestyle, behavior and manner of life." In other words, win him or her over by your words and actions. Your life should be an open book that reflects the character of Christ, and one after which your spouse can pattern his or her life.

Wives, there are specific verses for you to model your life after. First Peter 3:1-2 says, *"... be in subjection to your own husbands; that, if any obey not the word, they also may without the word be won by the conversation of the wives; While they behold your chaste conversation coupled with fear* [respect]." Your actions can win your husband to the Lord. Pray for him, bind evil spirits and believe for his salvation in private. How you treat your husband openly is what counts. The Bible says to live a good life before him and be loving. He will eventually feel so loved and cherished that he can't help but turn to God.

For example, greet your husband at the door with a big kiss. Surprise him with a candlelight dinner. Recognize the good things he does, then praise him for it. And don't gossip to others about him. Your goal should be to live as the virtuous woman of Proverbs 31. Your spouse won't have any complaints, especially concerning your church attendance or zeal for God. In fact, he'll eventually support you because he sees the positive results of your godly lifestyle. With each loving and thoughtful act, you draw him closer to the God in you.

By the same token, husbands, you can win your wife over to the Lord by your godly lifestyle (1 Timothy 4:12; James 3:13). Make her feel special. Love her as you love yourself. Be a good provider and always believe the best about her. Keep yourself looking and smelling nice. Clean the house, spend time with your children and shower her with affection. When she thinks you're irresistible, realize that she is only a step away from finding out how irresistible God is! Believe me, this works. It's a spiritual principle that never fails.

The more honorably you live, the more God's presence will infuse and change your marriage. The devil's power is weakened when you don't give in to his antics, because he'll see that you are committed to obeying God *despite* your spouse's spiritual condition. The enemy cannot hang around very long when you act on the Word and submit yourself to God.

Represent Him Well

The devil runs when you begin acting like Jesus. He sees that before you do anything where your life and marriage are concerned, you always consider what Jesus would do.

Second Corinthians 5:20 tells us that we are *"...ambassadors for Christ...."* An *ambassador* is simply a representative acting on behalf of the one who sent him. For instance, an ambassador is not the president of the United States, but he *represents* the president. And in order for him to be an effective ambassador, he must carry himself *like* the president.

As a born-again Christian, you should not carry yourself poorly because you represent the King of kings. Because you are an ambassador of Christ, the Anointed One, you also *represent* His anointing. That means you have the right to operate in His anointing—His burden-removing, yoke-destroying power—even in your home. And because of that, you can also expect change to take place.

Remember what 1 Peter 3:1 says about husbands being won over by the lifestyles of

> *If you want to see your husband or wife saved so you can be happier, that's selfish. Ask yourself, "What is my motive?"*

their wives? The Philips translation of that verse states, *"...that they also may without the Word be won by the lifestyle or the way one carries [her] self."*

As a representative for Jesus, you *must* demonstrate Who Christ is to your mate. Your preaching and nagging won't help. When you carry yourself as an ambassador of Christ, your spouse will see that your relationship with God is real, and that Jesus truly lives inside of you. Each time you are faced with a trying situation, ask yourself how Jesus would respond, then carry yourself in that way.

When you represent heaven in a good way, your unsaved husband or wife can't help but notice. That is what they need to see—a manifestation of God's love through *you*.

Look Good Inside and Out

First Peter 3:3 says, *"Whose adorning let it not be that outward adorning of plaiting the hair, and of wearing of gold, or of putting on of apparel; But let it be the hidden man of the heart, in that which is not corruptible, even the ornament of a meek and quiet* (*teachable*) *spirit, which is in the sight of God of great price."* It takes more than outward adornment to win your spouse to the Lord. Looking good on the outside is wonderful, but it will take internal *and* external beauty to please him or her.

God loves your spouse and wants him or her saved even more than you do.

Have you ever met someone who looked gorgeous, but was really ugly on the inside. Remember the girl or guy you had a crush on growing up—the one who seemed so perfect. But when you finally met them, they turned out to be an arrogant, ill-mannered and condescending person. It was then that you recognized their flaws. You probably learned that her nice, long eyelashes were stick-ons and his smooth, silky hair was actually purchased in a store!

What's on the inside of a person affects their outside. Your character can either attract people to you, or repel them. You must present yourself in a way that is going to *sincerely* minister to your unsaved spouse. They'll be able to tell if your relationship with God is not real. Work on your inward beauty, as well as your outward beauty.

Give a Little Respect

Ephesians 5:33 says that a husband is to love his wife as himself, but it also says for the wife to *see to it* that she reverences (respects) her husband. Respect is a very important issue, especially for a man. Show me a man who feels respected by his wife, and I'll show you a man who feels loved. A man without respect feels worthless. He loses self-esteem, ambition and ultimately his desire to go on living, and vice-versa.

Respect is a basic need. If that need isn't fulfilled, an individual has no basic foundation on which to build. When he or she is not honored, they may develop such self-hatred that they will project it onto others. It's one thing to be disrespected in the workplace or in public, but quite another in your own house. Your house should be a refuge; it's your sanctuary. Therefore, show your spouse some respect. If you don't show your husband or wife the respect they deserve at home or anywhere else, don't expect too much from them by way of change.

Respect your mate with words. It is so important to watch what you say. Avoid making threats or saying things in anger. Even if you're sorry later, those words have already pierced your spouse's heart. Put a guard over your mouth so there can be peace in your home.

And one more thing: Don't try to replace the Holy Spirit. In other words, don't hound your unsaved spouse about going to church or reading the Bible and praying. It's human nature to resist what is being forced on you. They probably already know what they're supposed to be doing.

I meet too many people who feel it is their mission in life to plan different ways to get their husbands or wives born again. There is a problem with that kind of thinking: they become so overbearing that their unsaved spouses learn to resent God. Forget your plans and begin treating them just as God would. He assigned the Holy Spirit to draw your spouse unto Him. God has a way of orchestrating events and sending just the right person to convince your unsaved loved one that it's time to get born again. You don't have to figure it all out on your own; God has *the* plan. Just continue to do your part and allow God to do His. Be sure to keep doing what you know to do, even when you don't feel like it. Consistency is the key to your breakthrough!

Respect your mate enough to allow God to draw him. Respect is more than an emotion. It's an attitude of the heart. It may not be easy, especially if he or she is acting in an ugly manner toward you. But remember, God will help you.

> *No matter how ugly the actions of your unsaved spouse, it is not him or her you are fighting, but the devil.*

Also keep in mind how your husband or wife feels. From his or her point of view, you are in love with a God Who is invisible; Someone with whom they can't compete. This leaves them feeling helpless, frustrated and even jealous. All of a sudden, you are born again, going to church, spending time in prayer and in the Word, and your spouse feels cheated because you're in a relationship with the Invisible Man. That's a hard pill to swallow.

Show Them the Love!

There are a variety of reasons for one spouse being saved while the other is not. Many times a husband or wife accepts Christ as his or her Savior after they have been married for some time. Or perhaps one spouse disregarded the biblical warning not to be "unequally yoked" with an unbeliever. Whatever the case may be, your vows are binding, and divorce is not an option!

Because Christianity often produces a radical change in an individual's life, your spouse needs to know that you still love them. They may feel cheated by your new lifestyle. Don't allow your zeal for God to push your spouse away. He or she is your partner for life just as God is. Therefore, take the initiative to make them feel like they are number one. Start by organizing your schedule to include spending quality time with them. "Date" your loved one more often than you associate with fellow church members. The time you spend attending to your mate's needs may be the ticket to their salvation!

How do you prevent your spouse from feeling cheated? By keeping your priorities straight. Yes, put God first. But don't neglect your family. That's called living a balanced Christian life. If you're out of order, you're in trouble. Ask the Lord to help you establish boundaries and practice time management. That, too, shows respect for your spouse.

*   *   *   *   *

There are no magic potions or miracle products to make your unsaved spouse come to Jesus. The truth is, even if you're the world's most perfect and submitted mate, that does not guarantee your husband or wife will ever become a Christian. They have a free will. They are free moral agents who must choose God for themselves.

The hope of your mate's salvation should not be your motivating factor for being a loving and devoted partner. You should act that way because the Lord commands you to do so—period. Your attitude should be, "I'm going to be loving, devoted and submissive to my spouse because I want to obey God." It's not about your spouse; it's all about Him.

Respond to everything in your marriage with unconditional love, just as the Father responds to you. By doing so you not only transform your heart and revolutionize your marriage, you ultimately win your unsaved spouse to God!

Having an unsaved spouse is not reason enough to divorce them. Your lifestyle, coupled with God's ability and love, is the key to bringing them into the Kingdom of God.

Find scriptures that mention salvation and God's desire for people to know Him intimately, such as John 3:15-16, Acts 2:27-39 and 1 Timothy 2:1-4. Recite them aloud during your prayer time. For example, you may say something like the following:

"Father, I thank You that You love me and [spouse's name] so much that You sent Jesus to earth to die for our sins (John 3:16). You desire for everyone to know You intimately and live with You forever in heaven (1 Timothy 2:1-4). Because of that, I thank You in advance that [spouse's name] loves and serves You wholeheartedly. You have rescued them from eternity in hell, and because of their commitment to You, they enjoy the good life here on earth (John 10:10)."

In addition, make it a point to show love to your spouse by showering them with affection, surprising them with a love note or small token, or spending time with them. It's okay to love your spouse, even if they have yet to commit themselves to God. By allowing His love to flow through you, you make it that much easier for them to draw close!

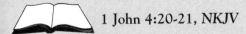

1 John 4:20-21, NKJV

"If someone says, 'I love God,' and hates his brother, he is a liar; for he who does not love his brother whom he has seen, how can he love God whom he has not seen? And this commandment we have from Him: that he who loves God must love his brother also."

16

THE JUDAS KISS
Dealing With Adultery and Betrayal

Adultery can be a spouse's worst nightmare. To say the least, the effects of it can be devastating. Although you expect to encounter a few speed bumps on the road to a successful marriage, nothing prepares you for the emotional fallout caused by betrayal. You immediately experience a whirlwind of emotions that range from anger and guilt to hurt and shame, and you are often unsure of what to do next.

Regardless of whether you were the betrayer or the betrayed, it's vital to understand that there is absolutely *no justification* for adultery. Despite the circumstances or who and what is to blame, infidelity is not justified, especially in the eyes of God. Simply put, it is a copout—a failure to follow through on a commitment to remain faithful to your spouse. It's an internal problem that drastically affects the external. For both of you, it now boils down to one question: "Where do we go from here?"

Now What?

This chapter has been written to help you and your spouse answer that question. Where *do* you go from here? You have several options: ignore the problem, call it quits or work it out. But what good are the first two options? Putting your problems in a closet only serves to set the stage for future difficulties, since skeletons have a way of making a lot of noise. A divorce doesn't resolve problems either; it only serves to add more pain to an already difficult situation.

At the moment your heart may be shattered or hardened, and what I'm about to say may sound crazy; but whether you believe it or not, it *is possible* for you to reconcile with your mate. You *can* operate in forgiveness and enjoy a successful, fulfilling relationship with him or her, even after adultery. In order to arrive at that level, however, you must be willing to examine yourself carefully, including past hurts and disappointments, even if you were the one who was betrayed. Honesty, openness and communication are the first steps in rebuilding the trust, love and loyalty that has not only been lost, but that belongs in a marriage.

Of course this is easier than it sounds. The journey toward healing and restoration is a difficult one. But keep in mind that success doesn't come cheap; there is *always* a price to pay. Whatever the cost, rest assured that it is *definitely* worth it.

Helping you to succeed in your marriage is our goal. Therefore, we must deal with the heart of the matter by examining the factors that contribute to infidelity. In addition, we will share the steps necessary for either overcoming the temptation to cheat or dealing with the emotional residue adultery often generates. The aim is to give you the information you need to heal a wounded marriage in spite of the situations that are working to destroy it.

To help you obtain victory over adultery, you are challenged to do the following:

1. **Make a decision to change and follow through on your commitment.**
2. **Deal with any feelings of anger, guilt, hurt and shame you may be experiencing.**
3. **Forgive yourself for the part you have played in the situation. Be sure to forgive your spouse also.**
4. **Forget the past.**
5. **Trust God's way of doing things over your own.**

Decision is the open door to reality. God has a perfect plan for your relationship with your spouse. To experience the reality and benefits of His plan, you must make up your mind not to allow *anything* to hold you back. This decision is then reflected in an attitude that says, "Adultery won't stop me. Unforgiveness won't stop me—nothing will. My marriage belongs to God. I trust Him, and that settles it!"

It's impossible to be defeated with this kind of "can do" mindset. I'm sure you've heard the old saying, "Winners never quit and quitters never win." The same principle is true regarding your marriage. God has already paved the way for healing and restoration through His Word, so adjust your thinking and lifestyle! Remember, without a firm commitment to change your thoughts and actions, there can be no true change in your relationship. As Taffi and I like to say, "Change isn't change until *you've* changed!"

That Cheating Heart

There are many underlying reasons for infidelity, such as:

- Lack of sexual fulfillment
- Seduction (getting caught up in the moment)
- Unrealistic expectations
- Lack of respect for one's spouse
- Insecurity (the need to prove oneself)
- Feeling trapped (a need for freedom)
- Lack of maturity (giving in to youthful lusts)
- Revenge
- An intentional way out of the marriage
- No moral values (adultery is "the" thing to do)

A person experiences a wide range of emotions when he or she discovers that their spouse is having an affair. Often the initial reaction is shock. You may think or say something like, "It can't be true. I can't believe this is happening to me. Not *my* marriage!" There may even be a tendency to deny the truth. But if you are honest with yourself, you'll begin to experience a deep, numbing hurt because, in a moment, your entire world—the dynamic of your relationship with your spouse—suddenly changes. The trust and confidence you had in him or her is now shattered, and your love and commitment is now in jeopardy. Your masculinity or femininity has also been challenged and damaged. It may even feel as if you've been living a lie or that you don't really know your spouse.

At this moment, it's *very* important to be rational. Although you are shocked, angry, hurt and disappointed, calm yourself. Don't harm your spouse or the person with whom he or she is involved. In fact, it isn't your responsibility to put the other person in his or her place. Your spouse made the mistake, so keep your focus on them. Don't make any rash decisions about your marriage and future at this time. Just hold yourself together until God can minister to you.

A cooling period is necessary before dealing with a situation like this. Trying to handle the problem while you are still upset will only make things worse. You may be tempted to pack your bags and leave, which is an understandable reaction. But don't ever assume that divorce and separation are the answers. Your spouse may not have held on to or understood the sanctity of your marriage vows, but that doesn't mean they are not still sacred to you. By *you* holding on to the meaning of that commitment, it lays the groundwork for unconditional love, repentance and restoration.

Consider the fact that it may have been an isolated incident, and that your spouse is remorseful that it happened and is willing to work things out. Calmly talk with him or her about the situation. Be honest about your feelings. You must communicate in order for reconciliation to take place. This means finding out from your spouse what led him or her to betray you. Let them know that you're willing to do your part to make things better. Reconciliation won't happen overnight, but with effective communication, things can and will work out.

As with all things, it's going to take some time for trust to be re-established. But it begins by agreeing that you will both do *whatever* it takes to ensure that future infidelity will not take place—*it must end right now!* Establish a system of accountability for a set period of time. Your spouse should tell you where they are going, how long they will be gone and when to expect them back. However, don't police their every move in an attempt to control them. The goal is to rebuild trust.

You can learn from Jesus and how He handled betrayal. His closest friends left him in His time of need (Matthew 26:47-56). Peter denied knowing Jesus (vv. 69-75). And for 30 pieces of silver, Judas turned Him over to the authorities, which meant certain death (vv. 14-16; 47-50).

Imagine the hurt and offense Jesus could have carried against Peter, Judas and the other disciples. His love *for* them, however, was greater than anything they had done *against* Him. It's going to take loving your spouse *in the very same way* to move beyond the hurt and pain their adultery has caused.

The following segment outlines others factors that play key roles in infidelity, as well as a course of action to take if your marriage is challenged in any of these areas.

Attention Deficit Syndrome

When a husband or wife fails to spend quality time with their significant other, their spouse may seek attention from others. This usually occurs in cases where the husband works long hours and rarely fulfills his wife's number one need—attention and affection. When he is at home, he is focused either on the television or on work. He is too busy for his wife. This may also be true for a wife with a busy lifestyle. She may spend a considerable amount of time at work, with friends or completing errands and may be too distracted to notice that her husband needs her attention.

In such cases, adultery is a scapegoat. The husband or wife begins looking for outlets to express his or her frustration. They begin thinking about another man or woman who is readily available: *"So and so doesn't treat me this way. She cares about me and tells me so,"* or *"So and so really listens to me. He's always there when I need him."*

Your spouse needs your undivided attention. When you're too busy to attend to their need for attention and affection, you communicate a lack of concern for them. That also communicates a lack of genuine love.

Take the time to turn off the television, unplug the phone and put work aside. Those things will still be there tomorrow. Do whatever it takes to show your husband or wife that you care. Don't push him or her away. You may be unknowingly pushing them into the arms of another.

Your thought life plays a key role in adultery. Whatever you think on the most is what you will eventually do.

On the other hand, If your spouse isn't paying you any or enough attention, *don't* seek out someone else to give it to you! You're deceiving yourself if you think the relationship will remain platonic; you are simply placing your marriage on the road to destruction. It's not worth it. If you could hear the heartbreaking stories I've heard and seen the lives I've seen that have been shattered by this self-deception, you would know that *nothing* is worth risking the loss of your marriage and family.

Approach your mate in love and let him or her know how you feel. You may have to do it several times, but keep on the issue until the matter is resolved. Communication is the key to a solid marriage. Without it, you can be easily deceived and seduced by others.

A Tight Squeeze

Some people are unable to function well under pressure. Problems at home or on the job drive them to seek various means of relieving stress. Some exercise, take time off or turn to drinking, drugs and abuse. Others commit adultery.

This method of escape ignores the issues at hand. Some people have affairs to escape the constant nagging and complaining they endure from their spouse. Others do so to measure their self-worth. In addition, they may feel inadequate or insecure, but an illicit sexual encounter boosts their self-esteem. In reality, the time they spend with their lover only offers them temporary relief from the outside pressure that is coming against them. They still have to go back home or to the job and face what they tried to ignore. It's a continuous cycle.

Why waste your time on a temporary fix? Instead, address the problem that lies inside your heart. If you are unhappy with your job, change it! If you are unhappy at home, do your part to work things out. Take up a new hobby or other method of relieving stress that will not place you in a compromising position with another person. Many state colleges offer free or inexpensive courses at night or on the weekends which may be of interest to you, and that may foster unity between you and your spouse.

Your lover can't do a thing for you except offer you a temporary escape and ruin your life and marriage. Although this individual may not be stressing you out at the moment, it's only a matter of time before they will. No one is ever content to play second fiddle. At some point in time they begin pressuring you to leave your spouse. What will you do then—find *another* lover?

Adultery is a dangerous, high-stakes game. You have nothing to win but everything to lose! Adultery is *not* your answer. It's only a temporary bandage for a wounded heart and poor self-image. Seek to change yourself by asking for God's help. In doing so, you'll receive the answers you need.

Welcome to Fantasy Island

Your thought life plays a major role in adultery. For instance, you may see someone at the grocery store and something about him or her piques your interest—probably their appearance. Or you have stopped your car at a stoplight only to look out your side window to see someone of the opposite sex in another car looking at you and smiling seductively.

If you don't forget about that momentary interest right away, it won't take but a few minutes for you to become intrigued and forget the fact that you're married. Your attention is now drawn to a complete stranger and your thoughts run wild. You create "what if" scenarios in your mind: *What if I was with that person instead of my spouse? I wonder if he (or she) wants me? What would life be like then?*

When the "what if" seed of adultery is planted in the soil of your mind and heart, it will produce a harvest.

Thoughts are like seeds. When a "what if" seed of adultery is planted in the soil of your mind and heart, it will produce a harvest. That is what Jesus meant when He said, "*...whosoever looketh on a woman to lust after her **hath committed adultery with her already in his heart**"* (Matthew 5:28, emphasis added). In other words, you don't have to actually sleep with someone other than your spouse to commit adultery. The very thought of doing it *is* adultery.

What you imagine affects the condition of your heart. And if you keep entertaining those thoughts, it won't be long before you'll begin acting out what you've spent so much time imagining.

Nimrod and his followers imagined themselves building a city and tower that would reach toward heaven (Genesis 11). After seeing what Nimrod purposed in his heart to do, God put a stop to his plans. Why? Because "...*nothing will be restrained from them, which they have imagined to do*" (verse 6). There is power in imagination.

Even if you never cheat physically, simply strategizing and rehearsing how, when and with whom you would cheat if given the opportunity, is committing adultery. You may think that you are not being unfaithful, but like Jesus said, your thoughts indict you.

Thoughts of unfaithfulness are blueprints to the tower of adultery. Like an architect, your first step in the building process is to draw a blueprint, or *inner image*, of what you desire to be constructed. All you need is an opportunity to find yourself involved in an affair.

To overcome thoughts of adultery, you must avoid situations that will cause your mind to wander. Soap operas, secular romance novels, pornographic magazines and videos and certain Internet sites are things you should stay away from because they will trigger ungodly fantasies. Before you know it, your mind will be consumed with uncontrollable, lustful thoughts.

You don't have to sleep with someone other than your spouse to commit adultery. The very thought of doing it is adultery.

Do not fight thoughts with thoughts; you'll lose every time. Instead, fight thoughts with words—more specifically, the Word of God. The Bible is your greatest weapon. It says to cast down and destroy the stronghold of thoughts contrary to the knowledge of the Word of God (2 Corinthians 10:4-5). When an adulterous thought enters your mind, open your mouth and obliterate it by confessing, or speaking, what God says about the subject.

For example, you can personalize Proverbs 5:18-21 in *The Amplified Bible* and say, "I choose to rejoice with my spouse. He (or she) satisfies me physically and emotionally. I will not become infatuated and embrace another. God watches over me and I choose to live a life that is pleasing to Him."

If you want to see a change in your spouse's life, begin by *sowing* change. You reap what you sow (Galatians 6:7). That may mean changing the way you speak and act toward him or her. Don't allow suspicion to cause you to doubt their faithfulness. Unfounded jealousy can ruin a relationship. Believe the best. Your spouse is innocent until proven guilty.

Change begins with a quality decision to speak the life-changing truths of God's Word. Therefore, guard your heart because it is fertile soil. What you watch, listen to and speak affects the condition of your heart and ultimately determines the kind of harvest you receive. Remember, your family's future depends on the decisions you make today. Don't do *anything* that will negatively affect future generations.

Break Free

David and Solomon were father and son. Both reigned over Israel and had something in common—a lust problem. They loved women and had numerous wives and concubines. Talk about "Like father, like son!"

Many men suffer the stings of *generational curses*—habits or addictive behaviors passed down from one generation to the next. It is a perpetuation of the like father, like son syndrome. For example, you may see this in cases where a father abuses his son, then the son abuses his son and so on until someone breaks the cycle.

The generational curses of lust and adultery are no different. Solomon lusted after women just as his father did. The Bible refers to generational curses as *iniquity* (Exodus 20:5). *Iniquity* means "to bend or distort the heart." It's simply a distortion, redirection or turning of your heart. Iniquity also implies a certain weakness or predisposition toward a certain sin. When a man or woman *continues* indulging in a particular sin, iniquity is birthed. It is practiced until, in certain situations, it eventually becomes a spontaneous reaction. When placed in a compromising situation, you simply give in.

Unresolved iniquity will invariably be passed down to your children. Here are several principles you must live by to break a generational curse in your family.

1. Recognize that there is a weakness in your lineage.

Don't dismiss the possibility that you may have inherited a generational curse of adultery. Does your family have a history of unfaithfulness in marriage? The point is to find out where the sin of adultery began in your family. Once you find the root, you can dig it out and destroy it.

2. Refuse to accept ownership of the curse of infidelity.

Avoid making excuses by saying things like, "That's just how I was raised."

That's a copout against change. Once born again, you are a *new* person in Christ (2 Corinthians 5:17). The old you with its lifestyle of sin has now passed away; however, it's up to you to make sure it stays away. You don't have to commit adultery if you don't want to. Rather than perpetuate a life of ungodliness, stand in your righteousness—your right-standing and ability in God—to overcome adulterous tendencies.

3. Live by the Word of God.

Don't try to overcome adultery in your own strength. You can't. That's the worst thing you could try to do. Although your will is involved, you need the supernatural strength of God and His Word to support you. An individual who was once an alcoholic may be able to refrain from alcohol on his own, but it's easier to do when he has the help of others.

Study what the Bible says concerning adultery. Study it until it becomes a part of your thought life. When you're tempted to be unfaithful, remember what you've learned. A good place to begin is Proverbs 5-8. These chapters will give you wisdom on what to do when you're tempted. Allow the cry, or pleadings, of wisdom to ring louder in your ears than the cry of adultery (Proverbs 8:14).

The Grass Isn't Greener

It goes without saying that adultery will ruin your life and family. It's not worth the hurt and pain it causes. When you married, you vowed to love and protect your spouse and not allow *anything* to come between you. Your wedding ring is a token of that commitment. It symbolizes a circle of love, unity, peace and faithfulness. Why throw that away for a few lustful moments with a lover?

The Word of God instructs us to love our *own* wife or husband (1 Corinthians 7:2). We have no business going into someone else's yard, so to speak. The grass may look greener on the other side, but it's what lies beneath the grass that counts. That pasture may be covering a septic tank! The affair you may be involved in might seem more exciting and fulfilling than your marriage, but corruption and deception lie in wait just beneath the surface.

The seventh commandment, "Thou shalt not commit adultery," was given to us so that we could understand God's perspective of marriage. The Ten commandments are still valid today. Every principle Jesus stood for is tied to those mandates. When He joins you to your spouse, He is establising a covenant—a solemn oath and agreement—between the two of you. It is a contract that is not only written on earth, but in heaven also. To commit adultery is to neglect to fulfill your part of the contract. In fact, it's a slap in God's face.

God is against the sin of adultery because it is equated with idolatry (Jeremiah 5:7; 7:9; 29:23). *Idolatry* is the worship of anything other than God, which He forbids (Exodus 20:3-5). Your lover can be your idol. The women or men you lust after in magazines, Web sites or on television can become idols that you lust after. When you commit adultery, you set yourself up to worship someone other than God. Think about it. You're drawn to that person to the point that you would do anything to be with him or her, even in your fantasies. You attempt to satisfy your lustful cravings in the arms of another or in your mind, rather than enjoying the love of your spouse. That's breaking your covenant, and dishonoring God and all that He stands for.

Where Do You Go From Here?

You must discipline yourself to be faithful first to God and then your spouse. If you are faithful in living by His Word by allowing it to be the final authority in your life, you won't have a problem with infidelity. That is true whether you or your spouse is involved in an adulterous affair. The Word must have the final say in how you live.

Perhaps you've known for years that your mate has been unfaithful. You have done all you know to do to change his or her ways. Realize that *you* can't change your spouse. We don't have the power to change anyone but ourselves. Don't allow yourself to feel inadequate or to develop low self-esteem. And don't allow your spouse's sin to affect the way you think about yourself. It is clear that their problem is emotional or spiritual. It either stems from your mate's unresolved past hurts, uncommunicated needs or a generational curse.

What you *can* do is love him or her as Jesus loves you. Like Him, be willing to love your spouse despite the wrong they have done. Love is a conquering force. It will conquer infidelity if you give it an opportunity. If you need professional counseling, then be sure to get it. In addition, love should always motivate you to pray for your spouse. Prayer really does change circumstances. Therefore, pray according to God's Word, which is His will, and He will answer you (1 John 5:14-15).

You can't fight a spiritual war with natural weapons (2 Corinthians 10:4, *The Amplified Bible*). Lust and adultery are spiritual forces that can only be conquered through the supernatural forces of love and prayer.

If you're having an affair, love yourself and your family enough to stop immediately! Use the principles that you've read in this chapter as a springboard to freedom. If you and your mate can't work through it alone, seek counseling. Sometimes we need the help of others to work through our web of problems or fears.

*   *   *   *   *

Faithfulness in marriage is the will of God for you. He promises that a faithful man or woman will be overtaken by His blessing (Proverb 28:20). That *blessing* is an empowerment to prosper and succeed in every area of your life. Your marriage has a right to prosper and succeed!

Be faithful regardless of what has happened in the past or what's going on right now. You have nothing to lose by being faithful, but everything to gain. Your relationship deserves the best. Never forget that! Do your part to forgive and forget, and strive toward true reconciliation with your partner. Remember, faithfulness is a solid investment in your marriage, its future and the generations to come.

Communication, understanding, effort and a commitment to remain faithful are the keys to victory over adultery and reconciliation.

Divorce-proof your home and solidify your commitment to your spouse by setting aside quality time each day to spend with him or her. Express your needs clearly and offer suggestions on how your spouse can meet those needs. Allow him or her to do the same with you. In addition, take a few moments to examine your thought life and lineage. Is there a predisposition for adultery in your family line? Are you focusing too much attention on sexually-charged media, such as magazines, videos, television shows or Internet sites? Together with your spouse, break the generational curses that have been passed down to you. Speak the blessing of God over your marriage and children, and purpose in your hearts to forgive one another of any past hurts. If necessary, seek counseling for further understanding and help with accountability.

1 Corinthians 13:7-8, NKJV

[Love] bears all things, believes all things, hopes all things, endures all things. Love never fails...."

Part III

Family
Planning
and
Children

17

BE FRUITFUL AND MULTIPLY
God's Purpose for Children

H ow do you view children? Do you see them as little aggravations that always seem to be either needing or asking for something? Are they an annoying interruption to the plans you have made and the goals you have set for yourself? Or do you see children as little angels from heaven?

Unfortunately, not everyone has a positive view of children, although they were once children themselves! This stems from a variety of reasons, such as a bad experience with a screaming baby, inquisitive toddler or rebellious teenager. Fear may also be a motivating factor, such as the fear of a lifestyle change, high-risk pregnancy, difficult childbirth or concern about the child's future. With all this in mind, it's easy to see why an individual may shy away from having children. They simply do not see children as God does.

Psalm 127:3 makes it clear that children are gifts from God. *"Lo, children are an heritage of the Lord and the fruit of the womb is his reward."* This scripture has a two-fold meaning. First, it speaks of the value of children, and then it tells of the blessing they are.

A Special Assignment

One of the definitions of the Hebrew word *heritage* is *assignment.* Did you realize that children are assignments given by God? That verse actually says, *"Lo, children are an **assignment** of the Lord"* (emphasis added). This adds value to children and changes the way in which they should be viewed.

Do you remember when you had a project assigned to you in school? You were careful to plan beforehand, then gather your supplies, put it together and make sure it was ready for presentation on the day it was due. In fact, that project often made up a large percentage of your final grade.

Children are just as important as your old school assignments—even more so, because they are given to you by God. As a parent, your job is

Children are gifts from God.

to build up, train, invest in and shape them in preparation for the future. When they are finally ready to leave home, your children will be equipped to follow God and fulfill His will for their lives. How well they are able to do this is your presentation to Him. In other words, the strength of their character and walk with God will have much to do with your "final grade."

Not only are children an assignment, they are an inheritance as well. An inheritance involves possession, much like an estate. It's something that is placed in another's care until the rightful owner comes back to claim it. Your children are your estate. They belong to God, but He's entrusted *you* to manage them for Him. He gave them to you to care for until He returns for them. That means your stewardship of them will be evaluated.

A Heavenly Reward

Psalm 127:3 also says, "*...the fruit of the womb is his reward.*" This simply means that your children are rewards to you from God. He has empowered you to create life in order to perpetuate the human race. In fact, the same instruction God gave to Adam and Eve still applies to us today. He told them to "be fruitful and multiply" (Genesis 1:28). In other words, He wanted them to have children to populate the earth.

Although you do not have to populate a planet, you *do* have a right to have children. God did not design for a man or woman to be barren. Infertility, though a reality for some, is not of God. How do I know? God loves to build up and create, not tear down and destroy. He imparted His creative ability into you and me when He gave Adam dominion over the earth. That meant Adam was not only able to have children, he was also equipped with the wisdom and creativity to name every animal (Genesis 2:20; 4:1-2, 25). If you've ever watched *National Geographic*, you know how creative Adam became—some of the names are so long and outrageous, it's hard to imagine how he came up with or even remembered them all!

Fight for Your Right

As a result of Adam and Eve's fall from grace, sin entered the world, corrupting all that God had intended for our pleasure. Pregnancy and childbirth are your God-given rights. It shouldn't be a difficult process to have children. No one should have to go through the agonizing delays and red tape associated with adoption, in vitro fertilization or fertility drugs! But because we live in an imperfect world where sin and the effects of it run rampant, some couples must fight for their right to have children.

If this is you, take heart! Don't despair. The doctor may have given you one report, but that doesn't mean you have to believe it. The Word of God can change your situation for the better. But you must do your part to make it happen. This takes boldness and confidence.

Go through the Bible and write down every scripture you find that pertains to childbirth and your right to have children. Speak them over yourself several times daily, until you receive the manifestation of your heart's desire. For example, you can say something like this: "Father, in Genesis 1:28 You commanded me to be fruitful and multiply. I thank You right now that I am able to do so. I declare that my husband's sperm is fertile and that my body is able to conceive and give birth. I thank You for the manifestation of our heart's desire and believe that I have what I say."

Remember to maintain a positive attitude even when it seems as if nothing is happening. It may take a little time, but rest assured, you *will* be a parent!

God gives you children as a reward. He not only wants to give you joy and a sense of accomplishment, He also believes you will be faithful to love and care for your children properly. He has entrusted the precious life of a child to your stewardship and protection. If you follow the guidelines outlined in His Word, that assignment will bring you joy.

As a part of that reward, God desires to use your children to minister to you and others, just as the Prophet Samuel was able to minister to his mother, Hannah, and all of Israel (1 Samuel 1-4:1). He has an awesome plan for their lives and wants them to be shining examples of what it means to have an intimate relationship with God. That ought to excite you!

When you cherish your children, they "reward" *your* relationship with the Lord. This happens in two different ways. First, it becomes easier to understand God's involvement in your life. The relationship a parent has with his or her child often parallels the relationship he or she has with God. God is a father, and you are His child. Everything He says and does is for your benefit, just like the things you do for your child. Biblical principles come into focus and take on a new meaning.

Second, children have a way of improving your character. For example, have you ever noticed how they have a way of making you look at the world in a new light, or bring things out of you, such as patience, love and self-control? They can show you which of those qualities you are lacking so you can make a change in your life! That's a wonderful reward, and you can thank your child for it.

God enjoys giving gifts; His best gift to you is your children. The fruit of the womb is His generous legacy—the fulfillment of a promise He gave to Abraham centuries ago.

A Serious Commitment

When God made a covenant with Abraham, then known as Abram, He said, *"...I will make thee exceeding fruitful, and I will make nations of thee, and kings shall*

You have a right to

have children.

come out of thee. And I will establish my covenant between me and thee and thy seed after thee in their generations for an everlasting covenant, to be a God unto thee, and to thy seed after thee" (Genesis 17:6-7).

Your children are a part of this promise. When God told Abraham, *"I will make thee exceeding fruitful, and I will make nations of thee,"* He was talking about giving birth to children. After this, God swore He would extend this promise to future generations, meaning that He would be the same God to them as He was to Abraham!

The agreement between God and Abraham was all about you and me. In other words, God looked into the future and saw you and your children. That's when He vowed to continue being the same God to your family as He was to Abraham's. What a promise!

You may say, "I'm not any relation to Abraham!" If you have accepted Jesus Christ as your Lord and Savior, then you have been adopted into God's family, making you "kin" to Abraham (Galatians 3:7). That's why it's not enough for you to be saved and then let your children make up their own minds about God. *No way!* God has given you the responsibility to train your children and direct them to the path that leads to the Promised Land—the will of God for their lives.

By seeing children from God's perspective, you learn to cherish, or treasure them. You will understand the importance of investing time and energy into making sure they know the ways of God and His promises. You'll make sure they know how to fight the enemy and win every time. A child's training will show whether his or her parents treasure them. God says that when they are old, they will not depart from what they know (Proverbs 22:6).

A Hidden Arsenal

Psalm 127 says something else very interesting about children. Right after God described them as an assignment and a reward, He then referred to them as "arrows:" Verses 4-5 say, *"As arrows are in the hand of a mighty man; so are children of the youth. Happy is the man that hath his quiver full of them: they shall not be ashamed, but they shall speak* (meet head-on) *with the enemies in the gate."*

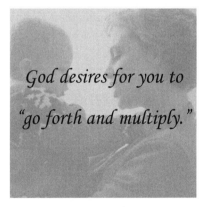

God desires for you to "go forth and multiply."

What does a soldier do with an arrow when confronted by an enemy? He takes his bow, loads an arrow onto it and fires away; the arrow then goes forth seeking the target. For centuries arrows were preferred weapons simply because the archer could stand a great distance away from the battle and shoot at the enemy without danger of being killed by a sword, axe or ball and chain. The greater the distance, the longer the bow and arrow. Commanders often used this weapon to confuse the enemy. It's hard to fight a battle successfully and efficiently when you have to continually look into the sky and duck or run for cover. A wound from an arrow is extremely painful, and can be fatal.

God said that children are like arrows that are prepared for use in battle. By instilling biblical principles in their lives, they are able to go forth and accomplish the mission God has for them without fear. Notice verse 4 says, *"As arrows are in the hand of a mighty man..."* (emphasis added). It doesn't say, *"As arrows that are not in your possession...."* Your arrows (children) are to be under your control, close at hand. if you can't control your children, you can't train or guide them in the truths of the Word.

Something else to keep in mind is this: arrows have sharp points. Those sharp points are what enable them to do their job: hit the target. Likewise, children sharpened with the Word are able to do the jobs they were created to do: fulfill the will of God for their lives by carrying out the assignments He has specifically for them. In addition, they will have the strength and determination not to be swayed from their mission, but will overcome obstacles and meet the enemy head on!

Give 'Em the Basics

Do you know what your goal should be? To raise supernatural children—children who know, love and serve God wholeheartedly, and effectively carry out the principles outlined in His Word. Although you may look at your child and think, "I need help! I can't even get him (or her) to wash the dishes without a fight!" That's okay. It's not too late to start training them. *Carpe diem*—seize the day (or the moment)—and begin imparting the Word of God into their lives. Make the most of every opportunity. Taffi and I love to use something called "situational teaching." When a situation arises, we use it as an opportunity to weave in or reinforce a biblical principle. This way, the Bible is explained to them in a way that they understand and which is easy to remember.

Make the most of every opportunity to weave the Word of God into their lives

But don't just concentrate on spiritual principles; be practical also. Of course your children should know about healing, deliverance, salvation, prosperity and the gifts of the Spirit. But they should also know how to manage money, change a tire and be a savvy shopper. Teach them life skills so they'll know how to function in the real world.

In addition, build them up mentally. Equip them with confidence and help them to develop a positive self-image. When you send your children off to school, tell them that they can do all things through Christ (Philippians 4:13). As a result, they can get an "A" on their test or win the relay race in Physical Education class. Let them know they have the wisdom of God working on the inside of them. When your children believe those things, their grades remain high and their work output steady. They won't be fighting with other children in school or bringing home a report card filled with Ds and Fs. It's your job as a parent to encourage them so they won't feel inadequate or inferior.

Most importantly, children must learn to fear, or respect, God and His Word. Psalm 1 tells us that the person who delights in the Lord and meditates on His Word is blessed, or empowered to prosper and excel. You can't expect children to respect God's ways if they see you disrespecting them yourself by the words you speak and the things you do. Actions speak much louder than your words. Children are remarkable little magnets. They are quick to pick up on things, whether they are positive or negative. Remember that the next time you're inclined to dishonor your spouse! You are a role model for your children. They will reflect the time and effort you put into them. If you don't want to see your negative traits passed on to them, make a quality decision to change your ways. It's that simple.

Also keep in mind that it's *okay* to say "no" to your children! Many parents make the mistake of wanting to be friends with their children more than caregivers. So they compromise, bargain or relax established rules and principles to gain their affection. While this may provide a temporary bonding, it will eventually come back to haunt you in the form of rebellion and self-centeredness.

Saying no doesn't make you a bad parent, but a *good* one. Your children have plenty of friends, believe me. What they need is an authoritative figure who gives them structure, stability and discipline. Although they fuss about it, children feel most loved when their parents enforce established rules and boundaries. It's not going to end your child's life if you say no to something that's not good for them. Remember, those "arrows" *must* remain under your control until it's time to release them. It often helps to explain the reason for your decision, and by weaving in the Word, they will also gain a greater understanding that you have their best interests at heart.

Celebrate!

Proverbs 23:24 says, *"The father of the righteous shall greatly rejoice: and he that begetteth a wise child shall have joy of him. Thy father and thy mother shall be glad, and she that bare thee shall rejoice."* These parents are able to rejoice because of the wisdom and knowledge present in their child. In other words, their son or daughter is so well-trained in the ways of God that he or she does nothing to shame them; on the contrary, everything they do prospers!

When your children live their lives according to the Word and make it their final authority in everything they do, that's a reason to celebrate! It means that you have seen them from God's perspective and perceived that

He has a plan for them. Because of your love, encouragement, discipline and training, they are now a credit to you and to God.

Proverbs 29:17 says, *"Correct thy son, and he shall give thee rest...."* Wouldn't you like a little rest? I don't know of any parent who would turn down the opportunity to take a break! If you've given your children proper home training, you can rest assured they are equipped to handle any situation. You don't have to worry about them losing their virginity in the back seat of a car. You don't have to worry about them drinking or doing drugs at some party. You don't have to worry about them flunking out of college. You can rest!

If you haven't done so already, say this prayer aloud right now and commit your children to the Lord:

"Father, I thank You that my family is established on Your promises. Thank You that my children are godly, holy and submitted to Your will for their lives. I thank You that they love Your Word and make it their final authority. I declare that their names are written in the Lamb's Book of Life and that angels are encamped about them every minute of the day. Today I choose to build my house on Your Word by treating my children as an inheritance and a blessing from You. I will do my part to train and teach them as You would have me to do. In Jesus' name, Amen."

By doing as God commands and laying hold of your right to have children and raise them in His ways, you fulfill the promise given to Abraham in Genesis 12 and position yourself for the greatest adventure and most pleasurable rewards ever!

God desires for you to have children. He has equipped you for that purpose by instilling within you His creative ability. It is a God-given right that should not be ignored or taken lightly.

Begin to see children as blessings instead of aggravations. If possible, volunteer one hour a week at a nursery or day care center, or offer your services as a babysitter to your friends and relatives. The more time you spend with a child, the more you will be challenged to change your present mindset and see them as

God sees them. In addition, you will develop higher levels of patience and self-control, while gaining a greater understanding of what it takes to be a parent. By renewing your mind to what the Word of God has to say about children and spending time with them, the better off you will be when it comes time to have children of your own!

 **Genesis 1:27-28**

"So God created man in his own image, in the image of God created he him; male and female created he them. And God blessed them, and God said unto them, Be fruitful, and multiply, and replenish the earth, and subdue it...."

18

SUPERNATURAL CHILDBIRTH
The Solution to Infertility, Miscarriages and High-Risk Pregnancy

So, you want to have a baby. You and your spouse have tried to conceive on numerous occasions, but so far every attempt has failed. You've done everything in the book to get pregnant. Relatives and friends have given you all kinds of advice: "Do this. Try that. It worked for me." You may have even visited fertility specialists and undergone a variety of treatments, from in vitro fertilization to the latest fertility drugs—but nothing has worked.

Perhaps conception isn't the problem; repeated miscarriages or being unable to carry a child to full term may be the issues. I'm sure it hasn't been easy for you to find out that you're pregnant only to miscarry weeks later, or having to be hospitalized because you or the baby are in distress. The specialists may have diagnosed you as being high risk or prone to miscarriages.

With all that you have gone through, you may feel like the woman with the issue of blood before she was made whole (Mark 5:25-34). You've invested quite a bit of your finances in seeking help and feel like you have wasted your time and money. Months and years have gone by without results. At this point, you and your spouse may be thinking, "We might as well give up! There's no hope."

Hope Floats

There *is* hope! Regardless of the fact that you have not conceived, have had repeated miscarriages, or have been labeled as high risk, don't give up on your dreams! This may sound cliché, but since you've tried the rest and nothing has worked, now it's time to try the *best*. I'm talking about doing things God's way—trusting Him to the point that you're willing to do whatever He says because His methods guarantee results. What do you have to lose? *Absolutely nothing!*

Years ago when Taffi and I first decided to have children, we experienced a few challenges. For a while I thought something was seriously wrong. We tried to conceive but were unsuccessful. I asked my grandmother, Big Mama, for advice and she simply said, "Just relax. Don't try so hard." Her statement, though seemingly insignificant, was full of wisdom.

Trusting God was at the heart of what she said to me. In essence, Big Mama was telling me that Taffi and I should stop worrying about the fact that she hadn't yet conceived. Human nature tends to push God aside, saying, "Lord, I can handle things on my own. I don't need Your help." By worrying, you actually crown yourself as God.

My grandmother's advice to relax and trust in the Lord is what the Bible calls "entering into His rest" (Hebrews 4:1-11). This involves becoming fully persuaded—resting assured—that you have a right to the promises of God. It means that you stop worrying and trying to do things *your* way and instead begin doing things God's way. Just as you would rest after working all day, you must *rest*, trust, in the fact that He is in control.

The Bible is full of God's promises—promises that have to come to pass. In fact, God took care of His end of the bargain before you were ever born—before the foundation of the world (Ephesians 2:10; Hebrews 4:3). It's now up to you to do your part and trust Him so you can see your dream of having children come to pass.

Don't accept the report that says you can't have a baby. You wear God's blessing, which means you are empowered to be fruitful and multiply.

Taffi and I entered God's rest where giving birth was concerned. We didn't do anything magical like hopping backwards on one foot. We simply studied what the Bible has to say about the subject and believed beyond a shadow of a doubt that it is our right to bear children. We made the Word of God the final authority in our lives by placing it *above* what anyone else had to say. Taffi and I then prayed in accordance with those scriptures.

In the name of Jesus and with His authority, we exercised our dominion over everything that was hindering conception from taking place. We declared that our physical bodies, including our organs and tissues, were aligned with the truth of God's Word. We covered everything that pertained to our reproductive systems. In doing so, we put heaven and hell on notice that we intended to see God's promises come to pass in our lives. It wasn't long before we found out that Taffi was pregnant. I'll never forget the day she told me she was carrying our first-born daughter, Jordan. I was so happy!

Our testimony should encourage you to allow patience to work its perfection in your situation. James 1:4 says, *"But let patience have her perfect work, that ye may* *be perfect and entire, **wanting nothing**"* (emphasis added). God wants you to be whole, with nothing missing or broken in your life. That *includes* having children. He wants to perfect, or bring to completion, the things that concern you (Psalm 138:8). Miscarriages, infertility and high-risk pregnancy are signs of imperfection that He wants to reverse. Therefore, trust Him and His Word.

Entering God's rest requires patience. That does not mean you should sit around hoping and wishing things would be different. True patience involves being consistent in what you desire from God; that is, being consistent in *doing* what He instructs you to do. In simple terms, you "keep on keeping on" until you get whatever it is you're after. You must be aggressive and not quit until His promises become a reality in your life. That's what I call "violent faith."

A Dream Come True

Abraham, the father of faith, believed God to the point that he didn't waver concerning God's promises (Romans 4:20-21). He was perfectly aware of his age and the fact that his wife, Sarah, was past the age of childbearing. In spite of this, he remained fully persuaded that the Lord is a promise-keeping God.

Genesis 12:2-3 tells us that God promised to bless Abraham and his offspring, making them a great nation. Because of that promise, Abraham would in turn bless mankind. Verse two says he was blessed *to be* a blessing. The *blessing* on Abraham was an empowerment to prosper and excel in every area of his life. This prosperity included financial, emotional, social, mental and physical well-being. In fact, he had a track record of excelling in everything he did, wherever he went.

To solidify His promise to Abraham, God appeared to him in a vision and established a covenant, or agreement, between them (Genesis 15). In it, He and Abraham agreed to each do their part to ensure God's promises to the human race would come to pass. God said to Abraham, *"...Fear not, Abram: I am your Shield, your abundant compensation, and your reward shall be exceedingly great"* (verse 1, AMP). In essence, Abraham responded by saying, "Lord, I believe You. But what will You give Sarah and me as a token of Your covenant, seeing that we don't a have child of our own?" (verse 2).

You have to understand Abraham and Sarah's situation. They were *well beyond* childbearing years. In addition, Sarah was barren (Genesis 18). When Abraham was 99 years old, God promised to make him a "father of many nations" (Genesis 17:4-7). It would take a supernatural intervention from heaven to make this promise a reality! But that's exactly what happened. The Lord came through on His promise, and Sarah gave birth to Isaac (Genesis 21:1-7).

The key to Abraham and Sarah receiving Isaac (the manifestation of God's promise), was Abraham's *obedience*. Obedience is the key to transformation. God transformed, or reversed, a natural dilemma—their inability to bear children. Isaac wasn't a surprise to Abraham, because he knew that trusting and obeying God has its rewards. Isaac's birth was a supernatural reward.

This tells me that children are a reward from heaven. The Bible says that the fruit (offspring) of the womb is the Lord's reward to His people (Psalm 127:3). Based on this truth, why would He withhold children from you? He won't. He would *never* hold back the gift of children from you (Psalm 84:11; James 1:17).

Make It Real

There's no question that the Lord will remain true to His Word. Therefore, it's up to you to know His promises concerning your right to have children. You cannot have the mentality that *God will do it for others, but He won't do it for me*. That's not how He operates; He doesn't play favorites (Acts 10:34). Like Abraham and Sarah, as well as the many other couples in Scripture, you too, have a right to give birth and have children.

Study the Bible for yourself and you will discover that many of God's people experienced supernatural childbirth. Take Samson's mother for instance (Judges 13). Although she was barren, an angel appeared to her and declared that she would one day give birth to a son (vv. 3-5). When she told her husband, Manoah, what the angel had said, he asked the Lord to allow the angel to reappear and teach them what they needed to do to raise their son. The Lord answered Manoah's prayer and "*...the woman [in due time] bore a son and called his name Samson; and the child grew and the Lord blessed him*" (verse 24, AMP).

What about Hannah's situation? You can read her story in the first chapter of 1 Samuel. Hannah was barren, and to make things worse, her husband, Elkanah, had another wife, Peninnah, who gave birth to many children. For years, Peninnah ridiculed Hannah for not having children (vv. 4-7). Imagine what Hannah went through. She must have been embarrassed and angry. There came a time, however, when she had enough hurt and humiliation. Hannah prayed to the Lord and made a vow:

> *...O Lord of hosts, if thou wilt indeed look on the affliction of thine hand-*
> *maid, and remember me, and not forget thine handmaid, but wilt give*
> *unto thine handmaid a man child, then I will give him unto the Lord all*
> *the days of his life, and there shall no razor come upon his head*
> (verse 11).

Hannah meant business! She poured out her soul to the Lord. Heartfelt prayer got heaven's attention and connected her to God's supernatural power. That makes perfect sense. James 5:16 tells us that the *"...earnest (heartfelt, continued) prayer of a righteous man makes tremendous power available [dynamic in its working]"* (*AMP*).

Hannah's prayer tapped into God's supernatural ability, giving her womb the ability to conceive what it could not conceive before (1 Samuel 1:19-20). Heaven's dynamic, explosive power was released in her physical body and she later gave birth to Samuel, who became a mighty prophet of God.

Stop and think for a moment. Are you any different from these women? No. Don't you think God can empower you with the ability to give birth to the next mighty man or woman of God? He can!

Your and your child's destiny is in God's hands, just as Hannah's and Samuel's were. Hannah understood this, but she also understood a simple key to receiving her petition. She didn't wonder *if* the Lord could empower her; she was simply *convinced* that He would! That's why she honored her vow after Samuel was born. She brought him to the temple and presented him to Eli the priest to be dedicated to the Lord (vv. 24-28). She basically said, "I prayed for this child and the Lord answered my prayer. Therefore, I'm dedicating his life to God so that he may serve Him for the rest of his life."

Eli later blessed Elkanah and Hannah because of what she did. That blessing empowered her to give birth to three more sons *and* two daughters. Talk about a breakthrough! Hannah's faithfulness with dedicating her *firstborn* to God released an overflow of His power. Like my good friend in the ministry, Dr. Leroy Thompson Sr. would say, Hannah tapped into a "gusher!"

In each of these cases, we see that God reversed infertility. Allow this to stir your faith in what He can do for *you*. You, too, can tap into God's power to make conception, childbirth and children a reality in your life. No, God doesn't have to send an angel to you. He doesn't have to do anything miraculous like giving you a burning bush. Your willingness to act with faith in His Word is more than enough.

Mary, the mother of Jesus, understood this principle of faith in His Word. When an angel told her, a virgin, that she would give birth, she said *"...be it unto me **according to thy word**"* (Luke 1:38, emphasis added). That "word" concerned her giving birth to the Son of God by the supernatural power of the Holy Spirit coming on her (verse 35).

It is interesting to note that the angel told Mary that her cousin, Elisabeth, had conceived a son in her old age (verse 36)—John the Baptist. The angel was confirming something powerful to Mary. In essence, he was saying that the same Holy Spirit power and ability that enabled her cousin to conceive was the same Holy Spirit power and ability that would cause her to conceive. Mary *received* that prophetic word. In other words, she accepted God's promise, and the rest is history!

Tap Into the Power

You have every right to see manifestation where children are concerned. The supernatural power of God is available to you. His power can reverse your infertility, proneness to miscarriages or high-risk pregnancy. But you must do your part in order to experience manifestation. Like Mary, you must *receive* what the Word of God says concerning your situation; you *must* accept His promises.

In Deuteronomy 7:14, God promises that *"You shall be blessed above all people: there shall not be male or female barren among you, or among your cattle" (AMP)*. This promise overrides what the doctors have told you. God promised to bless you with an empowerment to succeed in life—and that includes giving birth. His only condition is that you listen to His instructions and carry them out. *"And all these blessings shall come on thee, and overtake thee, if thou shalt hearken unto the voice of the Lord thy God...Blessed shall be the fruit* (offspring) *of thy body..."* (Deuteronomy 28:2, 4, emphasis added). This means that infertility and miscarriages are powerless when God's blessing is on you.

Keep in mind that the natural and the supernatural work hand in hand. So allow God's super to work with your natural.

How do you tap into the power of the blessing for childbirth? You might be surprised at the answer: through your tithes. In Malachi 3:10-11, God commands us to bring 10 percent of our income into His house (the Church) so that there may be a sufficiency of resources. However, when you tithe, not only are the resources of the local church strengthened, but God opens the windows of heaven and pours out a *blessing on you* as well. That blessing is not a car, money or anything material. Instead, He pours out an overflowing empowerment so great you can't contain it.

The tithe is a covenant connector. It connects you to the same power and ability that was promised to Abraham. No wonder he and Sarah prospered and were able to conceive Isaac supernaturally; Abraham was a tither (Genesis 14:20)!

God also promised that when you tithe, He will *"rebuke the devourer"* (Malachi 3:11), which represents *anything* that attempts to hinder you from receiving the manifestation of His promises in your life. Barrenness is a devourer, and so are miscarriages. But when the blessing is upon you, your vine (body) will not cast (miscarry) its fruit (offspring) before the time in the field (the full-term pregnancy).

Taffi and I made sure we tithed consistently. That's how much we wanted children. Now examine your life. Have you and your spouse been tithing consistently? If not, make the adjustment. Begin tithing in your local church or wherever God directs you; however, make sure you're tithing into a ministry that operates by the Word of God. It will make a tremendous difference in your life and situation. The tithing issue may *seem* irrelevant in the case of giving birth. But trust the Word, and you'll see that a manifestation is guaranteed (2 Peter 1:19).

Don't Overlook the Natural

Up to this point, I've only discussed supernatural manifestations. But it is very important that you don't completely disregard the natural facts concerning your inability to have children.

Often people can be so spiritually minded that they neglect to do what's necessary in the natural. They refuse sound medical advice and suffer for it. There is nothing wrong with doing what the doctor orders, as long as you have God's okay. Keep in mind that the *natural* and *supernatural* work hand in hand. So allow God's *super* to work with your *natural*.

If your doctor has diagnosed the problem, pay attention. For example, if he or she says that there is a problem with genetic abnormalities or bacterial infections, at least you know what to pray against. You can now be specific when asking God to correct the symptoms. You may be surprised to hear that a simple surgery or adjustment in your diet and exercise routine will resolve the problem. You may even discover that a stress-free lifestyle can also reverse infertility. God can use a doctor to share His wisdom with you. Remember, however, that their advice should always line up with His Word.

Allow God to guide you in your decision-making. That's what a young couple in our church did. After several miscarriages, they prayed and received wisdom from the Lord *and* the doctors. Now they have a handsome baby boy. Yes, I prayed and laid hands on them. But that wasn't the total solution. I simply joined my faith with theirs. They did what they needed to do in the natural in order to see manifestation. Imagine if they had been overly spiritual. I honestly believe they would still be childless to this day. Thank God that's not the case!

Make Way for the Stork!

I encourage you and your spouse to come into agreement right now. Power is made available when a husband and wife, covenant partners, get together and pray (Matthew 18:19).

First, thank God for His goodness. Thank Him for what He has already done in your lives. Thank Him for blessing your bodies with the power to produce offspring. Next, remind Him of His promises to you concerning having children. Vow that if He proves faithful to His Word, you will raise your children to serve Him all the days of their lives. After you've prayed and settled in your heart that you *will* give birth, begin acting like it. Confess, or recite aloud, scriptures that deal with healthy childbirth. Keep the Word on your mouth daily and it won't be long before you see the manifestation of your confessions.

In addition, your corresponding action of faith may be to start preparing for the arrival of your unborn child. Visit hospital nursery and delivery rooms. Begin skimming through catalogs for pictures of baby clothes and furniture. Invest in a pair of baby booties or shoes to help you develop an inner image of life with a child, rather than life without one. All it takes is for you to receive God's promises and your corresponding action for conception to take place. And don't forget to do what's necessary in the natural!

---

* * * * *

From now on, every time you and your spouse come together sexually for the purpose of conception, remember to invite God to join in on your lovemaking experience. He wants to be a part of your life in every way. Together with Him, you and your mate *will* create a life!

Have faith in God and His Word concerning conception, childbirth and children, and He'll reward you for it.

Search the Bible for scriptures that talk about children and childbirth and begin confessing them at least three times a day until you have delivered a healthy baby girl or boy! As an added bonus, recruit your spouse or a close friend or family member to partner with you in prayer, confessions and faith. It won't be long before you have your heart's desire!

Hebrews 11:1

"Now faith is the substance of things hoped for, the evidence of things not seen."

19

LITTLE ORPHAN ANNIE
Adoption

S omeone once asked me if I believed in adoption. I said, "Well, I'd better. It's a biblical principle—and I've already adopted my son!"
Did you know that adoption is mentioned in the Scriptures? Two of my favorite verses are Ephesians 1:4-5. In *The Amplified Bible* they read, "*Even as [in His love] He chose us [actually picked us out for Himself as His own]...For He foreordained us (destined us, planned in love for us)* **to be adopted** *(revealed) as His own children through Jesus Christ...*" (emphasis added).

When you become born again, you are adopted into God's royal family. He is now your heavenly Father, and you are an heir to all that is His. Your family in the blood of Jesus grafts you into that family tree (Romans 8:15-17). You have been chosen by God to be His extension in the earth. As a result, you are able to operate in His authority. Angels move and circumstances improve when you speak His Word in faith. If that doesn't make you want to shout, you need to check yourself for a pulse!

Spiritual adoption is a very exciting subject and is our foundation for Christian living. But this chapter wasn't written solely from a spiritual slant, but a practical one as well for those of you who are interested in adoption.

The Right Choice

As I said before, if you are born again, you know that you have been spiritually adopted. You are able to exercise the same rights and privileges as your Father; as a result, your life is filled with blessings, hope, forgiveness, healing and prosperity. It's a great joy to be God's child.

Here on earth, there is also a natural adoption. Many times, those who are naturally adopted don't have the opportunity to feel as special as a child who was born into a family. These children simply don't realize that they were specially chosen to be a son or a daughter.

If you are the adoptive parent, you can change that kind of thinking. You can allow your compassion and patience to create a special bond. If you remain stable and consistent, using the Word as your guide, you will create a beautiful and successful family.

I speak from experience because years ago I adopted a 13-year-old Caucasian boy from a psychiatric unit. Why did I do that? Compassion. He was very special to me and I chose him because of my compassion for him. That compassion grew into love. Today, I am so proud of him. He is married and has children of his own now. In addition, he is serving God, and is a godly husband raising godly kids. He even came to work for me for a while and totally transformed our television ministry with his energy and creativity.

Although Greg has matured into a strong man, let me tell you, it wasn't an easy journey. When Taffi and I adopted him, he had already been in the world for thirteen years, living under *his own* set of rules. His independent streak was almost out of control because he had spent years having to look after and fend for himself. We had to totally transform his way of thinking.

I remember the day everything came to a head. I put my face about one inch from Greg's nose and said, "You need to get this straight. You are not my partner. The responsibility is not equal in this house. I am the head, and there's only one head in this house. You are the one submitted to the head. When you don't do what I say to do, I will get you every single time."

> *You are an adopted child. On the day you become born again, God adopts you into His royal family, making you His heir.*

I had to be tough—Greg was already a teenager—and consistent, because he was constantly testing me to see if I would do what I said. I had sought God for wisdom on how to raise this child, and "tough love" was the direction I was given. I didn't like being so hard on Greg, but I was doing it because I cared so much for him.

Oh, but there were days—days when I thought I had ruined my life. In fact, every day for about the first two and a half years, I had nothing but questions, problems and complaints all the time. Greg gave Taffi and me such trouble! In fact, he ran away *three* times. One time, we were so aggravated at him that we even helped him pack! When we got home from church the next morning, he was sitting on the porch like a little whipped puppy. I walked by and said, "Hi, how are you?"

He said, "Dad, can I come home?"

I replied, "Yes, but you know there are rules and regulations that you have to follow."

"Will I be punished for this?" he asked, fiddling with his suitcase.

"Yep," I said.

He *already* knew the answer. I had to be a tough disciplinarian and stick to my guns because for the most part, Greg was too old for a spanking, although I did apply the rod sometimes. Do you know what I said the whole time I was using it? "I love you, boy. I love you too much to let you act like this."

It was a difficult situation, but God's way worked. After those rounds of rebellion, Greg never gave me one bit of trouble. I had a near-perfect teenager. I didn't have to worry about him getting into trouble in school or doing things behind my back. Eventually, Greg went into the Army for a little while. He's made us very proud of him.

Although there were times that I wanted to throw in the towel and give up, I didn't. I couldn't, because God has never given up on me. Taffi and I refused to compromise where Greg was concerned. Day after day, we kept feeding him the Word of God and praying for him. I believed the scripture that said children were a blessing and a heritage of the Lord (Psalm 127:3), and I would quote that over and over.

Did Greg seem like a blessing all the time? By no means! Any parent will tell you that a child can run you into the ground. But faith doesn't operate by what is seen; instead, it's what you know. Taffi and I knew that Greg would one day be a godly man and a blessing. Have you ever heard someone say, "I know it in my knower," or "I know that I know?" Well, I was absolutely certain of it. *I just knew*, and I was right.

I share this experience because you're probably reading this chapter to get information on adopting a child. I wanted to give you just a sampling of what could be in store for you, as well as the end result, because adoption isn't going to be easy. There will be trying times and beautiful times. With firm direction from the Lord and the absolute assurance that you are doing His will, nothing will be impossible for you.

In fact, you can even make something supernatural out of a natural adoption by taking your family tree and grafting another branch on to it. Then, by training that child to be whoever God desires for him to be, you start an entire new and godly generation! That's what God did with you and what Taffi and I did with Greg.

Assess Your Motives

Parents go through a dramatic change when an adoptive child enters their lives. If they did their "internal homework" and evaluated their reasons for adopting, then that change was for the better.

Before you begin the process of adoption, I strongly recommend that you first stop and evaluate your own situation. For instance, if you're not able to have children and are interested in adopting because of the pressure you feel from other people, don't do it. You are not ready. Wait until *you* are emotionally, physically and mentally prepared to take on this responsibility without pressure from loved ones.

If you're thinking that adoption will make your marriage better, stop! Children, whether birthed into a family or brought in by adoption, are not the solution to your marital difficulties. Children can place incredible pressure on your marriage. In addition, many people who divorce often use their children as leverage against their spouses. That is a no-win situation for everyone involved.

You must also consider your age—how old will you be when the child graduates from high school and college? You must take your family's feelings into consideration. Will they accept the adopted child as if he or she had been born into the family?

Adoption is not something to be taken lightly. Aside from marriage, it is probably the most important decision you'll ever make. With it there is no such thing as a "divorce." Children are forever. There are no refunds or exchanges when they aggravate, challenge or tire you out. You can't look at adoption as something that will fill a void in your life. To adopt means that you are totally on the giving end, just as all parents should be. You will give and give, and at times, your patience will be worked until you feel you have nothing left. So be sure you're ready to give this child all the love and support he or she will need.

Adoption also means a radical transformation. You will change from a set lifestyle to an instant family, and the transformation can be dramatic if you're not prepared for it. It will take most of your time and resources to obtain the child and continue meeting his or her needs. This means financial preparation and good management are key issues. If your financial picture is shaky, or you have trouble managing money, think twice before bringing a child into your life.

Where to Begin

Congratulations! Now that you have assessed your motives, weighed the pros and cons, examined your ability to provide, and determined you are ready to take the next step, it's time to think ahead to the actual adoption process. Ask yourself these questions:

- Do you want an *open adoption* (where you meet and stay in contact with the birth parents) or a *closed adoption* (no contact with birth parents)?

- Do you want to adopt a special-needs child?
- Do you want a newborn?
- Are you willing to adopt siblings?
- Do you want to adopt a child from overseas?
- Are you financially ready to adopt?
- Do you want to use an adoption attorney?
- Do you want to adopt through an agency?

Adoption Basics

Most prospective parents desire a healthy child, often with a background similar to their own. Caucasian, African-American, Hispanic, and mixed-race infants are available through private adoption agencies, and some public ones. The Caucasian infants make up the smallest percentage available, and are placed only through private agencies and independent adoptions.

The adoption of Native American children of all ages by non-Native Americans is strictly limited by the Federal Indian Welfare Act. If the child is a registered tribal member, at any time the child's Tribal Council can step in and protest the adoption or seek a court order to stop it. If you are interested in adopting a Native American child, you will need to check the state laws concerning the requirements.

Children with special needs are also available. These children may be older (grade school through teens) and have a physical, emotional or mental disability. At times, siblings will be placed in this category so they can be adopted together. Usually these children live within the state foster care program. However, both public and private agencies place children with special needs.

When you adopt a child, it is forever.

An advantage to adopting children with special needs is the national, regional and statewide adoption exchanges. These exchanges usually have a photo listing and description of available children. A particular Web site, *www.AdoptionDirectory.com*, is the world's largest and the Internet's most popular photo listing of children awaiting adoption.

In many cases, state financial assistance in the form of adoption subsidies is also available. These subsidies help to cover the legal costs and medical care expenses associated with adopting a special-needs child. The subsidies can also cover any living costs incurred. Before adopting a special-needs child, ask your agency about any available subsidies. If you desire more information on this subject, call the National Adoption Assistance Training, Resource and Information Network (NAATRIN) at 1-800-470-6665.

Adopting children from another country has been a growing trend, especially in America. Russia, China, India, Korea and several countries in Eastern Europe, Central America and South America are the sources for most out of country adoptive children. If you are considering adopting a child from another country, let me forewarn you of the challenges you will almost certainly encounter. There are very strict immigration laws, as well as substantial agency fees. In addition, you must also take into account transportation expenses, legal fees and any medical costs. Whereas a child may take up to a year to adopt within America, it can take up to three or more years for a child born abroad.

You should also carefully consider the emotional and social implications that come with adopting a child of another nationality. Remember, you are adopting the child's culture as well. If you are not willing to help the child learn about and appreciate his or her native culture, the agency will not consider you as a prospective parent.

Get the 411

This chapter only covers the basics of adoption. If you desire to know more about it, community colleges, hospitals, religious groups, local YMCAs, adoption agencies and other organizations may offer preparation programs. There is also a wealth of information you can obtain from the National Adoption Information Clearinghouse and its Web site: *www.calib.com\naic*. There you can find information on reputable adoption organizations and attorneys, as well as guidebooks, fact sheets and lists of support groups.

In addition, if you have acquaintances, friends, coworkers or relatives who have adopted a child, don't be shy about talking to them to gain knowledge and information. The more you know, the better off you'll be!

Who Can Adopt?

There are requirements for prospective parents, and it varies from agency to agency. It becomes even stricter when an infant is involved.

For the most part, adoptive parents can be married *or* single. Sometimes an adoptive child prefers a single parent, especially if the child has experienced abuse at the hands of a parent. You can also be childless or already parenting other children. Having a disability does not disqualify prospective parents. However, those will disabilities must be able to prove they can care for the child and meet his or her needs throughout childhood.

Divorce or a history of marital or personal counseling does not automatically eliminate you as a candidate, either. In addition, you are not required to be a homeowner or have a high income in order to meet the needs of the child.

Adoption will add a depth and dimension to your life you can't imagine.

What you must do is be able to prove that you can provide permanence, stability and a lifetime commitment to the child. You must show that the child will be a welcome addition to your family. Agencies aren't concerned with whether or not you are a "perfect" parent—they just want to know and be shown that you will be caring and committed.

For infant adoptions, however, the agency criteria are much more restrictive. Often agencies will only consider couples married at least one to three years, between the ages of 25 and 40, with a very stable employment history and income. However, some agencies will accept an applicant older than 40. In addition, some require that the couple have no other children and be unable to bear them. Others require that one parent not work outside the home for at least six months after the adoption.

Private Agencies

There are both private and public adoption agencies. A private adoption agency is supported by private funds and should be licensed or approved by the state in which it operates. To use a private agency, look under "Adoption

Agencies" or "Social Services" in the Yellow Pages. You can obtain a free copy of your state's agency listings via Internet by visiting the National Adoption Information Clearinghouse (NAIC) at *www.calib.com\naic*. Once there, you should access the National Adoption Directory site.

Always check with the Better Business Bureau and the State Attorney General's office to investigate whether any complaints have been recorded against a particular agency. You may also want to check with a local adoptive parent support group for their recommendations of reputable agencies.

If you are searching the Internet for adoption agencies, *please* use caution. The NAIC Web site gives invaluable information on how to detect a scam. There are many details to consider when accessing an adoption site—many you've probably never thought of—so be sure to do your homework and study their precautionary advice before considering any Internet agency.

Keep in mind that private agencies handle both domestic and foreign adoptions, with fees ranging from $5,000 to more than $30,000. Exercise wisdom by asking what the fees are and what the payment schedule will be. Find out what services are covered in that fee and which are not. Most will allow you to pay in installments, but be sure that you understand the payment plan and everything it covers. Then have it put in writing.

Public Agencies

A public adoption agency is the local branch of your state Social Service Agency. Most public agencies handle only special-needs children, not infants or foreign adoptions. Children in the custody of a public agency are usually children who have been abused, neglected or abandoned by their birth parents.

Adoption will definitely change you, and that change lasts for the rest of your life.

Abuse, neglect and desertion can leave very deep, emotional scars. Be sure to discuss all aspects of the child's history with the social worker. Know beforehand what counseling services are available just in case they might be needed.

Public agencies are listed in the government section of your telephone book. Look under "Department of Social Services" or "Department of Public Welfare." If your state organizes the agencies by county, call the county office and ask to speak to the adoption specialist. If they can't help you, ask to be referred to the regional or state office.

Public agencies accept applications from families wanting to adopt older children, siblings, or children with special needs. Because they are funded by State and Federal taxes, the adoption services are usually free or available for a modest fee. If the child does not have any special needs, the family may be asked to pay a modest legal fee. In some cases, even if the child has no special needs, subsidies pay for these legal fees. Adoptions from a public agency can range anywhere from $0 to $2,500.

Another option that public agencies offer is the ability to become a *foster parent*. Children are placed with foster parents to give the birth parents a chance to improve their situations. During this time, the birth parents are offered counseling and other services to help them. Foster parents receive a monthly stipend for the child's living expenses.

For the most part, the goal of the foster care program is to reunite the child with the birth parents. Unfortunately, this doesn't always happen. To prevent these children from floating from one foster home to another, many states are requiring birth parents to relinquish their parental rights if they are unable to care for the children.

In light of this, the agency will ask you if you want to be considered only as a foster parent, adoptive parent or foster-adoptive parent. Foster-adoptive parents are willing to be foster parents while the child is waiting to be reunited with his or her birth parents. They understand that the agency will do everything possible to reunite the child with the birth parents. However, if the child is free to be adopted, then the foster-adoptive parents are given priority consideration as the child's adoptive parents.

If you choose to be a foster-adoptive parent, you must prepare yourself emotionally. Of course the best interest of the child would be to reunite him or her with the birth parents, so you must genuinely work toward that goal. If the reunion is successful, you must be prepared to handle the sense of grief that may accompany the loss of the child.

Independent Adoptions

Adoptions can sometimes be arranged outside of an agency. An independent adoption is when the contacts are made between a pregnant woman and the adoptive parents. Independent adoptions are legal in all but a few states.

If you pursue this approach, retain an experienced adoption attorney and discuss the laws in your state. Become familiar with the Interstate Compact on the Placement of Children (ICPC), because in interstate adoptions, you will be required to comply with the adoption laws of both states. You don't want the adoption challenged because of failure to comply with a law.

To initiate an independent adoption, you must first locate a birth mother interested in giving up her child. You can advertise on your own, but if you use the newspaper, make sure this type of advertising is legal. You can also use a national adoption advertising consultant or send an introductory letter, photo and resumé describing your family life, home, job, hobbies and interests to crisis pregnancy centers. This packet can also be submitted to obstetricians and friends or colleagues—basically anyone who might lead you to the right person.

Finding the birth mother is only one step. You must also know about the birth father. States have now recognized the right of the birth father to have a say in whether the child is adopted or not. Several high-profile lawsuits have involved contested adoptions where the birth fathers were not notified.

The expenses vary for independent adoptions. It is always customary to pay the birth mother's medical and legal expenses, in addition to your own. Some states require the birth parents to undergo counseling to make sure they understand what is taking place. The adoptive parents will usually incur that expense as well. The required home study, conducted by a Social Worker or a licensed child-placing agency, also carries a fee. Sometimes the adoptive parents help out with the birth mother's living and clothing expenses.

For an independent adoption, you can expect the cost to range from $8,000 to $30,000 and above. Again, the laws vary from state to state, and only a good adoption attorney can educate you.

Pre-Placement Inquiry

Once you've decided on an agency, you may be invited to an orientation to learn the agency's procedures and what children are available. From there you will receive an application form. The agency will review your application to determine whether or not to accept you as a client. If accepted, you will probably have to pay a registration fee.

The next step is the pre-placement inquiry known as the "home study" or the "family assessment." Required by law, it consists of an evaluation of you, as a prospective parent, and of the physical and emotional environment in which the adoptive child will be placed.

There are also several interviews conducted by a social worker, with at least one of these conducted in your home. During this interview, the social worker discusses all aspects of adoptive parenting and identifies the type of child you wish to adopt. Many of the questions asked are very personal and may seem intrusive if you're not prepared for them. Remember, these questions are necessary for the social worker's evaluation. You will also be asked to take a physical exam to ensure your good health. Most states now require a fingerprint and background check to make sure you don't have a felony conviction for domestic violence or child abuse.

The home study is usually completed within a few months, depending on the size of the agency and the number of clients.

Hurry Up and Wait

Adopting a child always requires a waiting period, and often it's a long one. For example, if you are looking to adopt a Caucasian infant, be prepared to wait at least one year after the home study is completed, and sometimes it's a wait of two to five years. Out-of-country adoptions can take even longer. If you wish to adopt an African-American or Hispanic infant, the wait is shorter—probably six months.

Once your child has "arrived," he or she will live with you for at least six months before the adoption is finalized. The social worker may visit several times to make sure the child is being well cared for and to write the required court reports. After this period, the adoption agency will submit a written recommendation of their approval to the court. Afterward, you or your attorney can then file with the court to complete the adoption.

Foreign adoptions require much more paperwork. Finalization of the adoption depends on the type of visa the child has and the laws in your state. The actual adoption is just *one of a series* of legal processes required. You must also fulfill the U.S. Immigration and Naturalization Service's (INS) requirements and then proceed to naturalize your child as a citizen of the United States. Make sure that you have a competent attorney to lead you through all of these segments.

* * * * *

As with anything in life, seek first the will of God before adopting a child. Trust Him to lead and guide you. He will assist you in avoiding common pitfalls or alert you to any difficulties that may arise so you can avoid the hurt and regret that come from poor decision-making. Seek Him for the peace you need when the wait seems long.

God has a beautiful plan for you and the child you are soon to adopt. Remember, He knew that child before he or she was formed in their mother's womb (Jeremiah 1:5). As your heavenly Father, He knew that you could be trusted to love, protect, nurture and guide that little person into adulthood and the fullness of His will for their lives. What a compliment!

Adoption is a biblical principle and a wonderful option for mature, loving and responsible adults wanting to care for a child.

Take a moment to evaluate your motives for adoption. Make a list of pros and cons and discuss them with a spouse, close friend or relative. Fast and pray concerning your desire to adopt. When you are ready, gather as much information as possible by visiting a private or state agency or speaking with parents who have gone through the adoption process. Be sure to take your time and evaluate all the facts before making your final decision.

Romans 11:16-18, The Message

"Behind and underneath all this there is a holy, God-planted, God-tended root. If the primary root of the tree is holy, there's bound to be some holy fruit. Some of the tree's branches were pruned and you wild olive shoots were grafted in. Yet the fact that you are now fed by that rich and holy root gives you no cause to crow...Remember, you aren't feeding the root; the root is feeding you."

20

TAKE GOOD CARE OF MY BABY
Keys to Effective Parenting

Children are *gifts* from God. Did you realize that? Sure, there are days when you probably think otherwise, but nevertheless, the Bible says they are a reward, assignment and a heritage from the Lord (Psalm 127:3).

While they are in your possession you have the opportunity to impart biblical principles that will enable them to fulfill their destiny and succeed in life. Children are like little sponges, soaking up everything you say and do, whether positive or negative. When you understand how much information they are able to retain at one time, it changes the way you approach parenting.

Isaiah 8:18 says, *"...I and the children whom the Lord hath given me are for signs and for wonders in Israel from the Lord of hosts...."* Despite the hassle you go through just to get your children to brush their teeth, bathe, keep their clothes clean or eat their vegetables, you should not forget that God desires to use them as signs and wonders in these last days.

As a parent, He wants you to perceive your children correctly. This means that you are able to see the gifts and callings He has placed within each of them. When you get the Word on the inside of them, they will develop a God-consciousness which will increase their levels of faith and the ability to operate in His supernatural power. As a result, they'll begin to demonstrate to others what it means to be joined with and blessed of the Father. That should excite you!

You must assume the responsibility to train and prepare your children to be the signs and wonders they are meant to be. They don't have to wait until they're older to be used of God! Samson, Samuel and Jesus were only boys when they began demonstrating God's power. Size and age are irrelevant. Encourage your children to see themselves laying hands on the sick and seeing them recover. Help them create an inner image of God using them to prophesy, teach, intercede and operate under the anointing of the Holy Spirit. Train them to be a part of God's plan, and let them see that you honor the call of God on their lives.

Good Old-Fashioned Home Training

Proverbs 22:6 says, *"Train up a child in the way he should go: and when he is old, he will not depart from it."* To train means, "to mold character; to instruct by exercise," and "to drill." As you can see from the definition, there's a difference between teaching and training. You can teach little Johnny the importance of personal hygiene by explaining the importance of brushing his teeth. But "to train" him in that area requires that you *make* little Johnny get up every morning at the same time and go through the personal hygiene procedures. Do you see the difference? Training reinforces what you've taught.

Parents need to return to good, old-fashioned home training. For example, it's important that you train your children to show respect to those in places of authority by saying "Yes, Ma'am" and "No, Ma'am," and "Yes, Sir" and "No, Sir" when spoken to. Terms like "please" "excuse me" and "thank you" should be grafted into their vocabulary. Good personal hygiene, table manners and speech should be taught in the home, not learned on the street.

You must assume the responsibility to train and prepare your children to be the signs and wonders they are meant to be.

In addition, you must train your children to control themselves, because nothing can be imparted into children who are out of control. A child who is out of control in public is out of control in the home. If the principal of your child's school calls to let you know what he or she did, don't accuse him of negligence and ask what the school is going to do about it! The only thing that matters is what *you* do about it. Don't point the finger at someone else. Look in the mirror. It's your responsibility as a parent to keep your children under control so that you can train them in the Lord.

When you fail to impart and train, your child will get into trouble. This is evident in the story of Eli. First Samuel 3:13-14 says, *"For I have told him that I will judge his house for ever for the iniquity which he knoweth; because his sons made themselves vile, and he restrained them not. And therefore I have sworn unto the house of Eli, that the iniquity of Eli's house shall not be purged with sacrifice nor offering for ever."*

Eli allowed his sons to sin before God by sleeping with prostitutes in God's house and eating the sacrificial portions that were holy. Eli's passive parenting angered God. As a result, he and his sons lost their place as priests in the temple and died.

When you knowingly allow your children to get involved in wrongdoing, you open the door for their actions to bring a curse, or empowerment to fail, on themselves *and* the entire household. Why the entire household? You are the ultimate authority over your children. By turning a blind eye to their actions, it was as if you yourself had opened the door for the negative consequences to be poured into your household. God holds you, the parent, responsible.

You can't afford to have a curse on your home. There's enough in the world to deal with as it is. So, when your children get into sin, you must deal with it right then and there—and sometimes that requires chastisement and correction. That doesn't sound enjoyable but it is absolutely vital if you want to raise children of whom you can be proud.

Spare the Rod, Spoil the Child

Don't allow your children to despise chastisement and correction (Proverbs 3:11). Be positive when correcting your children, and let them know that chastening is an act of love. That may mean continually reinforcing the fact that your correction *now* will benefit them *later*. Of course when your child sees the paddle, he or she will not believe that statement! But tell them anyway. You are planting seeds of love that they will one day understand.

There is a difference between correction and punishment. Correction is rooted in affection and concern. It is designed to restore honor and focus. Correction says, "I'm going to show you the right way because I'm concerned about you." Punishment, on the other hand, is for revenge and to satisfy the need to control. It says, "I'm gonna get you, boy, because it makes me feel better." Some parents don't believe in spanking, but Creflo and I do because the Bible does. Proverbs 29:15 says that discipline gives wisdom. A child left to his or her own devices will always bring shame to their parents.

Children must be taught self-control, because nothing can be imparted into children who are out of control.

That doesn't give you the right, however, to beat your kids. Bruises are not a sign of discipline, but abuse. You know your own strength. A light tap won't do much for your child, and neither will what Creflo calls "a beat-down."

A spanking should hurt enough to leave a mark on your child's conscience, not on his or her body. But don't be afraid to use the rod, either. When necessary, be willing to spank your children—but do it in love, not anger. Harshness and cruelty make for bad parenting. Show me cruel parents, and I'll show you poorly-behaved children. Creflo and I believe in spanking, but we don't misuse it because the Bible also commands parents not to provoke their children (Ephesians 6:4).

For further information on this subject, read chapters 21 and 22. In them, we share our experiences with discipline and the proper way in which to carry it out.

The V-Word

Sex is one of the most avoided topics in parenting. You'd be surprised at the number of parents who prefer that their children learn about sex in school or on their own. That's a big mistake, because they are more likely to get into trouble that way. Buying condoms and other methods of birth control is not the answer, and neither is relying on someone else to teach your children about sex. The best solution is for you, the parent, to take the initiative.

You may feel uncomfortable talking about this subject with your children, but that's a discomfort you'll have to get over. There are too many kids sitting in the pew on Sunday morning that have been in the backseat of someone's car the night before. In addition, these same children are not only getting pregnant and having abortions, they are contracting and spreading sexually transmitted diseases.

The irony is that many of them had no business dating in the first place. They were too young and ill-prepared to handle the sexual temptation that accompanies one-on-one dating. Parents, hear me well: Just

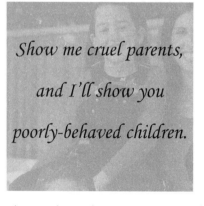

Show me cruel parents, and I'll show you poorly-behaved children.

because all of their friends are dating doesn't mean your child is ready to do the same. It is a shame and a dishonor when parents willingly throw their children into the arena with the opposite sex. It's not "cute" for your 13-year-old daughter to be left alone in a compromising situation with a boy the same age or older. Their bodies may be maturing rapidly, but their minds have a long way to go.

Setting age-appropriate and Word-based boundaries will prevent your children from placing themselves in situations where they can be easily tempted. For instance, allow them to "group date" rather than "single date" until you're confident they are equipped to handle sexual temptation. And don't allow your kids to watch TV shows or movies that show heavy petting and promote promiscuity. If you are lax about it, your children will grow up thinking heavy petting and sexual intercourse are *supposed to* happen on dates.

Children must be taught to control their urges and understand what happens to their bodies as they mature. Self-control is vital (1 Thessalonians 4:3-5). Virginity is a treasure. Sex outside of marriage is against God's Word, and there is no such thing as "safe sex" with birth control. The only truly safe sex is abstinence. If you need help with how to present this topic, refer to chapter 23, which gives you several good ideas.

As a parent, one of your strongest weapons in this battle is prayer. Pray for the protection of your children. Pray and believe God for his or her virginity. Pray that your children develop self-control and the other fruits of the Spirit (Galatians 5:22-23). Pray that they have the mind of Christ and make wise decisions. Pray for your children's future spouses. Pray fervently!

Second, there is training and education. By teaching your children that sex is reserved for marriage and God is glorified and honored through virginity, you protect them from the negative consequences of fornication. If they see sex as God sees it, it will become sacred to them—not just something to try for curiosity's sake.

Third, there is the weapon of unconditional love. When you show your children the God-kind of love you have been given by your heavenly Father, they won't have to go looking for love in all the wrong places. Encourage your children in the things of God so they'll have that love on the inside of them. When they're filled with that kind of love, it leaves no void for a counterfeit to fill.

Go the Distance!

There's nothing like raising a child who isn't your own flesh and blood. Creflo and I have done that twice, and one was of a different race! We made a commitment before the court and before God to raise Greg as our own. And I'm here to tell you that there were times I wanted to quit. Before adopting him, he was already experienced in doing things, which made it tough for Creflo and me.

From the beginning we fed him the Word, but he refused to comply. That didn't mean we quit doing it. Creflo and I knew consistency was the key. We wouldn't compromise where he was concerned. We continued praying for and loving him. In addition, we made the positive confession that he was a strong man of God, although that seemed the furthest thing from reality.

We were almost ready to throw in the towel when we got an early morning phone call. It was Greg. He was crying.

"What's wrong, son?" Creflo asked.

"I don't know what's going on with me," he said. "All I know is that the presence of God is on me. I fell out under the power of God in front of my television watching Benny Hinn. It seemed like the scales fell off my eyes. Now, all I want is Jesus. I want His Word, and I want to ask you to forgive me. I'm sorry for everything that I did." I'll never forget that morning as long as I live.

It's worth it all to see your child turn from hell and make it into the Kingdom of God because you chose to stand in the gap for him or her and not quit when things became difficult and they jumped on your last nerve. Today, Greg has children of his own into which he's imparting biblical principles. He enlisted in the Army, and when he got out, he came to work for Creflo and me for a little while and radically improved our television ministry.

You may be thinking, "It worked for your family, but you and Dr. Dollar are preachers." It doesn't matter that we are ministers. God is no respecter of persons (Romans 2:11). What He did for us, He'll do for you and your children. But you don't have to take my word for it; take God's Word for it.

No one said that parenting would be easy. Having a child does not automatically make you a good parent. You learn as you go. Raising godly children requires sacrifices on your part, but your love for them will motivate you to make them. You may want to come home after work and relax, but your teenage son has a baseball game at six o'clock. Consequently, you only have time to change clothes and get to the field, where you'll cheer all night while the mosquitoes eat you alive. Those little sacrifices are all a part of good parenting.

* * * * *

Children are a big commitment. It takes time, energy, love and prayer to raise them properly. But you aren't doing it alone! God is with you every step of the way. Purpose to do your part in training your children the right way. Teach them to be responsible, respectful and compassionate people who know the will of God for their lives and are willing to follow it at any cost. Believe me, they will thank you for it later.

Commitment, consistency, discipline and love are the basic ingredients of good parenting.

Make it a point to show your child how much you love him or her. Set time aside today to shower them with hugs and kisses, give encouragement and praise and listen to their stories. Involve yourself in his or her life by asking open-ended questions, such as "Did anything good happen to you today?" Don't settle for one-word answers, and refuse to compromise in the area of discipline when it is needed. By investing your time, energy and effort, you reinforce your commitment to your children.

 **Ephesians 6:4**

"And, ye fathers, provoke not your children to wrath: but bring them up in the nurture and admonition of the Lord.

21

GOOD COP, BAD COP
God's System for Disciplining Children

arenting isn't a piece of cake. It's hard work. While some people work hard at being good parents, others work smarter. *Smart* parenting—parenting according to God's Word—is absolutely essential in raising mature, responsible and considerate children today.

Parents desire the best things in life for their children—good health, a sound financial future, quality education and loving relationships, to name a few. It is your job to provide them with whatever they need to succeed in these areas. That's what "good" parents do: they go the extra mile to ensure a higher quality of life for their children.

Preparing your children for the future is important. The world can be a tough place for an adult who, as a child, was never properly trained to function in this fast-paced society. For instance, an individual who is not taught the value of saving money at a young age will more than likely develop a money management problem. Once he or she obtains employment, they'll end up spending their money foolishly. Their lack of discipline in the area of finances will ruin them.

Or what about a child whose parents rarely assigned chores for him to do around the house? Rather than enforce their rules, they continued to clean up after him while he played or watched television all day. As an adult, he's lazy and unable to hold a steady job. Lazy adults never succeed in life. That's a hard but true reality.

Who's Raising Your Kids?

Often parents have false assumptions when it comes to their child's development. They think that because their child attends a good public or private school or is involved in church activities, he or she is being taught the right things. That isn't always the case. Some children adopt certain negative behaviors no matter where they are. Years later the parents realize that their child grew up learning all the wrong things. In some cases, it's almost too late to do anything about it. The child, now a young adult, has developed the attitude that "This is my life and I'll do what *I* want with it!"

So I ask you: *Who* is raising *your* kids?

Before you can answer that question, you'll have to honestly assess your parenting. Just because your children are home in front of the television or the computer doesn't necessarily mean *you're* raising them. Yes, you may spend some time with your kids, but is it *quality* time? Are you imparting to them the values of life and the principles of success?

That brings up another point. What is the atmosphere like in your home? Is it full of strife, anger and rebellion? Parents should strive to create an atmosphere where their children are exposed to godly things. More importantly, they need to learn from *your* example of godliness. They must see you reading the Bible, praying and living a life that is pleasing to God. Children are like computers. The type of software (training) you install in them determines their output. If you put junk in, junk comes out. It's that simple.

It's impossible and dysfunctional to completely isolate your children.

In today's society, television, the Internet and the "street" have become many children's most influential teachers. Who ever thought that one day children would look to secular music artists, supermodels, athletes, celebrities and even gang leaders as role models? There used to be a time when most kids wanted to be like their parents. Some wanted to become doctors, lawyers, teachers and engineers just like mom and dad. Show-and-Tell at school was their opportunity to let everyone know "My mom and dad are my heroes!"

Now things have changed so much that many parents feel powerless against these outside influences. If this describes your situation, don't be discouraged. There is hope—and it's found in the Word of God! Throughout countless generations these truths have conquered every challenging situation known to parents with positive results. This generation is no different.

It's All About the Blessing

If you are born again, your *hope* should be in the personal relationship you have with Almighty God through His Son, Jesus Christ. That relationship, and the blessings that stem from it, affects every area of our lives, including raising children. When you raise your children God's way, you can rest assured that they *will* turn out right!

Hope is an interesting word defined as "favorable and confident expectation describing the anticipation of good; earnest expectation." We can narrow this definition to "an earnest expectation with an outstretched neck."

Picture yourself looking out from your front door with an outstretched neck, expecting a package to be delivered. You eagerly await its arrival because you *know* it's on the way. The same is true with raising your children according to biblical principles. When your faith and trust are grounded in God's Word, you develop an earnest expectation that what He promised concerning your children *will* come to pass. Simply knowing that He promised good things for you and your children should increase your hope in the fulfillment of His Word. With an outstretched heart (neck), you earnestly expect the Bible-kind of results.

We know that God is covenant-minded. In other words, His entire focus is on making sure He does His part to ensure your family reaps the benefits of His promises. What is a *covenant*? It is "an agreement between two or more parties to carry out the terms agreed on." It is an oath or contract that simply states, "I agree to do whatever it takes to get the job done. God and I are in this together!" That is God's attitude when it comes to His covenant relationship with your family.

God chose a man named Abram, or Abraham, to fulfill His covenant promises toward the Israelites, His chosen people (Genesis 12). As you read the terms of this agreement below, think about how it relates to you and your family.

> *...Get thee out of thy country, and from thy kindred, and from thy father's house, unto a land that I will show thee: And I will make of thee a great nation, and I will bless thee, and make thy name great; and thou shalt be a blessing: And I will bless them that bless thee, and curse him that curseth thee: and in thee shall all families of the earth be blessed* (vv.1-3).

Notice that these terms required Abraham to leave a place he was familiar with and move to wherever God now wanted him to live. Obedience on Abraham's part was the only requirement. In simple terms God said, "Abraham, do what I say and I will bless your household and all the families of the earth through you."

The *blessing* that God promised Abraham and his offspring was an empowerment to prosper and succeed in every area of life. It was an endowment of power for success, which was evident throughout Abraham's life. Everything he did prospered.

Why did God choose to establish a covenant with Abraham and teach him

His ways? He knew that Abraham would teach his children about the importance of being in covenant with God. Genesis 18:17-19 says:

> ...Shall I hide from Abraham that thing which I do; Seeing that Abraham shall surely become a great and mighty nation, and all the nations of the earth shall be blessed in him? **For I know him, that he will command his children and his household after him, and they shall keep the way of the Lord, to do justice and judgment; that the Lord may bring upon Abraham that which he hath spoken of him** (emphasis added).

That is a powerful compliment! The Lord knew Abraham would keep his end of the bargain so He blessed him and his household as a result.

The verses you've just read aren't some fable or fairy tale. The same agreement established between God and Abraham applies to you today. God wants your family blessed in every area just as Abraham and his family were blessed.

It's important for you to understand that as a Christian, you are related to Abraham spiritually and have a right to this covenant of success (Galatians 3:29). That also means you have a responsibility to teach your children about having a relationship with God so they can experience the God-kind of results in their lives. Their obedience to Him will determine their prosperity.

Solidify Your Lesson Plan

The world has a system for raising children, and so does God. But which produces positive, long-lasting results? There's no doubt about it—parenting according to biblical principles has proven to be the most effective system (2 Samuel 22:31).

God gave us His Word so you can make it the final authority in the way you raise your sons and daughters. Despite the opinions of child psychologists, friends and relatives, the Bible must have the last word. You must dismiss anything that contradicts what it teaches and not waver from this stance when it comes to raising children.

The Word of God admonishes us to "...bring [your children] up in the nurture and admonition of the Lord" (Ephesians 6:4). The Amplified Bible says to "...rear them [tenderly] in the training and discipline and the counsel and admonition of the Lord." In other words, apply the Word when training your kids, regardless of the situation.

Let's zero in on the word "training." This is a key to effective parenting. When you train your children God's way, it pleases Him and compels Him to overwhelm your household with His goodness.

You may have heard the saying, "Daddy knows best." In this case, God, as our heavenly Father, knows what is best for your kids. That's why Proverbs 22:6 says, *"Train up a child in the way he should go: and when he is old, he will not depart from it."* This "way" is God's way, God's plan. You must train your kids while they are young so they won't depart from what they've learned when they get older. They'll grow up to be responsible in everything they do because of it.

Training and teaching are different. *Teaching* involves the giving of information. *Training*, on the other hand, involves making your children do what you teach them. You're molding their character through exercise and regimentation.

For example, a football coach does not simply draw plays on a chalkboard and expect his players to automatically execute them when it's game time. The Xs and Os on the chalkboard won't do the team any good until the players move them from the chalkboard to the practice field. The coach has to train his team over and over until they know how to run those plays proficiently, and he won't quit until they do.

> *When you train your children God's way, it pleases Him and compels Him to overwhelm your household with His goodness.*

Another example is a clean room. Children must be trained to clean up after themselves. If you've been a parent for very long, you know that a clean room doesn't *just happen!* You can't just tell the child to clean his or her room, or even teach them why a room should be cleaned. Instead, you must take the time to train the child *how* to clean the room. That means going in there, picking things up one at a time and showing them how to put it in its place. This includes how to hang up their clothes, dust the furniture and so on. You may have to show them over and over again. In your training, you can even make a game out of it; soon they'll know what to do on their own.

Make sure you have the proper perspective on training. I don't recommend that you force your son or daughter to do something just because *you* want them to. Many parents make that mistake. They force their children to play an instrument or get involved in a sport to fulfill *their* dreams, not the child's. Your child may not be inclined to "follow in your footsteps." Not only that, the activities you want them to be a part of may not line up with God's ultimate will for their lives.

I can recognize the different gifts that my children have within them, from singing, preaching and business administration to housekeeping. It's very important that you see those things in order to encourage them to cultivate those gifts and abilities. If you don't recognize the gifts within your children, then pray for God to show them to you. Rest assured that He will, because He's entrusted them to your care. Future generations rely on what you instill into your children today.

Do yourself a favor: don't get offended and hurt because your child doesn't share your interests and goals. Although he or she sprang from your loins, God has an individual purpose for your son or daughter. You can break their spirit by crushing their enthusiasm and zeal for life, if you force them to like something just because you like it.

As I've said before, it's your job as a parent to train your children. If you don't know what to do in a given situation, look to God for direction, and He will help you.

Three Types of Parenting Methods...You Choose

Trusting God may not always be the easiest thing to do as a parent, but it is the *best* thing. You may not always understand or agree with His methods, but remember, your goal is to help fulfill His will for your child. Therefore, allow the Lord to direct you and you will have success.

Here are three types of parenting methods you need to be aware of. The first two occur when you don't trust God. All parents should strive to execute the third method, which guarantees positive results.

1. Isolation.

When some parents are fearful of what goes on in society, they tend to isolate their children from contact with others aside from school and church. Many times they don't even allow them to play with neighborhood children. In this case, the home becomes a closet of isolation and the children are stifled by the parents' fears.

It's impossible and dysfunctional to completely isolate your children. When a challenging situation presents itself from outside influences, use it as an example. Take the Word and weave the scriptures into your child's thinking, teaching him or her what is right and wrong. When the negative influences come, turn them around and use the circumstance to plant the Word of God into your child. If you'll do that, you'll soon discover that your children are equipped to make correct decisions by what you've instilled in them.

Homeschooling: Good or Bad?

Evaluate your motives before making the decision to homeschool your children. Make sure you are not isolating your child out of fear. Place your son or daughter in homeschooling pools and events where they can interact with other children. Homeschooling support groups offer a variety of activities, so there's no reason why you should not encourage your child to participate in them. In this way you conquer fear and focus on a well-rounded education and lifestyle for your child.

---

2. Passivity.

These parents often live defeated lives and have a quitter's mentality. As a result, they have given up hope of influencing their children amid what goes on in society. They cave in under pressure and allow their children to be influenced by others.

Passive parents neither engage in purposeful training nor plan for their children's future. They only make excuses like, "I'm going to allow them to decide what they want to do." Or, "I don't want to interfere with their life." Sadly, the children often suffer because of the poor choices they make and the negative consequences of their actions.

Passivity and parenthood are opposite words with opposite meanings. As a parent, you must point your children in the right direction. You can't give up or cave in just because they don't want to do something, or because it's easier to quit.

3. Training.

Although we discussed this method in the previous section and will expound on it in the next section, let's briefly deal with it at this point.

Parents who train their children God's way don't allow the cares of the world to govern their lives. They take *active* responsibility for their children. They don't isolate them from everyone, but are selective of the other children they allow their kids to associate with. These parents are confident that they are instilling in their sons and daughters the necessary values that will help them to make the right decisions in life.

The Ingredients of Parenthood

God's system for raising your children must begin at home. Think of it as good old-fashioned "home training." What your child learns at home—politeness, courtesy, table manners and respect for adults and authority figures—will determine their behavior outside of the home.

There are several practical ways to hometrain your child according to God's system. It's like baking a cake. Once you have the proper ingredients and follow the instructions, the cake will turn out the way it's supposed to. Although at the moment your child may be rebellious, or having issues with complaining, fighting, or being bitter or slothful, by following the ingredients for effective discipline, you'll see a tremendous change.

Ingredient #1: Establish the rules.

Depending on the age of your children, establish specific rules to which each child must adhere. But don't expect your 4-year-old to abide by the rules for your 9-year-old. Be reasonable in what you expect from your children.

Make sure your rules are written down and clearly understood. Tape them to your kids' bedroom doors or in a location that you've designated as the "Discipline/Time-Out Room." This list will serve as a reminder to you and your children that the rules *will be* enforced. Your children won't take you seriously if you make rules that you're not willing to enforce. Keep in mind that it will take time to train your children to abide by your rules; change won't happen overnight. Therefore, be persistent in enforcing your rules without being a drill sergeant.

Ingredient #2: Make sure your child understands.

When your child breaks the rules, deal with it *immediately* if possible. Take him or her to your designated area of discipline and explain what they did to displease you. Make sure they clearly understand why they are being disciplined. Let your son or daughter know what God's attitude is concerning their behavior by showing them what the Bible says about disobedience and rebellion (Deuteronomy 12:28; 1 Samuel 15:23; Proverbs 3:11-12; Ephesians 6:1-3; Colossians 3:20).

Always weave the Word of God in when you're correcting your child. Once he or she understands, then they are ready to be spanked.

Ingredient #3: Don't spare the rod.

The Bible clearly says, *"Apply thine heart unto instruction, and thine ears to the words of knowledge. Withhold not correction from the child: for if thou beatest him with the rod, he shall not die. Thou shalt beat him with the rod, and shalt deliver his soul from hell"* (Proverbs 23:12-14).

Some parents cringe when they read these scriptures. Their attitude is "I love my children too much to spank them. I'd rather talk to them. After all, spanking will make them more aggressive." Anyone who thinks this way is misguided. *Not* using the rod creates aggressive children because they know that you're only going to talk to them—not spank them.

If you truly love your children, you will spank them when they become unruly and need correction. The Word of God states that the rod is an instrument of love that must be used to drive out foolishness in the hearts of children (Proverbs 13:24; 22:15). When parents *misuse* the rod, aggression is born and abuse is inevitable. The rod should not be used to invoke fear or to injure your child. The objective is to deliver a message that disobedience will not be tolerated. Therefore, don't withhold correction from your children. You're saving their lives.

In addition, never spank your children out of anger. You may lose control and injure them. Always maintain control. Spanking them when you're angry also sends a message that they are getting spanked because you're mad about something. Your child may get the impression that they are the source of your frustration, or that if you're angry, they should expect a beating.

Take some time to cool down before you spank your child. In that way, you can always be in a position to clearly communicate your displeasure with their behavior *in love*. Sometimes you may need to use the rod in public, but don't embarrass your children. Pull them to the side for discipline.

A rod can be a belt, ruler or paddle. *Never* use your hands. Hands are for embracing, not for spanking. Also, never punch, kick, slap, push or throw things at your kids. That's child abuse! If you do, they'll do the same to their children in the future.

Ingredient #4: Know the difference between willful disobedience and childish behavior.

You should be able to tell when your children are being rebellious or simply exhibiting behavior suitable to their age. Be reasonable in your establishment of rules and expectations.

Ingredient #5: Pray.

Prayer should always follow spanking. This is a time of restoration—a time for your children to realize that you still love them. You may use this sample prayer:

"Father, in the name of Jesus, I thank You that I have used the rod according to Your Word. Help me to continue training and loving [your child's name] with the love of Christ. [your child's name] has received correction and instruction, and is ready to repent for being disobedient."

Allow your children the opportunity to pray as well. They may pray, *"Father God, please forgive me for breaking my parents' rules. Help me to obey them for this is right. I want to make You and my parents happy so I repent and won't be disobedient anymore. Thank You for forgiving me. In Jesus' name."*

Both of you should end the prayer and express your love for one another. Use some form of affection, such as hugging and kissing, which communicates volumes to your children. It tells them that you're willing to love and support them no matter what they do. It's a good thing to also reward them for their willingness to receive correction and repentance. You're not rewarding their disobedience; instead, you're rewarding their obedience to make things right.

*   *   *   *   *

Never forget that God's system for discipline and correction is based on *love*. Love your children enough to prepare them for the future. It may get rough at times, but all things are possible with God! You're not alone, even if you're a single parent having to raise your kids by yourself. The Word of God is the tool you need to succeed in being a good parent. Allow it to expand your capacity to love your children despite their behavior. Remember, love conquers all!

Love is the key to effective discipline.

Take a few moments to evaluate your method of parenting. Do you parent your children through isolation, passivity or training? In what areas are you weakest? Do you apply the rod sparingly, harshly or in love? Once you have determined which is your style, list the ways in which you can strengthen your skills.

If you are married, sit down with your spouse and agree on the methods you will now employ to avoid a "good cop, bad cop" scenario with your children where they play one parent (disciplinarian) against the other (contradictor). If you are a single parent, share your goals with your ex-spouse (if possible) or a close friend or relative. By voicing your commitment to apply biblical principles to your parenting, you help to maintain focus and guarantee success.

Proverbs 22:15

"Foolishness is bound in the heart of a child; but the rod of correction shall drive it far from him."

22

REBEL WITHOUT A CAUSE
Kicking Rebellion Out of Your Home

Many people have a tendency to exalt rebellion, which often takes the form of extreme independence and non-conformity. While having your own mind is wonderful, too much of a James Dean "loner" attitude is not. In fact, too much of anything good can be bad for you, and it goes without saying that a rebellious nature is a self-defeating one. The self-centered actions and often callous or tactless remarks that come out of the mouths of "free-thinkers" hurt the feelings of others and damage relationships.

In God's eyes, rebellion and obstinacy are in the same boat as witchcraft (the worship of occult powers), iniquity (habitual sin) and idolatry (replacing God with other things). In other words, it is an attitude that displeases God and moves you further away from Him.

Resistance Is Futile

Rebellion comes from the root word *rebel*, which simply means, "open resistance to," "the refusal to obey," and "to resist authority." When you resist someone or something you turn away from it to something else. You can resist things like food, the advances of an unwelcome suitor, the temptation to gossip or fornicate, or a thought or attitude. The ability to resist stems from your free will and the ability to think for yourself. As with many things in life, it can either protect or harm you, depending on what you resist.

For example, it's okay to resist illegal drugs if they are offered to you; it's *not* okay to resist arrest. Although you may not be guilty of a crime, the law makes it clear there is a penalty associated with resisting a police officer. The best thing to do is go with the flow until you can make a phone call, obtain an attorney and clear up the misunderstanding. To resist arrest not only makes you look guilty, it also makes it difficult to expedite the judicial process on your behalf. There is always a price to pay for rebellious actions.

It's important to understand that God is the ultimate authority. Psalm 91 describes Him as El Elyon, the Most High God. There is no one or nothing higher than He. Like any wise leader, He has delegated portions of His authority. These "portions" are actually *positions* of authority. Romans 13:1-7 tells us that He has commissioned, or given His authority, to the people in those positions. This means people such as police officers, city officials, civil authorities, senators, congressmen and heads of state have been commissioned by God to protect and lead you. If they don't do their jobs according to His Word, they will be judged accordingly. Although you may not respect the person in that position, *your* job is to respect the authority they carry. Your submission to that authority is what protects you.

Rebellion has one objective: to destroy.

When you don't respect those in authority, you are actually rebelling against God. To rebel against God is to resist His Word, and you *cannot* separate God from His Word. They are one and the same. If you look at what God has said in His Word and openly resist what He has set in order, you're operating in a *spirit* of rebellion.

A Dry Land

When you rebel against authority, you have chosen your course. Psalm 68:6 says, "*God setteth the solitary in families: he bringeth out those which are bound with chains: but the rebellious dwell in a dry land.*" This scripture tells us that God is able to provide a home for the outcast, and lead those who are lacking to abundance. However, He can't do a thing for the rebellious person because he or she is *choosing* to live in a dry land—a land without prosperity, peace, comfort or opportunity.

When you think of dry land, what do you envision? The first thing that comes to my mind is a desert, like the Sahara. If you've seen pictures of that place, you know that it is basically full of sand, and little else. Because the rainfall evaporates before it reaches the ground, very little, if anything, is able to take root and grow. When a person is in a dry land, nothing positive is able to manifest, or appear, in their lives, such as financial abundance, promotion or healthy relationships. A desert is the perfect representation of what rebellion breeds. I know this to be true because in the past I have experienced desert-like conditions in my life. It isn't fun.

Many years ago, I struggled with tithing. I didn't want to give the church 10 percent of the gross income I'd worked so hard to earn. I read the Word and found many places where it talked about tithing, but I'd say, "Tithing is not part of the New Testament, but the Old Testament, and it just isn't necessary to do so anymore."

One day while studying the Bible, I discovered that I was supposed to treat Jesus, the High Priest, just like Abraham treated Melchizedek, his priest. I closely examined the nature of the relationship between Abraham and Melchizedek and discovered that the tithing principle was mentioned each time their names came up. Abraham gave his tithe to Melchizedek.

I was stunned. Although it was there in black and white, the fact didn't change my attitude one bit. I flat-out decided that I wasn't going to obey what I had just read. I had unknowingly chosen to plunge head-long into desert-like conditions.

When you reject God's Word and resist change, you also resist growth. In fact, you open yourself up to all kinds of negativity. Everything in God's kingdom operates on the principle of seedtime and harvest (Galatians 6:7-9). Whatever you do comes back to you, whether positive or negative. Because I had disrespected God and His Word, I set myself up to be disrespected by someone else in return. And that's exactly what happened.

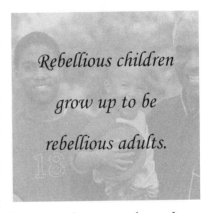

Rebellious children grow up to be rebellious adults.

I has just bought a brand new BMW. It hadn't even received its first washing yet. What happened? Somebody threw a brick through the window! Can you believe that? There was glass everywhere. I was so upset. I thought, "What is happening here?"

It didn't take me long to discover that I was dwelling in a dry land because of my rebellion. So I prayed, "Wait a minute, God. You mean just because I don't give you 10 percent of *my* income, You're going to allow someone to throw a brick through my new car window?" He replied, "It doesn't have anything to do with your money. It has everything to do with your obedience. When you rebel against Me, you submit yourself to the devil. What I'm trying to get you to do is to *rebel* against the *devil* and *submit* yourself to Me."

James 4:7-8 commands you to submit yourself to God. It also counsels you to resist the devil, which will make him flee. This scripture represents an "if-then" conditional statement. If you submit yourself to God, then the devil will flee. In other words, when you comply with God's Word, you become immune to negativity and temptation. But you can't rebel against God and try to resist the devil. Your rebellion is a magnet for unpleasant things!

Believe it or not, I *still* didn't change my tune. I continued to rebel against the Word and experience dry land conditions. After awhile, the spirit of rebellion that I had developed vertically toward God began to show up horizontally in my relationships with others—especially my pastor. At the time I was in charge of the youth choir in the church I was attending. One day the pastor approached me and said, "I want the choir to go with me over to Such and Such church and sing So and So..." I said, "Absolutely not. You should have let me know about this a little earlier. We can't go now. We're rehearsing. Thank you."

I can't tell you that I was anything other than foolish. That rebellion began trickling down into every area of my life. I was still seeking God on a regular basis. I loved Him and believed He had great things in store for me. But when I tried to begin my own ministry, it failed miserably. And I was probably the only one surprised about it!

If you want your children to have respect for authority, you must first have respect for authority.

I said, "Lord, what's wrong? I've been praying. I've been fasting. I've even been tithing every now and then...where is the fruit of my labor?"

He replied, "You're in the dry land! Fruit won't grow where *you're* living."

I knew what I had to do in order to get out of the dry land, and believe me; I was willing to do *anything* to leave that place! I began tithing faithfully and I repented to my pastor both privately and publicly. Almost instantaneously I began to see fruit, and lots of it. To this day, whenever God tells me to give financially or submit to authority, I do it willingly. Why? I had my fill of desert-like conditions in my life. That dry land has *nothing* that appeals to me.

Rebelling against God stops God from doing anything positive in your life. Submission is what will enable you to be successful in every area of your life. If you are rebellious, then your children will grow up to be rebellious just like you. Is that the kind of legacy you want to pass on to your kids?

No More Rebellion

Once you have examined your life and removed all traces of rebellion from it, you must also remove it from your home. Don't allow your children to rebel. When you receive reports from teachers, ministers or other adults that they are misbehaving, don't respond with, "What do you want *me* to do about it?" or "It's just a phase." Do what you need to do: explain to them why rebellion is dangerous and the consequences that will follow (such as a spanking) if they continue with that behavior.

It may seem harmless to you when your child sulks, pouts or throws a temper tantrum when he or she doesn't get their way at home. You may think they'll grow out of that behavior once they begin to mature into adults. That's faulty thinking. Rebellious children grow up to be rebellious adults. That cute little pout will transform itself into disrespect for laws. Your children will have difficulty holding down a steady job or receiving promotions because they have a problem submitting to their employer or other authorities. They'll live in that dry land the Bible talks about, having to struggle daily to make ends meet and overcome other challenges life sends their way.

Here are a few guidelines to help you rid your home of rebellion.

1. Make sure your children respect authority.

Whether you realize it or not, you are the primary example for your children. They watch everything you say and do. If want them to have respect for authority, *you* must first have respect for authority. Romans 13:1-3 says, *"Let every soul be subject unto the higher powers. For there is no power but of God: the powers that be are ordained of God. Whosoever therefore resisteth the power, resisteth the ordinance of God; and they that resist shall receive to themselves damnation."* Make sure your kids know that submission is not a dirty word.

2. Don't allow your children to constantly complain.

Numbers 11:1 says, *"And when the people complained, it displeased the Lord...."* No one enjoys a pessimist or a whiner. You can always count on people like that to bring others down. Don't allow your children to develop a negative outlook. By the same token, watch yourself. It's okay to blow off steam every once in a while, but not okay to be critical of everything all the time. Remember, what you do influences others. Where there are complaining children, there are complaining parents.

Taffi never allows our children to complain. When she tells them to do something, the last she wants to hear is a groan, sigh or comment. That doesn't mean they don't try to frown, roll their eyes or make a snide remark every now and then. If she sees it or hears it, Taffi quickly nips it in the bud. She is grooming our children for future success.

You need to do the very same thing. First, watch your own mouth. Then, train your children to obey you and others without complaint.

3. Don't allow your children to be bitter.

Teach your children to walk in forgiveness. Unresolved anger, bitterness and resentment only promote disharmony. Take the time to explain why they must forgive and what happens if they don't (Matthew 6:14-15; 18:21-35; Mark 11:25-26; Luke 6:37). Be a good example by being quick to forgive others. In addition, be the first to clear up misunderstandings. Teach your children to be the better person and say, "I'm sorry," "I was wrong" and "Please forgive me."

4. Establish and enforce the rules with love.

Don't act like a Marine Corps drill sergeant. Don't establish so many rules and regulations that you stifle your children or cause them to fear. In other words, be *reasonable*. Explain your rules. Communicate with your child so he or she can understand why you made the rules and the consequences of disobedience. Although they may fuss, your children will know that you love them by the guidelines you establish and the way in which they are enforced.

5. Make it plain.

Put the rules in writing and place them in a highly visible location, such as the refrigerator door or kitchen bulletin board. In this way, everyone clearly understands what is expected of them and what will happen if they refuse to comply with set guidelines. You may wish to give a copy to each child to post in his or her room.

6. Don't say it if you don't mean it.

Start out small and build from there. It doesn't make sense to set a guideline for your child's teen years when they haven't even turned 10. Make the rules age-appropriate and easy for you to enforce. Be prepared for your children to test you in this. The first few days you'll find yourself using the rod quite often, but it does get better! Consistent discipline is the key to well-mannered children. You'll see remarkable change and improvement if you stick with it.

Time Out!

Many people these days are in favor of "time out" when it comes to disciplining their children. This involves sitting a child in a corner and giving him or her time to reflect on their actions. While this sounds like a good idea, this practice only serves to foster rebellion.

Proverbs 22:15 clearly states that foolishness is bound in the heart of a child, and the rod is necessary to drive it out. In other words, a good spanking will get your child back in line and teach them that there are consequences to pay when they break the rules.

The next time your child disobeys, pull him or her aside and tell them what they have done wrong. Explain it to them in a way that is easy for them to understand, and then spank them hard enough to hurt, but not bruise. Afterward, hold them for awhile and show them that you love them.

Although your child may have trouble submitting to the punishment at first, he or she will eventually comply and come to realize that rules were not made to be broken, but rather obeyed. Years from now they will thank you for it!

---

7. Forget the past.

If your child breaks a rule and you neglect to punish them for it at the time it happens, don't bother. If you were too busy to punish them *then*, it's too late *now*. Let it go. Instead, thoroughly discuss the incident and warn them that if they break the rules again, they will have to experience the consequences for their actions.

8. Don't discipline your child in anger.

When you discipline your child in anger, you are reinforcing the idea that he or she is being punished because you are angry, not because what they did was wrong. The goal is for your child to respect you, not fear you. Before disciplining your children, take a moment to calm down. Then bring them to a special room in the home that you've designated for discipline, and ask them if they understand what they did wrong.

You must be calm. Don't lose control and shout, "What's wrong with you? How many times do I have to tell you not to do that!" When you say those things, you're simply spending a lot of energy accomplishing nothing. Instead, explain to your child *why* he or she is being disciplined, and then ask them to repeat what you said.

Once the child understands what he or she has done and why it was wrong, you can spank them. But don't go wild! This should be a very controlled, deliberate action. Train your child to submit willingly to the spanking and afterwards, tell them that you love them.

For more information regarding corporal punishment, refer to chapter 21.

A Natural Reaction

Rejection is one of the strongest negative forces on the planet. Regardless of your financial status, race or religious background, rejection is a reality for almost everyone on the planet.

You may not have realized that rebellion and rejection were related, but they are. Rejection makes people withdraw. Just as the body shuts down when it doesn't receive the proper nutrition, the spirit, or heart, shuts down when a person is rejected. Think about it: What happened the last time you were rejected? Did you run around, shouting for joy? Did you return for seconds? Or did you withdraw from the person and think about what just happened? More than likely you chose to do the latter, because rejection stings. No one likes to be turned down or turned away from something he or she wants. The only scriptural response to it is total forgiveness of the offending party, but that doesn't always happen because it's not an easy thing to do. When it doesn't, there's trouble.

Rebellion is the first reaction to rejection. In fact, rejection is always found at the root of rebellion, and rebellion rooted in rejection will produce a "tree" with branches of self-will, independence, pride, stubbornness, defiance, an inability to be taught and selfishness.

Bitterness is another reaction to rejection. Through repeated rejections, the root of bitterness grows stronger and produces hurt, anger, resentment, hatred, retaliation, violence and in extreme cases, murder. No one can get rid of bitterness for you. Only you can choose to forgive. When you don't, that root of bitterness eventually begins to affect your personality. You become moody, edgy, touchy and sullen. This, in turn, affects your ability to establish and maintain healthy relationships—with God and others. Hebrews 12:15 calls this being defiled, or corrupted. Once you have allowed bitterness to corrupt your life, it will also corrupt the lives of others around you.

Develop a zero tolerance rule and discipline your childrem when they disobey.

Children act the way they do because of what *their parents* are putting inside of them. Think about it for a minute. Who taught them to disrespect authority? Who taught them it was okay to cheat? Who taught them to be racist? By not teaching them positive life principles to live by, you are allowing someone else to do so. Children imitate what they see and hear at home. Don't try to blame it on the teachers or your relatives. *You* must take responsibility for their behavior and correct it today.

If you feel that you've had enough negativity and desire to experience peace in your home, pray this prayer right now:

> "Father, I declare that my family and I are free from rebellion. We will not continue to dwell in a dry land, but in a land of abundance. I repent of any rebellious thoughts, words, intentions or actions we have committed against You or the authority figures You have established over us. I declare that we are a disciplined family, free of bitterness and the sting of rejection. We always look to Your Word and believe the best of everyone and in every situation. Our home is rebellion-free, in Jesus' name Amen."

Do yourself and your family a favor and kick rebellion out of your home. Develop a zero tolerance rule and discipline your children when they get out of line. Instill in them the importance of submission to authority and then set an example for them to follow. You'll be amazed at the difference!

Rebellion is an attitude that, if left unchecked, will succeed in damaging relationships and undermining authority. It must be dealt with quickly and replaced with an attitude of submission.

Are you living in a desert or a rainforest? To find out, try this experiment: Take a moment to examine your life and choices over the past six months. Write down those instances where you chose to disobey rather than comply with set guidelines or authority figures, then list any consequences that followed, no matter how insignificant or trivial they may seem. Is there a pattern of negativity and challenges? If so, repent of your actions (make a 180° turn) and decide to do better in the future, no matter how difficult it may seem at first. In addition, evaluate yourself to see if there are any areas where anger, bitterness, resentment or rebellion may be lurking.

Do your best to rid yourself of these negative influences and instead purpose to develop a more positive outlook. Once you have finished examining yourself, have your children do the same regarding their own lives. Work together as a family to keep rebellion out of your home forever!

Proverbs 17:11

"An evil man seeketh only rebellion: therefore a cruel messenger shall be sent against him."

23

HOLY HORMONES!

Defeating Sexual Temptation

Sex. Just the mention of the word is enough to get most people's attention. It's the most talked-about subject on television, in print and in most of today's music and movies. The locker room humor or sensual thought-process behind these media degrade the sanctity and beauty of sex *within* marriage and downplay the negative repercussions of sex *outside* of it.

In fact, to most people, choosing abstinence is like trying to walk on water: impossible and foolish to try. Why abstain when you can indulge? Their attitude is: "If it feels good, do it." However, just because you really love a person and enjoy sexual relations with him or her doesn't make sex outside of marriage okay. Although it may *feel* good, it's *not* an acceptable practice in God's sight. First Corinthians 7:2 says, "*Nevertheless, to avoid fornication, let every man have his own wife, and let every woman have her own husband.*" Marriage is the *only* institution that makes sex legal. Feelings are temporary; commitment lasts forever.

If Jesus had followed His feelings, He would not have submitted himself to a humiliating, slow and painful death on a Roman cross (Luke 22:41-44). That type of punishment was reserved for criminals of the worst kind, and as Jesus had not broken the law, He was innocent. However, He was obedient to the will of God and placed His feelings under subjection to that will.

In his letter to the Corinthian church, Paul admonished them to "*Flee fornication. Every sin that a man doeth is without the body; but he that committeth fornication sinneth against his own body*" (1 Corinthians 6:18). When you commit sexual sin, you are defiling, or corrupting, the temple of the Holy Spirit (verse 19).

Most people regard a church building as a place that is set apart for God. You won't catch them telling a dirty joke or making out in the back pew! While the presence of God does indeed dwell in the building when His people are present, you must not forget that *your body* is the primary dwelling place of the Holy Spirit and should be treated with the same care and respect that is given to the most beautiful cathedral.

Two's Company

Living together has become the best option for some couples. They feel that they love one another enough to "try out" closer living arrangements without having to fully commitment themselves through marriage. In fact, some couples have lived together for so long that the government recognizes their relationship as a "common-law" marriage, meaning they have all the rights of a married couple without the hassle of paperwork and ceremony.

In God's eyes, marriage is the only institution that makes sex legal.

Because of this, many believers are anxious to try this type of living arrangement with their significant other. They ask, "Why do I have to have a marriage license? Can't we just make promises to one another in private, before God?" The answer is no!

Only God, through a civil authority, can unite two people in holy matrimony. In addition, you need others, usually family and close friends, to witness your exchange of vows. According to Matthew 18:16, this establishes, or cements, the words you speak. When you submit to God's will—His Word—and follow the guidelines and chain of authority He has established, a oneness is solidified in your union that you would otherwise be unable to experience if the two of you had simply chosen to live together.

Very little can stand up against a husband and wife who are united together with and by God (Ecclesiastes 4:12). However, if you're living "in sin," He cannot bless, or empower your union. When storms and challenges arise, you will be unable to stand up against them.

For example, take a dollar bill. In its simplest form, it's just a piece of paper. Some have tried to copy this piece of paper and pass it off as the real thing, but most counterfeiters get caught. Regardless of how *closely* the counterfeit money resembles the real thing, the U.S. Government does not sanction fake money. Although a counterfeit may *look* like the real thing, it's still a fake, no matter what. Sooner or later you will have to face the consequences that result from becoming entangled with it.

It amazes me that a man will get a license for his dog, but he won't make a commitment to his woman by marrying her. That is an indication that he only wants to jump in bed and use her to satisfy his sexual urges. Of course, this is not always the case; there are some women who refuse to get married for the same reason!

If you think that sleeping with a man or a woman will make them want to marry you, you are sadly mistaken. Do you remember the old saying, "Why buy the cow when you can get the milk for free?" That is so true! Why commit when you can enjoy sex outside of that commitment? Ladies and gentleman, your virginity is the most precious thing you have to give your spouse. Don't waste it on someone who won't fully commit to you. God's order is marriage *first* and the privileges of marriage *second*. If you're indulging in marital privileges *before* obtaining a license, you're going to lose that person. Remember, what you compromise to keep, you'll ultimately lose.

Self-control is not an impossible feat to achieve. You simply need to get your hormones under control. No one—especially the devil—can force you to jump in bed with someone you aren't married to. You do it because you allow yourself to think sensual thoughts, which puts your libido into overdrive. Instead of taking a cold shower and shifting your focus to something else, you indulge in whatever it is you are thinking about. This may be the result of what you were or were not taught about sex and sexual thoughts at home.

Sex Education

Most children today learn about sex in school, although it is the parents' responsibility to teach them. Many parents don't know what to say, so they don't say anything at all. That is a big mistake. You children will learn about sex *somewhere*, whether its behind the swing set on the playground or in the gym locker room. These stories are often told by an older student who is trying to "enlighten" his or her peers.

Make it a priority that your child's first lessons on sex will come from you. That is the only way that they will be able to adopt your values. They need to know what the Word says about sex *before* they read about it in romance novels or pornographic magazines. If you explain right and wrong to them according to the Word of God, those truths will grow and take root in their hearts. This equips them with self-control and the ability to defeat temptation in the future.

You will lose whatever you compromise to keep.

It's never too early to begin explaining sex to your children. In fact, if you take the time to talk to them about the "birds and the bees" and your feelings regarding pre-marital sex, they are less likely to experiment on their own or to listen to the advice of others. Calmly answer whatever question your child may ask, regardless of his or her age. You might think they are too young to be talking about sex, but if they're asking the question, they've heard about it somewhere.

When you allow yourself to become flustered or embarrassed at their questions, you send a subtle message that sex is dirty and they can't discuss the subject with you. Rather than come to you for advice, they will avoid mentioning the sexual pressure they feel among their classmates, or the fact that there is a baby on the way.

Feelings are temporary, but commitment lasts forever.

Age-Appropriate Language

Don't make your "sex talks" a one-time deal. Bring the subject up again and again, each time using different illustrations to make the point. Practice not only makes perfect, it also prepares your children for what lies ahead. Here are a few tips Creflo and I have learned over the past few years. They should help you talk to your children about sex in a manner they can understand.

1. Toddlers.

When your child is about a year old, begin teaching him or her the correct names for the parts of their body. You can point to their body and say, "This is your nose, this is your eye, this is your ear, etc." However, most parents never think to point to a child's genitals and say, "This is your penis," or "This is your vagina." Some parents will use cutesy, made-up names like "pee-pee" instead of the correct terminology.

Unfortunately, leaving out this area of the body or making up a name subtly conveys a message to the child that this area is different. They may even get the idea that their genitals are also "bad." Openly using the correct terminology without embarrassment assists the child in developing a healthy attitude about their entire body. As they get older, they will not be embarrassed to ask you questions about their private areas.

2. Preschoolers.

When your child asks you where babies come from, tell him or her the truth.

Babies are not brought to parents by storks; neither do they grow in cabbage patches. Again, use the correct terminology by telling your child that a baby grows in a uterus—not in mommy's tummy. Sooner or later, your child will find out the truth. When that happens, you want to make sure that they know you were giving them correct information. You can also answer their question by first asking, "What do you think?" That way, you will find out what your child already knows and be able to correct any misinformation that they have received.

Speak to your preschooler on his or her level. You don't have to go into explicit detail. You child probably wouldn't understand it anyway. For example, you may tell them that inside of women are egg cells and inside of men are sperm cells. When these two cells come together, a fetus is formed. The baby will then grow for nine months inside mommy's uterus before he or she is born.

Most kids this age will wonder how the two cells came together. If they ask, don't panic. Remember, you want your children to be able to talk to you about anything—especially sex. An easy-to-understand answer is that mommies and daddies love each other. Sometimes daddy will put his penis inside of mommy's vagina. Eventually sperm will come out of daddy's penis and travel to mommy's uterus through her vagina. If the sperm and the egg meet, then a fetus is started. Kids this age might think that what you are telling them is disgusting and that is o.k. When they are older they will better understand and accept the concept of sexual intercourse.

3. Preteens.

While your child may learn about the biological aspects of sex, family life and sexually transmitted diseases in school, they are not taught how to deal with the complexities of their emerging sexual feelings. Many schools today won't counsel your child to abstain from pre-marital sex. They will only inform students of the different types of birth control that are available to them.

Most schools send home a form for parents to sign giving permission for your child to attend a sex education class. Don't sign the form and then forget about it. Once your child starts the class, look for opportunities to discuss what he or she has learned. They may have questions about what is being discussed but are too embarrassed to ask in front of their classmates. This is a good opportunity for you to talk about romantic relationships, peer pressure, masturbation, pornography and abstinence.

Although teenagers are older and can basically take care of themselves, now is *not* the time to distance yourself from your child. Opportunities for them to drink, smoke cigarettes and experiment with drugs and sex abound at this time in their lives. You must set boundaries for your teens and be ready to enforce them, because they won't. Don't become lax on making them tell you where they are going and who they will be with just because they are older.

Some people think if they can make their children believe sex is dirty, they'll stay away from it. I've got news for them. They'll want to try it out for themselves! When those hormones kick in, they won't care what their parents said. If you take the "dirty" approach, what you are telling them is contrary to the Word of God. Everything He created was good (Genesis 1), including sex within the marriage. It was part of His plan from the beginning.

Like a Virgin

From the time your child is born, you need to stand in faith that he or she will remain a virgin until their wedding day. Some Christians may believe for new cars and houses but have never thought to believe for their child's virginity. If you've never made it a point to pray for your child's virginity, you need to start today. If you do this daily, you won't be on edge when the dating age approaches.

Along with prayer, it is important for you to show your children how precious their virginity is. According to Deuteronomy 6, it was the *parents'* responsibility to keep their children chaste so they could present them as virgins in holy matrimony. It brought honor before God and honor to the home.

You may be thinking, "That worked back in the Bible days, but that won't work today. That's just old-fashioned." It worked for them because more time was spent on hometraining and teaching. If you would take the time to invest in your child's understanding of sexual matters, it would work for you too. Unfortunately, most parents are too busy with their jobs or even in chauffeuring their children back and forth to different school activities. It's easier to blame the fornication problem on the present generation rather than take on the responsibility themselves.

You must do more than just tell your children to abstain from sex. We need to tell, teach, and train them *why* to abstain. If you give your child the option of condoms and other forms of birth control, they will probably take it. However, emphasize the importance of remaining pure until their wedding day. Tell them God's plan and why it's important to retain their virginity. Explain the spiritual laws of sex according to the Word. Teach them what happens when that law is broken and the adverse effects of a "soul tie," or emotional tie, through fornication (1 Corinthians 6:9-10, 18; 10:8; 2 Corinthians 12:21; Galatians 5:19; Ephesians 5:3; Colossians 3:5-6; and 1 Thessalonians 4:3). If you need help, refer to chapters 2 and 11, where it is explained in detail.

In addition, teach them about prayer and fasting. That's one of the biblical ways to counteract the flesh when it rises up. Not all children will fast, but some will. Pray with them openly and often about their virginity, and let them know you are keeping them covered in prayer. With love, openness, teaching and training, you can arm your children with spiritual weapons of warfare so they'll win sexual battles and remain pure until marriage.

Actions Speak Louder

Aside from teaching and training your children about sex and STDs, you also have additional responsibilities to carry out.

STDs

Too often young people have the idea that a sexually transmitted disease (STD) will happen to someone else and not to them. However, young people are the least likely to take precautionary measures. As a result, they often wind up with one of the following:

Genital Herpes – Is highly contagious and affects both sexes. It is caused by the herpes simplex virus (HSV) and is spread through sexual intercourse. Signs and symptoms include pain or itching in the skin around the genital area and water blisters or open sores. There is no cure for genital herpes although doctors can prescribe medication that may limit relapses and help to heal the sores.

Syphilis – A bacterial infection usually transmitted by sexual contact. It affects genitals, skin and mucous membranes and can also involve other parts of the body, such as the brain. Signs and symptoms include painless sores on the genitals, tongue or lips, enlarged lymph nodes in the groin, rash, fever, fatigue, discomfort, aching joints or bones, neurological problems (stroke, meningitis, personality changes, psychiatric illness, spinal damage) and cardiovascular problems (inflammation of blood vessels).

Gonorrhea – Is highly contagious and is caused by the bacterium *gonococcus*. It spreads through unprotected sexual contact and affects both men and women. Symptoms include a thick, cloudy discharge from the penis or vagina, pain or a burning sensation when urinating, pain during intercourse and a frequent need to urinate. Complications include *inflammation of the testicles*, *Pelvic Inflammatory Disease* (an infection that can cause scarring and infertility), *irritation of the throat and tonsils, eye inflammation* and *widespread infection* in the body.

Chlamydia – Is the most prevalent STD among teenagers and affects both men and women. It is difficult to detect because most individuals do not have symptoms that will cause them to seek medical attention. Signs and symptoms may include painful urination, lower abdominal pain, vaginal discharge in women or discharge from the penis in men. If left untreated, Chlamydia can also lead to the following: *Pelvic Inflammatory Disease, Epididymitis* (an inflammation in the coiled tube located beside the testicle), *Prostatitis* (bacteria in the prostate gland that causes fever, chills, painful urination and lower back pain) and *eye infections*.

HIV (human immunodeficiency virus) – HIV is the virus that causes AIDS (acquired immunodeficiency syndrome), a life-threatening condition. It is spread through sexual contact with an infected partner, as well as through infected blood and shared needles or syringes. Mothers with HIV can pass the infection to their babies during pregnancy, delivery or through breast milk. The virus destroys the cells of the body's immune system, which hinders your body from effectively fighting off other viruses and bacteria that cause disease. The virus can take up to 12 years to manifest with symptoms similar to the common cold. Complications such as pneumonia, meningitis and certain cancers eventually cause death.

When diagnosed early and treated with antibiotics, most bacteria-based diseases can be cured. In the case of viral-based diseases such as Herpes and HIV, there is no cure; available medications are only able to treat accompanying symptoms and illnesses, such as open sores or pneumonia.

For more information on sexually transmitted diseases, visit the Mayo

Actions Speak Louder

Aside from teaching and training your children about sex and STDs, you also have additional responsibilities to carry out.

1. Show affection.

This is especially true for fathers. The average father generally spends about 10 minutes a day with his children. That has to change! It's very sad to see young people getting into trouble sexually because they were looking for the love and attention they don't receive at home. Maintain an open level of communication with your child. They need to know that they can talk to you about anything at any time. Tell your children daily that you love them. Find out how their day went. Ask questions and then show interest as they tell you about it. If your child goes through a hard time, show concern. Let them know that you want to talk it through.

In addition, be affectionate with your spouse in front of your children. Let them see you hugging, kissing or holding hands with your spouse. It demonstrates what a godly marriage is supposed to be and how a marriage covenant works in the home.

Don't allow your children to watch or listen to anything that promotes premarital sex because the fantasy can overshadow what you've taught them.

2. Protect their associations.

You have a right to govern the associations of your children. Make sure their friends are a godly influence in their lives. If one of their friends is sexually active, that person is going to encourage your child to do the same thing. Make sure they aren't around other kids who might use drugs or alcohol. It's your job to protect your children by helping them make wise choices in regard to friendships. Read to them Psalm 119:63 which says, *"I am a companion of all them that fear thee, and of them that keep thy precepts."* Decide together that this scripture will be their foundation when searching for friends. Pray this scripture over your child, and believe it to be true in his or her life.

3. Keep them busy.

Kids are often tempted by promiscuity because they have too much free time on their hands. Keep them busy. If possible, avoid having them come home to an empty house. If someone is there to greet them, the opportunity to give in to temptation will be diminished.

In addition, you may wish to consider a "No Fly Zone" rule anytime you are away. This simply means that no one is allowed in the house when you or your spouse is not there. That includes friends of the same sex and especially members of the opposite sex. If one of their friends wants to use the restroom, get a drink of water or study, they will be forced to return home to do so. When they *do* want to get together with their friends, have their friends come to *your* house. It's easier to monitor and control what goes on under your own roof.

4. Monitor what they hear and see.

Don't allow your children to watch movies that promote premarital sex because the fantasy of a movie can overshadow what you've taught them. The movie may only be rated PG or PG-13, but if it's promoting principles contrary to the Word, your children have no business watching it.

Be cautious of the music that you allow inside your home. Listen to the words! If your children hear seductive words over and over, the words will become thoughts that eventually give way to corresponding actions. You may wish to preview CDs, video games or movies before allowing your children to buy, listen to or watch them. Many Web sites now provide lyrics to many of today's most popular songs while major retailers often allow you to listen to specific music selections or play segments of video games before purchasing the item. Do your homework and surprise your children with your music, video game and movie savvy.

It's your job as a parent to protect your children.

Although you may feel like the bad guy at first because you'll find yourself saying, "no" more than once, that's okay. There is nothing wrong with that. By taking a proactive stance, you teach your children that there are certain things they can and can't do. They might act like they don't like it, but deep down they know you have their best interest at heart. Your child will respect the stability you bring to their lives and the boundaries you establish for them even if they don't tell you so. Your parental protection shows them you care.

Take Them Out

You should only allow your children to "date" when they are emotionally, mentally and spiritually prepared to handle a dating situation. They shouldn't be allowed on a date until they understand what is and what is not supposed to happen.

The best way to prepare them is by "dating your children." Fathers, take your daughters out on the town. Show her how a man should treat a lady. Pay for everything and be courteous to her. Help her with her coat. Open door for hers. Use your best manners so she'll know what to expect. Mothers, take your sons on a date. Let him go in to your husband and act like he's meeting a girl's father. While you are out, show him how a lady is supposed to act with a man. Let him open doors for you and pay the bill. Allow your son to be the gentleman.

If you will be their first date and continue doing so throughout their childhood, those memories will leave an impression in their minds and set a standard for their future relationships.

Redirect Their Focus

As an added reminder, sit down and talk to your children about the kind of spouse they desire and the qualifications they should look for in a spouse. Doing so helps to protect them from fornication and from becoming involved with the wrong person.

Have you had that conversation with your children? If not, it's time. It's too late to talk about those things once they're already in love with the wrong person. So plant the seeds now! Explain to them that God will present many different choices for a mate, but that it will be up to them to decide. Also tell them of God's requirements. Since He forbids believers to be joined in marriage to unbelievers, help your child see that God won't present someone to them who is an unsaved or ill-mannered and selfish individual. Neither will He make his presentation in a nightclub or bar.

Plant in your child's heart the following requirements for a godly mate. He or she must:

1. Be born again.
2. Be filled with the Holy Spirit.
3. Love God more than anyone else.
4. Be attractive to them (but that shouldn't be the main qualification).
5. Treat his or her parents well.

If you sit down and make a list with your child using God's Word as the guideline, he or she will remember it when they are tempted to get off course!

*   *   *   *   *

Training your children to understand sexual relations is not always going to be easy, but you will be richly rewarded for doing so. Video games, sports equipment, automobiles and new clothes make great gifts, but the best ones to give are free. Shower your children with love by giving them the discipline, honesty and training they need to become mature, responsible adults. Invest in their future by taking time to invest in their present!

Children need to receive sex education from their parents in order to appreciate the sanctity and value of virginity and intercourse in marriage.

Take a moment to reflect on the information given in this chapter. Have you neglected to train your children properly regarding sexual temptation, fornication and abstinence? Are they aware of what the Word of God has to say concerning intercourse? If not, decide right now to act on the principles you have just learned. Take time out to thoroughly discuss this topic with them, and listen carefully to what they have to say. Combat any negative or erroneous stereotypes and ideas with scripture. Be forthright in your responses. Remember, the groundwork you lay today will build trust and enable them to feel comfortable coming to you in the future.

1 Thessalonians 4:2-5, 7, NKJV

"...for you know what commandments we gave you through the Lord Jesus. For this is the will of God, your sanctification: that you should abstain from sexual immorality; that each of you should know how to possess his own vessel in sanctification and honor, not in passion of lust...For God did not call us to uncleanness, but in holiness."

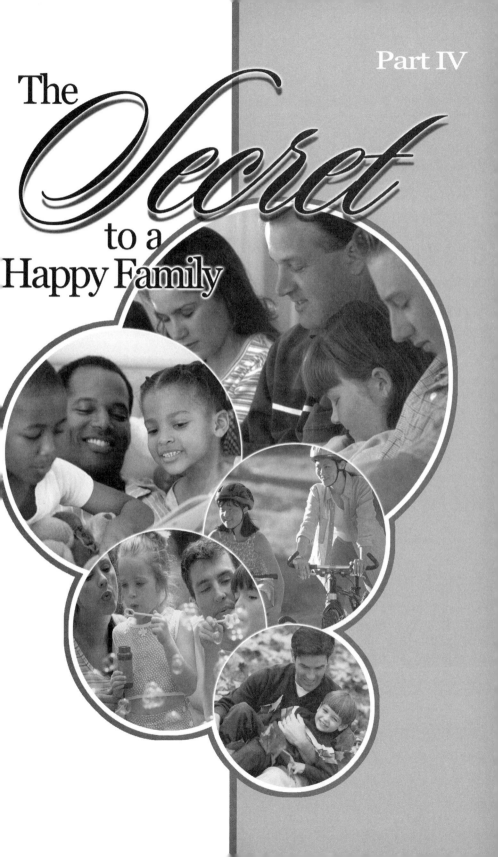

Part IV

The *Secret* to a
Happy Family

24

THE MASTER KEY
12 Steps to a Better You

I n order for a family to be successful, everyone must be willing to change. I say that because almost all of the challenges families face could be alleviated if only one or more people were willing to change their responses and behaviors toward one another. However, change doesn't always come easy. Sometimes it takes an extremely adverse circumstance to make a person realize that he or she *has* to change. For the born-again believer, a permanent change *cannot* occur unless he or she is willing to "turn over a new leaf" and transform their thinking.

God knows how difficult it can be for an individual to change certain thought patterns or set behaviors; however, He also knows that it is completely possible to do so. To help you accomplish this task, He has outlined the principles for "mind renewal" in His Word. Look at it as a success strategy for your life. Have you ever heard the saying, "You are what you eat?" The same thing applies to your mind: you are what you think (Proverbs 23:7).

Whether you realize it or not, the negative, ungodly thoughts you dwell on today will eventually become the things you do in the future. By changing the way you think, you change your actions. The more you meditate on, or think about, specific scriptures and apply them to your life daily, the more those biblical principles will transform you from the inside out. Without the Word of God providing the underlying force, any changes you attempt to make will not last.

Salvation 101

Before you can apply the process for change, you must first understand *why* you need to change. This requires a little Bible study.

Every person is divided into three parts: spirit, soul and body. You *are* a spirit. You *possess* a soul, and you *live* in a body. Your *spirit* is the part of you that lives forever. After you have taken your last breath, your body will eventually turn to dust;

however, your spirit lives on. If you have accepted Jesus Christ as your Lord and Savior, you will go to heaven when you die. If you have not, you will spend eternity in hell. When the Bible refers to the *heart* of a person, it is referring to your spirit. Your *soul* consists of your mind, will and emotions. The *body* is the physical portion of your being. It houses your spirit and soul.

In order for a family to be a successful, everyone must be willing to change.

Before you became born again, your spirit was "dead," or alienated from God by sin. Sin is simply a state of being that entered the world when Adam disobeyed God in the Garden of Eden (Genesis 2). After giving, or surrendering your life to Christ, your spirit was "reborn" and given new life. This is where we get the term "born again." Romans 12:1-2 says, *"I beseech you therefore, brethren, by the mercies of God, that ye present your bodies a living sacrifice, holy, acceptable unto God, which is your reasonable service. And be not conformed to this world:* **but be ye transformed by the renewing of your mind,** *that ye may prove what is that good, and acceptable, and perfect, will of God"* (emphasis added).

Although the condition of your spirit changes automatically when you accept Jesus, your soul and body *do not*. Some people think that just because they are now born again their thoughts and actions will automatically change. That's not true. You must make the effort to renew, or transform, your mind so that your thoughts agree with the Word of God. Only then will your mind, will, emotions and actions begin to line up with the desires of your spirit.

Until that transformation takes place, your mind will still think worldly thoughts, and you will continue to fall prey to the same temptations as before (James 1:13-15). Your actions will seem to deny the commitment you have made to follow after Christ. This is what leads others to believe that many Christians are hypocrites. It amazes me when people condemn Christians for messing up. Just because an individual fails to overcome temptation doesn't mean he or she isn't a Christian. It just means they have a long way to go on the journey to mind renewal.

Becoming a born-again Christian is not the end of the process for building a successful family and life for yourself. It's only the beginning! After accepting Jesus as your Lord and Savior, it's *imperative* that you study and apply the Word of God to your life *daily*. All areas of your life—spirit, soul and body—depend on you doing so.

Think about it. When you are sick and the doctor prescribes an antibiotic for your illness, do you only take one pill and put the rest away? Do you say, "It's not working!"? Of course not! You take the medicine until it's completely gone. If you don't, the symptoms may either return or never go away at all!

The same thing is true with the process of mind renewal. Before you became born again, your viewpoints were most often shaped by society, personal experience or the advice of others. Many of these views were in direct opposition to God and His Word. You were, therefore, in a state of sin, spiritually separated from God. In other words, you spirit was "sick." God, as the Great Physician, prescribes His Word as an antidote to your sickness. Your born-again status guarantees you eternal life in heaven, but not necessarily heaven on earth. To experience long-lasting success in life, you must know and apply the Word—God's cure—to every situation you face. After you learn and meditate on God's way of doing things, your mind will be changed, and you will not only begin to see things from His perspective, you'll also take on His characteristics!

The Bible is your instruction manual for successful living. Someone once put it this way, "It gives you "Basic Instructions Before Leaving Earth." From the principles outlined within, you learn how to speak, act, manage finances, raise children, enhance interpersonal communication skills, adopt a healthy lifestyle, position yourself for promotion and increase, and much more. Of course, there are many other good reading resources on these subjects, but the Bible was inspired by God Himself and contains His life-changing power. Every time you read it, you empower yourself.

What's Holding You Back?

Often the ability or willingness to change is hindered by the presence of strongholds in our lives. A stronghold is a thought pattern that has developed through the words you hear and speak, suggestions you entertain and mental images you create. These thoughts cause you to react automatically to certain stimuli. For example, a man or woman who has been taught that it is okay to hit others when they are angry will do just that when the opportunity arises. They have meditated so much on the fact that it's all right to hit others, they don't think twice about striking a family member who has upset them. They may justify it by saying, "They pushed me to do it," or "They deserved it."

Decision is the open door to reality.

Unfortunately, many people don't even recognize strongholds because they believe these thought patterns are normal or healthy. They've become so accustomed to a particular way of thinking that it has become a part of their personality. All information is automatically filtered through this thought pattern.

When you begin aligning your thoughts with God's thoughts (His Word), you will experience a season of inner conflict. You are breaking away from an established pattern and trying to develop a new one in your life. For years you have nurtured your stronghold with excuses and corresponding actions. You may have said, "That's just the way I am," or "Everyone thinks the same way." Tearing down those old patterns requires diligence and discipline.

Let God's Word serve as your spiritual mirror to reveal the changes you need to make.

You must understand that Satan *will* continue pushing your buttons—the ones that provoke the same old reactions within you before you discovered the knowledge of God. He loves to set up situations that will push you into negative thinking and corresponding reactions. If you are not careful to continue the mind renewal process daily, his button-pushing will overtake you, and you'll be right back where you started. Remember, transforming your mind is a life-long process. It doesn't happen automatically, and it certainly doesn't happen overnight! However, diligence, discipline and determination will eventually make the road a little easier to travel.

Identify Your Strongholds

How do you identify a stronghold in your life? Here's the test: If you find yourself constantly defending and justifying certain thoughts, opinions or actions, that's probably it. Here is a list of several of the most common strongholds. Take a moment to see if any of them have taken up residence in your mind.

1. **Unbelief:** You have trouble believing that the Word of God works.
2. **Cold love:** You do not have compassion, warmth or a tender heart.
3. **Fear:** You have a fear of failure, the unknown or present circumstances, or suffer from certain phobias.
4. **Pride:** You find it difficult or impossible to admit your

> mistakes. You also refuse to comply with biblical principles and guidelines.
> 5. **Unforgiveness:** You carry old hurts and allow bitterness and resentment to take root in your heart.
> 6. **Lust:** You struggle with, and often cave in to, strong appetites. These can include sex, food, money, knowl edge or power.
>
> Once you recognize a stronghold, get rid of it! Look up scriptures that pertain to your situation and confess, or speak them, aloud to combat those negative thoughts (2 Corinthians 10:5). Realize that it took more than one day for a stronghold to develop, and it may take more than one day to break free of them.
> The strongest person doesn't always win life's battles. However, the person who believes that he or she will win, always does. If you are experiencing inner conflict, rejoice! That confirms that you're at war with your old nature. Remember, victory is near: "*...in all these things we are more than conquerors through him that loved us*" (Romans 8:37)!

The 12-Step Process

Many people struggle with change because they are afraid of it. They are used to operating one way and are unsure of how to act in a new situation. Others would like to change, but they just don't know where to begin.

Here are 12 steps that I believe will assist you in reaching your goal of effecting a permanent change in your life. As you renew your mind with the truths of God's Word, you'll see a marked difference in yourself and your relationships with others.

1. Make a decision.

Until *you* make a decision to change, nothing will happen. Decision is the open door to reality. By that I mean you will never enter into the reality of a changed life until you've decided enough is enough and purposed in your heart to try something new. Once you've made your mind up, don't allow anyone or anything to take you off course.

2. Turn your will completely over to God.

This means that you must submit to whatever the Word of God tells you to do. The term submission simply means to "get under the will of another." In this case, you must place your will in subject to God. Isaiah 1:19 says, *"If ye be willing and obedient, ye shall eat the good of the land."* To eat the good of the land, you must set aside your plans and desires for God's.

3. Possess a strong desire to change.

Desire comes from whatever you pay the most attention to. If you drive by a sign that says, "Hot donuts" and get a strong yearning for them, it's because that sign caught and held your attention. You entertained the thought of eating a hot donut; as a result, you now want one. Desires are created by what we allow ourselves to be exposed to. If you hang around people who are talking about pornography all the time, pretty soon you'll want to indulge in pornographic magazines and movies too. Watch your influences and focus on positive, godly things.

4. Deepen your knowledge base.

Your level of knowledge must increase if you want to transform your life. For example, if you desire to eat right, but don't have any knowledge about what is good for you, you won't ever eat nutritious foods. Instead, you'll continue to eat the wrong things and love every minute of it. Your knowledge base is the foundation on which you are building. You can deepen this base through personal study of the Bible, correspondence courses, Internet resources, books, teaching tapes or by coming to church. Dig deep into the things of God. Knowledge is power.

5. Look into the Word as a mirror to change.

Allow the Word of God to measure your progress. Use it as a mirror to point out areas that still need to be adjusted or enhanced. Think about it. When you get up in the morning and look into the mirror, what do you see? Usually a scary sight: messy hair, oily skin and gritty teeth. The mirror is telling you that you could use a shower, comb and toothbrush! As a result, you make changes based on your reflection. In the same way, let God's Word serve as your spiritual mirror to reveal what needs to be changed.

6. Diligently apply the truths you've learned.

After you read a passage from the Bible, hear a sermon or listen to a teaching tape, apply what you have learned to your life. It helps to take notes as you listen or read, and then review and apply them until the principles are second nature to you. James 1:25 says that you will be blessed in your deeds if you are not a forgetful hearer.

7. Guard the entrances to your heart.

The entrances to your heart are your eyes (what you watch), ears (what you listen to) and mouth (what you say). So protect them! Proverbs 4:23 tells us *"To guard your heart with all diligence for out of it flows the issues of life."* This is a simple principle: garbage in, garbage out. Mind the things in which you indulge; they are not to your benefit.

8. Defend your mind against negative thoughts.

If the devil knows you can be tempted in one specific area, you can bet that's the button he will push. The Bible tells us to take every thought captive and bring it into submission to God's Word (2 Corinthians 10:3-5). In other words, allow the spoken Word to be the final authority over whatever is tempting you. If the devil sends you a thought like, "You've got cancer and you are going to die," don't give in to fear! Instead say, "Isaiah 53:5 says that by the stripes of Jesus I am healed, I am the healed protecting my health from sickness and disease. Cancer has a right to exist, but not in my body. I shall live and not die. I am healed in the name of Jesus."

9. Be selective of what you expose yourself to.

Watch who you hang around with. If you're a former drug user, don't continue to hang out with old drug dealing buddies. Watch where you go. If you're a recovering alcoholic, don't go to bars. It's easier to resist temptation when you're far from it. Do your best not to put yourself in compromising situations.

10. Disassociate from the past.

Philippians 3:13 says, *"Brethren, I count not myself to have apprehended: but this one thing I do, forgetting those things which are behind, and reaching forth unto those things which are before."* If you continue to live in the past, you'll never really grasp what God has set before you. Don't dredge up those old feelings of anger, regret, guilt or shame; they'll only keep you from enjoying the present and the progress you're making. In addition, you'll be tempted to make excuses or feel sorry for yourself. Forget the past. There are no "do-overs" in life. Press on!

11. Be open to correction and remain teachable.

If you're continually making excuses for, or justifying your behavior, and you refuse to learn from God's Word, you aren't ready for change. In fact, you're still acting like a child who refuses to grow up! Change is a process, and correction plays a key role in it. God corrects those He loves (Proverbs 3:12). He doesn't want you to have to reap any negative consequences. Be teachable and don't resist godly correction. It's good for you.

12. Depend on God and others for support.

You can't change yourself by yourself. Get off the phone and on your knees! Make God your primary source for encouragement and love. Then build a solid support base by surrounding yourself with mature believers. In doing so, you position yourself for lasting change.

*　*　*　*　*

Change is the master key to a successful family. By transforming negative thought and behavior patterns and establishing new ones based on the positive principles of God's Word, you are guaranteed success in every area of your life.

If you are serious about creating a better future for you and your family, pray this prayer aloud:

"God, I want to change. I believe that the more I study and apply Your principles to my life, the better off I am. I am being transformed from the inside out. My relationships with my family members are better than ever because I

am getting rid of my old thought patterns and replacing them new ones. Help me to continue on the path to self-improvement. In Jesus name, Amen."

In order for a family to be successful, everyone must be willing to change their thoughts, opinions and behaviors. This transformation can only be accomplished by the Word of God.

Take a moment to reflect on your thought life. What things do you dwell on the most? When you have diagnosed the problem areas, search the Bible for scriptures that pertain to your particular situation. Look in the concordance in the back of your bible for a complete listing of scriptures. When you have written them down, post them in several places where you will be able to reach them easily, including your car and wallet. When your mind begins to drift toward those thoughts, recite your list of scriptures aloud. Do this every time you feel your mind drifting into "forbidden territory." Before you know it, your mind will be free of those persistent, negative thoughts, because you will have replaced them with God's Word!

 **2 Corinthians 10:3-5**

"For though we walk after the flesh, we do not war after the flesh: (For the weapons of our warfare are not carnal, but mighty through God to the pulling down of strongholds;) casting down imaginations, and every high thing that exalteth itself against the knowledge of God, and bringing into captivity every thought to the obedience of Christ...."

25

KEEP YOUR SENSE OF HUMOR!
Defeating Stress and Adversity With Laughter

I am the first to admit that marriage and raising a family are very serious commitments. However, in dealing with the day-to-day demands of family life—homework, bills, errands and chores—it is important that you don't take things so seriously that you lose your sense of humor.

You can learn a lot about the humorous side of life from most television sitcoms. Have you ever noticed that the main characters never fail to find the humor in any given situation? This is probably why sitcoms are so popular. Not only are they a form of entertainment, they are also a tool that highlights the funny side of life while dealing with everyday issues. To avoid being overly stressed, it helps to be optimistic and see the brighter side of things even in the midst of severe adversity.

Don't Throw In the Towel

Whether you realize it or not, you have an enemy, and his name is Satan. He comes to kill, steal and destroy your family through adversity. *Adversity* is "an event or a series of events which oppose success or desire." It also means "calamity; affliction; distress;" and "a state of unhappiness." It is designed to stop you from succeeding in life by turning you away from your goals and to keep you from experiencing peace of mind.

Adversity accomplishes its goal by getting you to give up, cave in and quit. However quitting should never be an option. Just as a soldier has no other option but to press on in adverse, or even dangerous conditions, you should be able to do the same (2 Timothy 2:3, AMP). Endurance is vital. To *endure* simply means to outlast. When all hell is breaking loose in your home, that's not the time to quit. Rather than focus on the negative, you should look at opposition as an opportunity for God to demonstrate His power *through* you (1 John 4:4)!

When challenges arise, most people usually do one of two things—respond or react. Taffi and I have learned that it is much better to *respond* appropriately rather than to *react* inappropriately. When you have the right response, in accordance with the Word of God, you are able to overcome anything that gets in your way.

Joy and humor are great weapons in times of adversity (Psalm 31:7). Of course the last thing anyone feels like doing is rejoicing in the middle of a bleak situation, but if you maintain a positive attitude, you will be able to see beyond your present circumstances. The force of joy enables you to outlast the toughest situation. More importantly, when you rejoice, the Holy Spirit comes to your assistance. He is your Helper, and He will assist you if you continue to stand strong.

Joy to the World

Joy is much more than a feeling. It is a force that produces the power needed to endure during difficult times. Joy and strength are interchangeable; they cannot be separated. That is why the Bible says the joy of the Lord is your strength (Nehemiah 8:10). If you are without joy, you are also without the strength to endure.

Everyone should be able to find humor in everything—even in the midst of adversity.

Don't confuse joy with happiness. There is a distinct difference between the two. *Happiness* is temporary and depends on your physical, mental or emotional comfort. If everything feels good and goes smoothly, you are happy. For example, imagine that you've planned the Caribbean vacation of a lifetime. You've saved up the money, made the reservations, and prepared for your trip. You smile just thinking about the tropical breezes and crystal blue water. But when you arrive at the airport on the appointed day, the airline tells you that all flights to your destination have been cancelled due to a possible hurricane in the area. All of a sudden you're not so happy anymore. In fact, you're probably steaming!

On the other hand, *joy* is based on what you *know* or *understand*. It's not based on feelings. The 12 Apostles were able to endure multiple beatings because they not only knew God was with them and they were on the right track, they were also confident that there was a better life in store for them in heaven (Acts 5:12-41). Knowing, or understanding, is the key to joy (Proverbs 4:7). It is vital that you know what the Word of God has to say about your situation in order to build your strength and give you a firm foundation on which to stand.

Galatians 5:22 states that joy is a *fruit* of the Spirit, or a *spiritual force* that can change circumstances. Have you ever been involved in an argument with someone, and all of a sudden you or the other person begins to laugh? What happens then? Often the mood lifts and a potentially nasty situation is diffused. Circumstances can and will change, as will your level of happiness; however, your level of joy should remain the same.

Laughter *Is* the Best Medicine

You must purpose in your heart to keep your sense of humor regardless of what may be happening around you. Your children may be acting up, your spouse may be getting on your nerves, there may be challenges with your finances and the boss is giving you a hard time. In spite of all that, you still have the ability to exercise free will and choose to look on the bright side. That takes an unbelievable amount of character. It's easy to be a pessimist when things go wrong; but when you stand up and *choose* to be optimistic, that speaks volumes.

The Bible says a merry heart does the body good like medicine (Proverbs 17:22). The medical profession is finding evidence of this biblical truth. From their studies on laughter and the terminally ill, they are realizing that laughter is healing.

I remember reading about a man who was diagnosed with a deadly disease. His doctors had given him little chance of recovery. He didn't go home and prepare to die; instead, he watched videos of his favorite comedy shows and just laughed and laughed. Within eight days he had made a remarkable recovery. The man did not give up hope or lose his sense of humor in his day of adversity. Through the force of joy, he endured and came out victorious.

You must not forget to laugh. Stress has become one of the most serious health issues of our time, and humor is the quickest and most effective way to combat it. Laughter has many benefits. Not only does it make you feel better; it is also good for your heart. Although researchers are not completely sure *how* humor protects the heart, they have enough evidence to prove that a good chuckle reduces certain stress hormones that contribute to heart disease.

In addition, psychologists have found that laughter in the workplace contributes to creativity and diffuses tension, enabling employees to cope more easily with daily stressors. Some corporations even hire humor consultants to train their executives to loosen up. The executives are taught to take their work seriously without taking *themselves* too seriously.

What a Honeymoon!

My honeymoon night could have been a real disaster. Taffi and I arrived at our hotel in the Bahamas only to learn that there had been a mix up with our reservations—reservations that had been made *months* in advance.

The hotel clerk informed us that our double bed room was not available. All they had left in the hotel was a room with two single beds. I was extremely frustrated and upset. Taffi only aggravated the situation by suggesting that we push the single beds together. I said, "No! This is not supposed to be happening on *my* honeymoon." My happiness was nowhere to be found.

We took the room and it was awful. The chest of drawers was a mix-and-match set: dirt brown and olive green. When we turned the water on it didn't run out—it plopped out! Taffi and I sat down on one of the beds, looked at each other and started laughing. In fact, we fell on the floor and laughed to the point of tears. We finally snuggled up on one of the beds, laughing ourselves to sleep.

We were awakened first thing the next morning by a phone call from the manager. He said, "I apologize for the mix-up last night. One of the best suites in the hotel is available and I am calling to see if you want it." Of course Taffi and I jumped on the opportunity and spent the rest of our honeymoon in comfort.

By keeping our joy and composure in the midst of a troubling situation, things worked out in our favor. We could have easily gotten angry and yelled at everyone, including one another, but instead we found the humor in it all and didn't allow those adverse conditions to steal our joy!

In a recent staff meeting, I charged my staff to loosen up and look for something to laugh about daily. I want the people that work for me to enjoy their jobs and to look forward to coming to work, just as Solomon's servants did (1 Kings 10:4-8). We have even found that telling a good joke at the beginning of a meeting breaks the ice and enables everyone to relax.

Financial management is one task that seems to place more stress on marriages and families than any other. While it is important to manage your finances wisely, it is just as important that you set money aside for fun activities. Don't be afraid to do something that may seem impractical, like treating your family to a day of fun and relaxation. Everyone, including children, needs a break sometimes.

Keep in mind that it doesn't have to be anything expensive (like a two-week Disney vacation)—especially if your budget won't allow it. There are still many fun activities to enjoy that don't cost a lot of money, such as ice-skating or rollerblading, home movie night, picnics or long drives. Be creative and willing to find out what's available to you. Your goal is to do something that will help ease tension, strengthen relationships and give the entire family a sense of well-being.

Cut It Out!

When you are too stressed the following signs will appear:

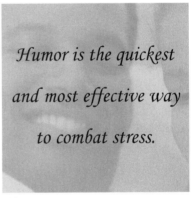

Humor is the quickest and most effective way to combat stress.

1. Irritability.
2. Loss of appetite or bingeing.
3. Insomnia or too much sleep.
4. Lack of joy.
5. Strained relationships.
6. Headaches, backaches and sore muscles.

The following 5 tips will help to reduce stress and keep your sense of humor alive and well.

1. Place in plain view a photo or cartoon that makes you smile or laugh.
2. Frequently expose yourself to what you think is funny.
3. Do something with family or friends in which no one is proficient, such as bowling, card playing or cooking. You'll end up laughing at yourselves and having a great time.
4. Learn to laugh at yourself. This not only shows tha you are human, it also takes the sting out of the negative things others may say.
5. Take your job seriously without taking yourself too seriously.

By incorporating these tips into your daily life, you will experience a renewed zest for life that will enable you to outwit and outlast even the toughest challenge!

A good sense of humor enables you to overcome adversity and promotes closeness and a sense of general well-being.

Lighten up! Search through the Sunday comics or Internet Web sites for cartoons, anecdotes, stories or phrases that tickle your funny bone. Share them with your family by posting them on the refrigerator, sending them through e-mail or retelling them over dinner. A laugh a day is sure to keep stress away!

Psalm 30:11

"Thou hast turned for me my mourning into dancing: thou hast put off my sackcloth, and girded me with gladness...."

26

TIME OUT FOR FAMILIES

Fun, Relationship-Building Activities

I once heard someone say, "Children spell love—T-I-M-E" and that's so true. Your children want your love, time and attention. Some of you probably thought that *your* kids spelled love, "M-O-N-E-Y" because of the way they're always asking for it! But that's not what matters most to them. They want *you*, and you need to make sure that's what they get—not the television, money or time at the mall. Just you!

I don't care how busy you are; you must set aside quality time for your family daily. If your job keeps you from spending time with your family, then change jobs. If volunteer work at the church keeps you from spending quality time with your children, resign from that position. It's all about priorities. If your priorities are out of line, make a quality decision to rearrange them. God comes first, then your spouse and children, church and *finally* your job. If you get one of those out of order, you'll find yourself in an awful mess.

Make sure your spouse and children know how important they are to you. Plan family outings and vacations together. Enjoy your children while they're young, because you'll never again have this time with them.

Great Ideas

Let's face it: kids like strange stuff! The stranger the adventure, the more they like it. Don't exclude yourself from an activity just because it's a new experience. You may find yourself enjoying it too! Just in case you are having difficulty coming up with ideas of your own, here are several projects to get you started on the path to all-out fun!

1. Build a blanket fort.

Take a few snack trays, card tables, chairs and some large blankets and—voila!—you have a fort. Grab some flashlights and a few favorite books and read stories together inside your creation. Once the creative juices are flowing, ask each child to make up a story and share it with the family, or begin a chain story. Here's how it works: one person begins the story and stops it at an interesting point. Then another family member picks up where the previous storyteller left off and adds some more. This goes on until the last family member takes the wild story and ends it. Get ready to giggle!

2. Have a puppet show.

Using old socks and markers, draw faces on sock puppets (it may help to place light bulbs in the toes to make it easier to draw on the material). Then, take some old yarn and glue the yarn to the sock puppets' heads. For a real nice touch, sew on buttons for eyes. Give each puppet a name, and make up a short play or have them lip sync to a popular song. Invite friends and other family members over for dinner and a pre-dinner puppet performance.

3. Plan a pancake day.

Fix pancakes for breakfast, lunch and dinner. For extra fun, use chocolate chips, two cherry halves and whipped cream to make a smiley-face pancake. You can also experiment with different syrups and fruit toppings at each meal.

4. Create your own bubbles.

Mix six cups of water, two cups of dishwashing liquid and 3/4 cup of corn syrup. Then, bend coat hangers and pipe cleaners into different shapes, dip them into the bubble formula and have a "Who can blow the biggest bubble?" contest.

5. Have a pajama day.

This is great for rainy weekends or vacation days. Simply declare,

"We're staying in our pajamas all day today," and watch your kids' eyes light up! Pop lots of popcorn and watch family movies, play board games or read favorite stories.

You may want to try creating a family "Trivial Pursuit" game for a fun, learning experience that will draw the family closer together. Ask questions such as: "What year did dad graduate from high school?" or "How did Mom and Dad meet?" or "What was Mom's maiden name?" If you can't do this for a whole day, just have a "pajama afternoon."

6. Get a makeover.

This is especially fun for little girls. Family members can give one another facials or style hair. Females can practice putting on eye shadow, blush and lipstick, or putting together different outfits to wear. For even more fun, have a fashion show, sporting their ensembles. You'll want to have the camera handy for this one!

Make Family Fitness Fun

Your children drag in from a long day at school, drop their backpacks at the front door, and head for the kitchen. A few minutes later, they emerge with chips and soda. Slowly they make their way into the living room, munching as they go. Then, with one swift click of the remote control, the television comes on and your children are in "The Spud Zone."

The United States is full of couch potato kids who are growing up to be physically inactive adults with health issues. Lifelong activities such as cycling, swimming, running and walking are great motivators for getting your spuds off the couch, into action and having fun. These activities promote physical fitness in a non-threatening way. Plus, you can bike, swim, run and walk as a family. Make a day of it!

Here are a few more family fitness suggestions for your consideration:

1. Take a hike in a nearby national park or woodland area.

Increase the fun factor by making it a scavenger hunt hike. List 10 things for your children to find on the hike: an oak leaf, an acorn, a bird's feather, a dandelion and so forth. Allow the winner of the scavenger hunt (the one who finds the most items) to choose next week's family fitness activity. Then reward the whole family with some frozen yogurt on the way home.

2. Have your own water Olympics.

If you have access to a pool, plan a day of water fun. You can get great exercise by having water relay races and "biggest splash" contests. In between the competitions, have your kids do some aerobic moves underwater—knee raises, arm circles or sidekicks. The natural resistance of the water guarantees a great workout. See who can do the most laps. Teach the children different kinds of kicks.

Take Care of Your Temple!

Before embarking on a family fitness program, take time to educate your children about their bodies being God's temple and the importance of taking care of them. You can do this by reading 1 Corinthians 6:19 and then discussing the passage with a question and answer session and practical example. Use the following as a guideline.

"The New King James Version of 1 Corinthians 6:19-20 says, 'Do you not know that your body is the temple of the Holy Spirit who is in you, whom you have [received] from God, and you are not your own? For you were bought at a price; therefore glorify God in your body....' How do you think we can honor God with our bodies? (Give them time to answer). By taking care of our bodies and keeping them in tip-top shape, God can better use us to fulfill His will for our lives.*

If we didn't keep our home in good condition by repainting the walls and fixing the roof, it wouldn't be a very nice place to live, would it? A run-down house wouldn't be doing its job of providing a good shelter for us. The same thing happens with our bodies. If we don't keep them in good shape, we won't be able to do the special jobs God has planned for us."

Close the lesson by offering a simple prayer over your upcoming family fitness time, and decide when to have the very first fitness day. Mark it on a calendar and place it somewhere everyone will see it.

---

3. Learn something new or join a team.

Have you always wanted to learn a certain sport or activity? Search your local community college newspapers or Web sites for classes the entire family would enjoy and then enroll in them. Local YMCAs are great family fitness centers, offering a wide variety of affordable classes for all skills and ages. In addition, you may also want to consider joining a community softball or volleyball team. This will promote teamwork and sportsmanship.

4. Horse around.

Running to catch a football or playing tag can be great exercise. Join in a game of hopscotch. Jump rope together. Toss a Frisbee. You can work up a sweat while enjoying the great outdoors. You can even find ways to make walking fun. For instance, encourage your young daughter to push her dolls in a stroller as you walk together or have your son walk the dog. If your children are older, buy each an inexpensive portable cassette or CD player to use during your weekend work-outs.

Let your kids see your positive attitude toward exercise. Remember: actions speak louder than words. As your children become more open and attracted to fitness, they'll spend less time on the couch and more time being active. More importantly, they will develop lifelong exercise habits while having fun with Mom and Dad.

Have a Family Night

Family night is a special time for everyone to get together and have fun without interruptions, conflicts or correction. If done correctly, it will foster unity and enhance feelings of security and trust. Try one or more of the following to help make this a time to look forward to.

- **Open the night with a song.** It can be a silly, made-up, sponta-neous or spiritual song. Singing is a good place to begin because it marks the beginning of family night and sets the mood for the rest of the evening.

- **Follow with prayer or positive affirmation.** Take turns saying a few words of prayer or a reason why you are grateful to God. You can also affirm one another by saying something like, "I think we are a great family because we stick up for one another." This works nicely if you stand in a circle and squeeze the hand of the person next to you when you're through with your portion. This encourages your children to be comfortable praying aloud and encouraging others.

- **Share a brief lesson.** "Brief" is the key word here. Don't take this opportunity to read a religious dissertation. Read a story from the Bible and discuss it, or share an account from your childhood. The purpose is to incorporate a moral principle in the telling. Try to teach only one main point each family night. A memory verse or reflective statement is an excellent way to end the lesson and reinforce your point. If you feel uncomfortable coming up with your own material, use a kid-friendly devotional book as an aid. Allow every family member the opportunity to share a lesson before beginning with you again.

- **Act out, don't stress out!** This does not necessarily involve arts and crafts. Take turns choosing the activity. If it is Johnny's night to choose and he chooses Hide and Seek, then the whole family plays Hide and Seek. If it's Dad's night to choose and he selects, "Watch NCAA basketball," then everyone watches NCAA basketball. The key is to go with whatever activity is chosen and make the most of it.

- **Serve snacks.** This is the highlight of the evening! The Nemours Foundation at *www.kidshealth.com* offers a plethora of low or non-fat, kid-friendly recipes that will be sure to satisfy everyone's appetite. Try a variety of familiar favorites, like nachos, hot dogs, ice cream floats and homemade pizza. Take requests and try to ful fill as many as possible in the future. You can even designate a snack person for each family night, enabling every member to cook.

Once you begin hosting family night in your home, you'll never want to miss it!

* * * * *

Wonderful memories begin at home. If you have neglected your family in the past, choose today to make them a priority. Work will always be there, but your children will not. The activities you indulge in daily or weekly will strengthen familial bonds and increase the levels of unity, love and stability in your home. It's a win-win situation for everyone involved!

It's important that adults prioritize their lives to allow time for rest and give their families the love and attention they deserve.

Brainstorm other ways in which you and your family can have fun together. Be sure to apply the following rules: (1) Strive to choose an activity that everyone will enjoy; (2) Make definite plans and stick to them; and (3) Have fun!

Psalm 133:1

"Behold, how good and how pleasant it is for brethren to dwell together in unity!"

27

BUILT ON A ROCK
Ideas for Devotions, Prayers and Confessions

G od intended for the family to be a strong institution, able to withstand a great amount of pressure and overcome any obstacle. Whether you are married or single, He desires for your relationships with one another to be built on a solid, spiritual foundation. The Bible is your blueprint for a peaceful, loving home. It provides you with a set of instructions by which you ought to live.

Deuteronomy 6:4-9 says you are to continually place God's Word in your mind and heart, and then teach those principles to your children. This is an awesome responsibility! God is counting on you to impart His values and spiritual truths into them, ultimately strengthening their faith, trust and confidence in Him.

Make Learning Fun

Conversations about the Word of God can be conducted in a scheduled family devotional time. Once a week or *more* often if your schedule permits, set aside time for everyone to come together and learn about the Bible—either through storytelling or the reading and discussion of scriptures. There are many age-appropriate study materials and illustrations available to help you make this time enjoyable.

Never allow your devotional time to become so structured that it becomes lifeless and boring! No one likes to feel obligated to do something. Be creative and think of special settings (such as a park, your backyard or a road trip) and activities you can do to keep the entire family interested.

For instance, if your discussion is about Noah and the Ark, ask everyone to imagine how the Ark looked and to draw a picture of it. Ask them how it would feel to look out of the Ark and see nothing but water. Plan a trip to the zoo to reinforce the lesson. If you teach about the Last Supper, pour some grape juice into Dixie Cups and set out saltine crackers. Show how the crackers are like the unleavened bread mentioned in the Bible and explain to your children what the juice and cracker symbolize. Then offer a simple prayer of thanksgiving for Jesus' sacrifice and take communion together. You may wish to visit your local grocery store and experiment with making homemade Jewish *matzo* bread.

Another topic to tackle is fear. Since the attacks on the World Trade Center and Pentagon in September 2001, doubt, suspicion, fear and worry have plagued many people. Teach your children that these feelings can be overcome with Psalm 91. Since this chapter might be too long to keep everyone's attention, divide it up into sections. Talk about a different section each devotional time. Allow each family member to discuss his or her fears, and then discuss the ways in which you can combat them.

For every subject that is chosen, think of a corresponding biblical principle and object lesson. When you do this, your family will not only begin to look forward to these devotional times, they will mature spiritually as well. Use your imagination to make it a fun experience for all.

Speak Up!

Your mouth is a powerful instrument. In fact, the words you speak have the ability to build up or tear down. Proverbs 18:21 makes it clear that your words have power—the power of life and death. Think about that for a moment. How many times have you been hurt or encouraged by the words of others?

God intended for the family to be a strong institution, able to withstand a great amount of pressure and overcome any obstacle.

When you speak God's Word, you put into action His creative ability. Just as He spoke everything into existence (Genesis 1; Hebrews 11:3), He has given you the power to do the same. In other words, your tongue has the power to deliver you out of tough times or make them worse. It is a funnel for God's power to work through you to change your life. Keep this principle in mind: "If you're not saying anything, you're not creating anything."

I firmly believe in the statement, *"The family that prays together, stays together."* Daily prayer and confessions are the perfect way to begin each day. No one should leave home without doing so. By speaking scriptures aloud, you build your level of faith and confidence in God. Always make your confessions fervently and expect results! God will bring what you say to pass. Isaiah 55:10-11 gives us this assurance.

For as the rain and snow come down from the heavens, and return not there again, but water the earth and make it bring forth and sprout, that it may give seed to the sower and bread to the eater, So shall My word be that goes forth out of My mouth: it shall not return to Me void [without producing any effect, useless], but it shall accomplish that which I please and purpose, and it shall prosper in the thing for which I sent it (AMP).

Never allow your devotional time to become so structured that it becomes lifeless and boring!

Utilize the following confessions as a guideline. You may wish to find a quiet spot and say them aloud by yourself, or have each member of the family take turns. The key is consistency. Continue making these confessions daily, even if it appears as though nothing is happening. Just as a plant takes time to grow because its roots must first grow down into the ground, so you must become rooted in the promises of God until your faith, confidence and expectation causes your desire to manifest.

Confessions for Women

1. My born-again status places me in right-standing with God (Romans 3:22). As such, I have the right to petition Him boldly and receive answers to my prayers.

2. I am being perfected by God's Word (Psalm 138:8) and am thoroughly equipped for all good works (2 Timothy 3:17).

3. I operate in the anointing, which is the burden-removing, yoke-destroying power of God (Isaiah 10:27). I am empowered with wisdom to resolve challenges because He gives me witty ideas, concepts and inventions (Proverbs 8:12).

4. I declare that I am a virtuous woman of God. I am endowed with

moral excellence and strength (Proverbs 31:17).

5. I constantly renew my mind to the Word of God, taking on the mind of Christ. Apart from Him I can do nothing (Romans 12:2; John 15:5).

6. I take excellent care of my body because it is the temple of the Holy Spirit. I exercise, eat nutritious meals and get the proper amount of sleep. I strive to glorify God in my body and spirit. (1 Corinthians 6:19-20).

7. I represent God; therefore, I dress appropriately because I am a godly woman and I respect myself. I maintain a clean and attractive appearance (1 Timothy 2:9).

8. I manage my household and affairs with godly wisdom (1 Corinthians 2:16).

9. I possess the power to get wealth (Deuteronomy 8:18). I am a money magnet, and money comes to me.

10. In the name of Jesus, I speak to the mountains of insufficiency, sickness and debt in my life and command them to be removed now (Mark 11:23)!

11. My words have creative ability (Proverbs 18:21), and in the name of Jesus I have what I say. I release most holy faith to bring these things to pass in my life. God, Your Word says, *"Let the redeemed of the Lord say so…"* (Psalm 107:2). I have been redeemed through faith in the blood of Jesus. Therefore, I declare these things to be so now, and I receive them in Jesus' name. Amen.

Confessions for Men

1. I declare that I am a man of God, in right-standing with Him. I am faithful, loving, patient and meek (1 Timothy 6:11).

2. I am being perfected by God's Word and am thoroughly equipped for every good work (2 Timothy 3:17).

3. The Word of God directs my life. It is my final authority on every

matter (Psalm 119:105; Proverbs 3:6; Colossians 1:9; 3:16).

4. I allow the Holy Spirit to lead me toward the good life (Ephesians 2:10, AMP).

5. I declare that my mind is renewed by God's Word (Romans 12:2). I dwell on things that are noble, just, pure, lovely, of good report, virtuous and praiseworthy (Philippians 4:8).

6. I know God's perfect will for me, and I walk worthy of the calling on my life. I please Him and am fruitful in every good work (Colossians 1:9-10).

7. I have put off the old man and put on the new, which is renewed in the knowledge of Him Who created me (Colossians 3:10).

8. God's purpose for me includes prosperity in every area of life—spirit, soul, body and finances (Psalm 35:27; 1 Thessalonians 5:23; 3 John 2).

9. I possess the power to get wealth, and declare that today is my day to receive financial abundance (Deuteronomy 8:18).

10. I speak to the mountains of insufficiency, sickness and debt and command then to be removed from my life right now (Mark 11:23)!

11. My words have creative ability (Proverbs 18:21), and in the name of Jesus I have what I say. I release most holy faith to bring these things to pass in my life. God, Your Word says, *"Let the redeemed of the Lord say so…"* (Psalm 107:2). I have been redeemed by faith in the blood of Jesus. Therefore I declare these things to be so now, and I receive them in Jesus' name. Amen.

Confessions for Wives

1. My husband is the undisputed head of our household and he leads us in godliness and with temperance (Ephesians 5:23; 1 Peter 5:6).

2. I love, honor and respect him, and speak well of my husband to others. I also speak kindly to him for his edification

(Proverbs 31:26).

3. My husband is faithful and true to me. He has no need to go else where, because I provide everything he needs and desires (Proverbs 5:18-19).

4. I was created to be a suitable helpmate for my husband. Everything he needs is in me. He lacks no good thing (Proverbs 31:12).

5. My husband's life is redeemed from destruction and no weapon formed against him prospers (Isaiah 54:17).

6. He is a mighty man of valor and protects, provides and leads our family in the perfect will of God for our lives (Judges 6:12).

7. God perfects those things that concern him (Psalm 138:8).

8. My husband handles money wisely. He is careful to pay tithes and offerings and give firstfruits (Malachi 3:8-11; Romans 11:16). Because of this, the windows of heaven remain open over our lives.

9. Because my husband is obedient to the Word of God, he shall live long and prosper all the days of his life (Proverbs 3:1-2).

10. My husband provides abundantly for our family as a result of God providing abundantly for him (1 Timothy 5:8).

11. My words have creative ability (Proverbs 18:21), and in the name of Jesus I have what I say. I release most holy faith to bring these things to pass in my life. God, Your Word says, *"Let the redeemed of the Lord say so..."* (Psalm 107:2). I have been redeemed by faith in the blood of Jesus. Therefore I declare these things to be so now, and I receive them in Jesus' name. Amen.

Confessions for Husbands

1. I am the head of my home. I lead my family in godliness and with temperance (Ephesians 5:23; 1 Peter 1:5-6).

2. My entire household is saved and serves the Lord
   (Joshua 24:15; Acts 16:31).

3. I declare that our lives are redeemed from destruction, sickness,
   poverty, debt and early death (Isaiah 54:14, 17).

4. God provides for and prospers me; therefore, I am able to provide
   for my household (1Timothy 5:8).

5. I choose to love my wife as Christ loves the Church by placing her
   first in my life and taking her into consideration in all that I do. I
   avoid anger, bitterness and strife at all costs (Ephesians 5:25;
   Colossians 3:19).

6. God has joined us together and no one can separate or defeat us
   (Matthew 19:6; Mark 10:9).

7. I give my wife the honor, respect, goodwill and kindness that is due
   to her (1 Corinthians 7:3, AMP).

8. My wife is a virtuous woman; she is my crown. I trust and submit
   to her and she trusts and submits to me (Proverbs 12:4; 31:11;
   Ephesians 5:21).

9. Alone, I can put a thousand to flight; however, when my wife and
   I are in agreement, we can put 10,000 to flight (Deuteronomy 32:30).
   Therefore I make a decision to stand in agreement with her.

10. My words have creative ability (Proverbs 18:21), and in the name
    of Jesus I have what I say. I release most holy faith to bring these
    things to pass in my life. God, Your Word says, *"Let the redeemed
    of the Lord say so…"* (Psalm 107:2). I have been redeemed by faith
    in the blood of Jesus. Therefore I declare these things to be so
    now, and I receive them in Jesus' name. Amen.

Confessions for Parents

1. I have the efficiency, ability and might to raise my children in the
   ways of God (Acts 1:8, AMP).

2. I will teach and impress His Word on their minds and hearts (Deuteronomy 6:7, AMP).

3. As I increase in the knowledge of God, I will raise my children according to His will. They walk worthy of His calling on their lives. Their lives are pleasing to Him and fruitful in every good work (Colossians 1:9-10).

4. I will live a life before my children that brings honor to God.

5. The wisdom of God operates within me and it directs my path regarding my children (Proverbs 3:6; Colossians 1:9, 3:16).

6. The Lord perfects that which concerns me. Therefore, He is perfecting every concern I have for my children (Psalm 138:8).

7. I will not irritate or provoke my children to anger, but will train, discipline and counsel them tenderly in the Lord (Ephesians 6:4, AMP).

8. I commit my children to God's care and remain confident that He is able to finish the work He has begun in their lives (Philippians 1:6).

9. My children are saved and serve the Lord (Joshua 24:15; Acts 16:31). Their lives are redeemed from destruction, sickness, debt, poverty and death (Isaiah 54:14, 17).

10. I declare that they obey me in all things according to God's Word (Colossians 3:20). My children also obey all those who are in authority over them (Ephesians 6:1-3).

11. No corrupt communication proceeds out of the mouths of my children (Ephesians 4:29).

12. My children walk in the favor of God and man (Psalm 5:12).

13. My sons have the spirit of Joseph, and they are successful in all that they do (Genesis 39:2). I declare that my daughters are virtuous according to Proverbs 31.

14. I bind anything that would try to destroy my children (Matthew 18:18; John 10:10). I loose the angels of God to go forth now and protect them (Psalm 91).

15. My words have creative ability (Proverbs 18:21), and in the name of Jesus I have what I say. I release most holy faith to bring these things to pass in my life. God, Your Word says, *"Let the redeemed of the Lord say so..."* (Psalm 107:2). I have been redeemed by faith in the blood of Jesus. Therefore I declare these things to be so now, and I receive them in Jesus' name. Amen.

Confessions for Children and Teens

1. I love the Lord with all my heart, soul, mind and strength, and I love others as myself (Luke 10:27).

2. I believe, according to Jeremiah 31:3, that the Lord loves me with an everlasting love. As a result, He does not remember anything I have done wrong (1 John 1:9; Hebrews 10:17).

3. I obey my parents and all those in authority over me because it is the right thing to do (Ephesians 6:1-3).

4. Because I seek the Lord first concerning my studies, I understand my assignments, and do well in all subjects (Proverbs 18:21). I do as God's Word commands me and I study to show myself approved (2 Timothy 2:15).

5. I am wise because I surround myself with wise people (Proverbs 13:20).

6. My body was not made to participate in any kind of sexual activity outside of marriage; instead, it was made to glorify God (1 Corinthians 6:13-20). My body belongs to Him because He purchased it with the blood of Jesus. As a result of my faith in Jesus, the Holy Spirit came to live inside of me, and I am now one with God. I will not defile this temple by having sex before marriage.

7. I choose not to look at or think of anyone in a lustful way (Matthew

5:28). I exercise self-control (Galatians 5:22-23). I abstain from sexual sin and honor God with my body (1Thessalonians 4:3-4).

8. I choose my friends carefully; as a result, I am not led astray by the ways of the wicked (Proverbs 12:26).

9. I let no one think less of me because I am young. I have the boldness to stand up for what is right, and to be an example for my peers (1 Timothy 4:12, AMP).

10. I fear nothing because God is with me. The Word of God and the Holy Spirit comfort me (Psalm 23). Greater is He Who is in me than he who is in the world (1 John 4:4).

11. I do not allow any corrupt communication to come out of my mouth, but only that which is encouraging for others to hear (Ephesians 4:29).

12. My words have creative ability (Proverbs 18:21), and I believe that I have what I say. I release my faith to bring these things to pass in my life. In Jesus' name. Amen.

* * * * *

Your family's spiritual health is just as important as their physical, mental and emotional development and well-being. People were made to fellowship with God. By having an intimate relationship with Him, and imparting its value into the lives of your children, you lay a firm foundation for their future—a foundation of stability, courage, self-assurance, peace and the knowledge that they are unconditionally loved by their Creator.

If you have neglected the spiritual development of your family, begin today to study and apply the principles of God's Word in your lives. It won't take long before you see positive results!

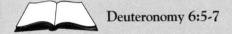

A family that remains rooted and grounded in the Word of God is empowered to withstand pressure and overcome any challenge.

Establish a time each day to read a Bible passage, pray and confess the Word of God over your family and individual lives. End each "session" with hugs and words of affirmation and love.

Deuteronomy 6:5-7

"And thou shalt love the Lord thy God with all thine heart, and with all thy soul, and with all thy might. And these words…shall be in thine heart: And thou shalt teach them diligently unto thy children, and shalt talk of them when thou sittest in thine house, and when thou walkest by the way, and when thou liest down, and when thou risest up."

Part V

Making a *Go* of It

28

GOD BLESS OUR BROKEN HOME

The Truth About Separation and Divorce

Imagine if there were absolutely no guidelines or criteria regarding marriage, separation and divorce. Instead of having to fill in the blank on the divorce decree with "irreconcilable differences," "adultery" or "abandonment," husbands could simply write "bad cook" and wives "continually late coming home from work." People would see marriage as a trial period and jump in and out of it at the slightest hint of discomfort or disagreement.

Unfortunately, many marriages break up because couples lack restraint and the willingness to change. When they encounter a problem or series of problems, their habit is to work it out only until their comfort level is threatened, and then throw in the towel rather than see things through. They do this because they lack determination, diligence and a solid understanding of commitment.

When you operate under healthy marital restraints, or guidelines, you don't think about separation or divorce. In fact, those words drop out of your vocabulary. Rather than give up when things get tough, you remember your vow to stand by your mate come hell or high water.

It's unrealistic to think that just because you and your spouse are Christians everything will be "hunky dory" in your marriage. That fantasy is found only in television sitcoms and movies. Any marriage will have differences of opinion and tense moments. At times there will be trouble. But you must decide right from the beginning that divorce is not an option. A good marriage doesn't just fall out of the sky and into your lap. As with anything else in life, it takes hard work to keep it alive and vibrant.

Sadly, too many couples don't understand this principle. As a result, one or both spouses unknowingly refuses to close their "exits." Somewhere in the back of their minds they still think there's a way out of the marriage if it doesn't seem to work out. For example, one will jokingly say to the other, "You'd better shape up or I'm going to trade you in for a newer model," or else they make idle threats in the heat of an argument, such as "That's it! I've had it! I want a divorce!"

Unfounded insecurities or unresolved anger over petty issues can crack, and even break, the strongest marital foundation if not dealt with immediately. Before you know it, you'll be filing for divorce over an accumulation of petty *nothings*. Don't fall into that trap. If your marriage is in trouble right now, don't even say the "d" word. Instead, try to be more sensitive to your mate.

Don't Be Insensitive!

A lack of sensitivity, or not being sensitive enough to the other person, is a prime cause of arguments. For example, one day I stayed home from work. Taffi, on the other hand, put in her eight hours at the office. While she was gone, I relaxed and enjoyed my time alone in the house. Although I knew the house could use some straightening up, I chose to let things be. When Taffi got home that evening, she noticed that the beds hadn't been made, the carpet wasn't vacuumed and dinner wasn't cooked. She took one look at the house and walked straight into the bedroom without saying a word. To make matters worse, I had the audacity to say, "Is something wrong?"

Taffi didn't say anything at first because she knew I was going out of town to preach that night. She wanted to keep it to herself and talk about it after I returned. Although I appreciated her thoughtfulness, I knew that my family had to come first. If my house isn't in order, I can't do anything for a congregation.

> *When couples encounter a problem or series of problems, their habit is to throw in the towel rather than work it out.*

I said, "Either we talk about what's wrong, or I'm not going to preach tonight. The congregation can preach to themselves. I'm staying right here."

Taffi said, "It's nothing major. I just came home after a long day and I saw that the beds weren't made and the house was a wreck. It just didn't seem like you took my feelings into account about my coming home to a situation like that."

Oh, I felt bad. The Holy Spirit reminded me of how Taffi always kept the house looking nice for me. I immediately repented and said, "God, forgive me for my insensitivity. Make me more sensitive to her needs."

I apologized to Taffi and straightaway began picking up around the house. I'd walk in front of her and ask, "Baby, what else needs to be done in here?" I didn't mind cleaning the house because she always cleans the house for *me*. I had been insensitive to her needs and feelings, and I was determined to make things right any way I could.

Insensitivity can occur anywhere at any time. For instance, you can be insensitive by speaking to your spouse in a condescending manner. It occurs when you belittle or make fun of your spouse in front of others or minimize their concerns. Most often, however, insensitivity happens in the bedroom, when one partner wants to make love and the other one doesn't. It does no good to assume that your spouse wants to have sex that night. Like I always say, assumption is the lowest form of knowledge. You must practice sensitivity toward your partner by communicating with him or her your desire to make love, and then listening to how they feel about it. It's vital that you learn to love your spouse with your *heart*, not just your body. Sensitivity is a heart issue.

> *A good marriage doesn't just fall out of the sky and into your lap. As with anything else in life, it takes hard work to keep it alive and vibrant.*

God's perfect will is for a man and woman to be joined for life. That's what I want— Plan A, not a contingency or secondary plan. There are no other options. I'm with Taffi for life. And if it's all right with Jesus, I'm going to spend eternity with her, too. I don't care what problem comes along or how crazy we act at times; I'm with her forever. We are stuck together.

That's the kind of determination you need to weather the tough times in your marriage. You need to work out your issues, as petty as they may seem. There is always room for compromise. Fight *for* your marriage, not *against* it! You *must* make the decision that divorce is not an option.

Although you may be willing to work things out and stick with your mate for life, he or she may not feel the same way. In addition, there may be other mitigating circumstances that are preventing your marriage from prospering as it should. Therefore, let's tale a closer look at what God has to say about separation and divorce.

There Are Exceptions

There has been great controversy in Christian circles when it comes to the topic of divorce. Erroneous teaching and the misinterpretation of scripture have kept many believers in bondage, hindering them from experiencing God's love and forgiveness to its fullest extent. Often divorcees stay away from church to avoid the stigma and discomfiture a broken relationship can bring.

Although the Bible makes it clear that God hates divorce (Malachi 2:16), there are some exceptions to the rule. First Corinthians 7:10-15 says:

> *And unto the married I command, yet not I, but the Lord, Let not the wife depart from her husband: But and if she depart, let her remain unmarried, or be reconciled to her husband: and let not the husband put away his wife. But to the rest speak I, not the Lord: if a brother hath a wife that believeth not, and she be pleased to dwell with him, let him not put her away. And the woman which hath an husband that believeth not, and if he be pleased to dwell with her, let her not leave him. For the unbelieving husband is sanctified by the wife, and the unbelieving wife is sanctified by the husband: else were your children unclean; but now are they holy. But if the unbelieving depart, let him depart. A brother or sister is not under bondage in such cases: but God hath called us to peace.*

In essence, this passage commands believers to remain with their spouses if at all possible. For example, you cannot get a divorce simply because your spouse snores at night. Neither can you divorce him or her if they want to stay in the marriage. However, verse 15 says, *"But if the unbelieving depart, let him depart. A brother or sister is not under bondage in such cases…."* In other words, if your spouse hardens his or her heart and leaves you, it's okay to let your spouse leave. You are no longer obligated to remain committed to that person.

Erroneous teaching and the misinterpretation of scripture have kept many believers in bondage, hindering them from experiencing God's love and forgiveness to its fullest extent.

Another exception is found in Matthew 19:8-9. In speaking to the Pharisees, Jesus said, *"…Moses because of the hardness of your hearts suffered you to put away your wives: but from the beginning it was not so. And I say unto you, Whosoever shall put away his wife, except it be for fornication…."* Fornication, in this scripture, actually means adultery. Therefore, if your spouse commits adultery, you have a right to divorce him or her—if you choose to do so. There is nothing wrong with trying to work through this issue; in fact, I know several couples who have been able to reconcile even *after* catching their spouse in a compromising position. But it's up to you to decide whether or not you want to go that route.

The third exception is abuse. John 10:10 says, *"The thief cometh not, but for to steal, and to kill, and to destroy: I am come that they might have life, and that they might have it more abundantly."* Getting beaten is not part of the abundant life

God desires for you to experience. Neither is verbal or sexual abuse or even marital rape. Don't let anyone tell you, "You've just got to take it and believe God for their salvation," or "That's just the way they are. Stick with it for better or for worse." If you or your children are being physically, sexually or verbally abused in any way, then you have a right to separate. God does not sanction abuse and He would *never* expect you to live under that kind of treatment.

I had to preach a funeral several years ago because a woman stayed with her abusive husband and was murdered by him. She left behind three little kids. Don't talk to me about your religious thinking concerning divorce until you've sat through a funeral like that.

No one has all the answers. Only God does. He is the only One Who can tell you if you're in a situation that's bad enough to merit a divorce. Follow the Holy Spirit's leading. He will give you the right answer for your marriage. One word of caution, however: make sure you have done all that could be done to save your marriage before opting for a divorce. I personally would never feel right about it unless I had done all that I knew to do. You'll avoid having to deal with regret, doubt and the "what ifs" simply by working your hardest and doing your best to improve the situation.

If you or your children are being physically, sexually or verbally abused in any way, then you have a right to separate.

If you have been divorced and are now remarried, keep in mind that there is no need to feel guilty about the choice you have made. It's amazing how many people live with feelings of guilt and condemnation because someone said that what they did was biblically wrong. Romans 8:1 says, *"There is therefore now no condemnation to them that are in Christ Jesus, who walk not after the flesh, but after the spirit."* Learn from your mistakes and own up to them. If you've repented, God will forgive. He isn't mad at you! He loves you more than you can comprehend and is eager to bless your new life and marriage. Just let go and press on!

Counseling, Anyone?

Often couples heading toward divorce will use counseling as a last-ditch effort to save their marriage. They face-off in the counselor's office and pour out their feelings of resentment, anger, bitterness, unforgiveness, hurt and sadness. Although in some cases this tactic may work to improve the situation, most couples end up separating anyway.

Rather than taking a defensive stance in regard to counseling, try taking an *offensive* one. If professional counseling is what you prefer, understand that it is not a quick-fix for your marital problems—in fact, things may get more troublesome as you openly discuss these issues. However, retain your resolve to overcome these challenges. Your counselor will act as a facilitator, assisting you and your spouse in discussions with one another.

In addition, you may wish to consider scouring your local library or the self-help section of a bookstore for resources to help you enhance your communication and conflict-resolution skills. Keep in mind that it's always a good idea to honestly evaluate your marriage periodically to clear up any underlying or unresolved issues. Ask each other: "How are we doing?" "How is our communication with one another?" "What areas need improvement?" "How am I at meeting your needs?" "Have I been insensitive recently?" Then apply one another's responses to your relationship.

Here are two tactics you can try at home:

- *Mirroring:* One partner speaks while the other listens attentively. When the speaker has finished, his or her partner (the receiver) repeats exactly what was said, and then asks, "Did I get everything you said?" If not, the exercise is repeated. This forces the receiver to listen to the speaker rather than trying to think of a response and missing what is being said. Once the receiver has successfully repeated the speaker, the roles are reversed.

- *Use a script:* If one or both partners finds it difficult to speak his or her mind clearly, it is a good idea to write it down on paper and then recite it aloud to their spouse. This script enables the individual to focus their attention on the issue and clearly relay what is on their mind.

If you are considering separation and divorce for reasons of physical, verbal or sexual abuse, contact your local women's shelter for free counseling and other emergency services. Don't remain in a dangerous situation, hoping things will get better. Instead, find a safe place to stay and use your time there to think things through, seek professional guidance and make a final decision. Remember, your life is precious!

Pick Up the Pieces

Many people who have experienced the trauma of a divorce or separation have also suffered feelings of sorrow, self-hatred and rejection. That's common. Separation and divorce are heart-rending situations that open the door to a variety of emotions. When the marriage ends, emotional ties are severed, leaving you feeling torn apart and empty.

This happens because those whom God has joined together cannot be easily separated; the agreement between the husband and wife is torn in two, ushering in hurt and pain. But God doesn't want you to be bound by those feelings for life. Although you may need to mourn the death of the relationship and its corresponding goals, dreams and emotional ties, you don't need to grieve forever. God can make you whole again, but you must trust Him and allow Him to restore you. Psalm 147:3 says, *"He healeth the broken in heart, and bindeth up their wounds."* Healing is a part of the abundant life God desires for you to experience. He wants you to be whole in heart so you can love another. All you have to do is ask for His help.

Children of Divorce

Adults are not the only people to feel pain when their marriage dies. On the contrary, the disintegration of a marriage reaches far, to include in-laws, extended relatives, friends, and most importantly, the children from that union. When one or both spouses agree to call it quits, that decision generates feelings of shock, abandonment, rejection and betrayal in their offspring, no matter what age they may be.

If you have been divorced and are now remarried, keep in mind that there is no need to feel guilty about the choice you have made.

Children are the innocent victims of divorce. If it is not made clear to them, they will often put the blame on themselves. They wear guilt, anger, hostility and fear like badges. They wonder, "If we'd been better kids, would our parents have split up?" It's an emotionally destructive line of thinking. If those children are not reassured that the divorce has nothing to do with them and shown love during the time of separation, they'll carry that emotional baggage into their future relationships.

You can nip this in the bud by reassuring your children that you love them unconditionally. Offer lots of hugs and tell them that the divorce wasn't their fault. Talk openly and truthfully about the divorce and answer any questions they may have. Don't ever speak negatively concerning your "ex" in front of or to your children. Most importantly, do not use them as weapons against your spouse. They are not leverage. Instead, encourage them to love the other parent and their spouse, when and if they remarry. This will enable the children to adapt quickly to change.

Allow God to help you and the children walk out your new lives together. Yes, life may seem strange and awkward for a while, but whatever you do, *never* look at God as the problem. He wasn't the cause of your divorce, and He didn't let you down; on the contrary, He was right by your side every step of the way!

* * * * *

God desires for you to have the best marriage possible; however, He knows that can only occur with both spouses working together toward a common goal. When one or both individuals are insensitive, unfaithful or unwilling to change or compromise, divorce is inevitable. However, there is good news. Although you and your spouse may miss the mark and separate, God is still with you (Isaiah 54:4-5), willing to help you through the situation.

Before deciding to call it quits, try applying the Word of God to your situation. In addition, review the exceptions for divorce and seek God for His wisdom and direction. Regardless of whether you choose to reconcile or separate, trust Him to meet your every need. You have a beautiful journey ahead of you, and *today* is the best day to begin it.

God does not sanction separation and divorce; however, there are biblical exceptions for both.

If you are considering divorce, take a moment to think about what God's Word has to say about it. Review the exceptions for divorce and seek God for guidance. If possible, share your findings with your spouse. If this is not possible, seek outside godly counsel from a trusted source. Make a final decision only after you are absolutely certain of the best course of action. If you are already divorced, maintain a lifestyle that is pleasing to God and rebuild your life using the principles outlined in His Word. If you have children, reassure them of your love and support. Know that the Holy Spirit is present to meet your every need, and be at peace in your heart.

Psalm 147:3

"He healeth the broken in heart and bindeth up their wounds."

29

HIS, HERS AND OURS

Remarriage and Blended Families

Today, thousands of children in the United States experience the trauma of their parents' divorce and the difficulty of adjusting to a stepfamily before the age of 18. The so-called "blended family" is no longer a wart on the face of the American society; rather, it's the norm.

Psychologists tell us that children in stepfamilies face a higher risk of emotional and behavioral problems and are less able to withstand stressful situations. While those may be the facts, they are not the truth. Facts are subject to change; the truth, however, is not. The truth comes from the Word of God. Psalm 112:2 says: "*His (Our) seed shall be mighty upon the earth: the generation of the upright shall be blessed.*" The term *blessed* means "empowered to prosper and excel." God empowers children to overcome adverse circumstances and adapt to new situations.

The good news is that this promise isn't reserved solely for families resembling the Cleavers in *Leave It to Beaver*; it is also for those who more closely resemble *The Brady Bunch*. Of course blended families come with their own set of challenges, but God is bigger than any problem. There is nothing too hard for Him to resolve.

Now What?

You've found love the second time around and pledged your life in marriage to a wonderful person who also has his or her own children. Now that the honeymoon is over, you wonder, *How in the world can this new family blend successfully?* Many people refuse to adopt the "his, hers and ours" mentality because it leaves room for arguments, debates and feelings of rejection or resentment. Instead, you, and others like you, would prefer the "ours" and "us" line of thinking. The next logical question is, "How do you get there?"

Here are some practical things you can do to help with the transition.

1. Your place or mine?

Moving into a new home is usually the best choice rather than moving into your or your spouse's prior residence. The new environment won't be labeled, "yours" or "mine," and it will be a completely different backdrop for building new memories. If possible, find a home that enables each child to have his or her own bedroom—especially if the children had their own rooms before the blending of your families.

2. Build your own family traditions.

The sooner you can implement some family traditions, the better. For instance, you may want to go out to breakfast every Saturday morning as a family, or establish "a family game night" each week. In addition, you may want to pool your resources and ask your new family members about the kinds of traditions they have celebrated in the past and which ones they would like to keep celebrating in the future. Implementing new and continuing old traditions will help to unify the family and build relationships in non-threatening ways.

3. Establish parenting roles.

Before marriage, you and your future spouse should have discussed disciplinary methods, house rules, expectations and specific parenting responsibilities. For instance, if you don't want your new spouse spanking your children, you had better speak up before the situation arises. If you and your spouse practice different parenting methods, sit down together and come up with a parenting plan.

Teamwork is absolutely essential. Children can sense dissention in the ranks and will do their best to "divide and conquer." Don't undermine one another's parenting skills in front of the children. If you're going to disagree, do it privately.

4. Settle the money issue.

Make sure you discuss financial management *before* you remarry. It's wise to establish a record-keeping system, spending boundaries and bill-paying strategies beforehand so there won't be any surprises after the ceremony. Follow the budgeting guidelines outlined in chapter 13. Don't allow a "This is my money, and I'll buy that if I want to" attitude to poison your family. Discuss all expenditures, and be considerate if someone makes an error. In addition, you may want to consider teaching your children jointly about financial matters to help them develop and enhance their problem-solving and communication skills.

5. Spend some time alone.

Although you're newlyweds, it may not feel like it if you have children around all the time. You may have to be creative and extremely organized to find time alone with your new spouse. No matter how difficult it may be to steal some private moments, find a way. You and your spouse need some "couple time." Schedule a date *at least* once a month. Place a lock on your bedroom door and don't be afraid to use it. Sneak in kisses and hugs at every opportunity.

Vive la Difference!

In this day and age it's not uncommon to see biracial or multi-ethnic families. Many people refuse to be limited by the color of another individual's skin or their cultural background. This is pleasing to God, who created mankind in His image (Genesis 1:27). However, rebellion against traditional ethnic practices or the reality of racism can place a strain on these marriages.

Instead of isolating yourself from family, friends or even society, present a unified front and face any challenges that may arise together, as one. Here are a few tips to help ease the pressure and strengthen the decision you have made.

• **Focus on the strong points.** Before introducing your future spouse to your friends and family members, warm them up by vocalizing his or her strengths. You may say something like, "Charles is a very good cook," or "Jessica is great with languages." Don't embellish; just emphasize the positive. You may also want to give your fiancé a "heads up" regarding any specific customs your family may follow, such

---

as removing the shoes before entering the house, compli-menting the cook after the meal or refraining from speaking on certain topics.

• **Celebrate your differences.** Try incorporating different ethnic elements into your wedding ceremony and household. For example, if your spouse is African American, you may wish to "jump the broom" at the end of the ceremony or "step on the glass," as is the Jewish custom. Try utilizing colors and patterns with specific meaning, such as red, white or plaid. Incorporate a variety of musical genres and dances. Once you are settled in your home, use art or decorative items to emphasize both of your cultural backgrounds.

• **Deck the halls.** Discuss with your spouse any typical eth-nic traditions he or she practiced while growing up and incor-porate them into your holiday celebrations. Go to your local library and research articles and books on whatever applies to your household, such as Kwanzaa, Hannukah, Epiphany, St. Nicholas Day, St. Lucia's Day or Los Posadas. Try your hand at a specific dish, decoration, song or activity, and share what you learn with your spouse and children.

Don't be discouraged if your family doesn't warm up to your new traditions right away. With time, diligence and prayer, they will adjust to the new situation and have fun celebrating you and your spouse's dif-ferences with you!]

Prayer must be the backbone of your marriage and your new family.

Be Prepared for Reality

Some blended families encounter addi-tional challenges that include custody issues, parental visitation, money problems and extended family battles. If your previous mar-riage or your spouse's previous marriage ended in an ugly divorce, chances are you're in the middle of legal battles with the "ex." In addition, legal expenses, alimony or child support payments may place an added strain on your finances, and emotions may be running high if you or your spouse lost custody of the children. Take each problem to the Lord and pray for wisdom. Prayer must be the backbone of your marriage and your new family—now more than ever. Be sure to communicate your frustrations with your new spouse. Allow him or her to be a sounding board for you, and listen to any words of encouragement or counsel they may give.

If you're in a situation where your spouse's children come to visit once a month or two weeks in the summer or every other holiday, try to make those times special and productive by building trust and understanding with each visit. Make sure that your spouse's children understand the house rules when visiting, and be ready to enforce them. If you don't, your children will resent your leniency with "the other kids," and you will cause strife and stress in the household.

There are no miracle answers for making these visits pleasurable, especially if your spouse's "ex" has poisoned the children's minds with negative talk about you and your new family. You, however, have the responsibility to show unconditional love. Take it slow and ask the Holy Spirit to help you gain their trust. Make the most of every opportunity to speak the Word into their lives, as you may be the only "Jesus" these children will ever see.

When your previous marriage ended, more people than just your immediate family were affected. The grandparents also took a hit. Your ex's parents may feel left out and disconnected from your children, so try to accommodate their visits. Make arrangements for regular "grandparent outings," and let your ex-in-laws know that you still want them in your children's lives.

No one said blending families would be easy, but God promises to be with you every step of the way. To keep Christ at the center of your marriage and your new family, it's important to have fun and implement regular family Bible studies. Set aside time each day for individual devotions and prayer, and make weekly church attendance mandatory. If you need help with activities and devotions, refer to chapters 26 and 27, where you'll find many creative ideas. Let everyone in the immediate and extended family know that as for your household, everyone will serve the Lord (Joshua 24:15).

Leave Your Baggage at the Door

Adults aren't the only ones who bring emotional baggage into a new household. Many times children carry some pretty large suitcases of their own.

For example, if your ex-spouse left your family for another person, your children may feel rejected, hurt, vulnerable and fearful. If you don't address those feelings, talk them out, pray over them and reassure your children of your love, they may resent your new spouse and fear rejection from that person, too.

Getting to Know You

Here are five activities that are guaranteed to produce fun-filled times as you blend your families together.

- **Have a picnic.** Let your kids help you make the sandwiches and prepare the picnic basket. Then enjoy your food at a park, in your backyard or under a tent made of sheets in your front room.

- **Take a hike.** Kids love the outdoors, so why not grab your hiking boots and hit the trails? You can get a good workout while appreciating the beauty of God's creation.

- **Play a game.** Take a trip to the local toy store and buy a new board game. Grab a pizza on the way home and make a night of it! Pizza and Monopoly, what's not to love?

- **Go bowling.** Even if you throw a gutter ball every time, you'll have a blast! Most kids love bowling, and you'll have fun cheering for one another and wearing ugly bowling shoes.

- **Try a video game.** Go to a local arcade, armed with lots of quarters. Let your children show you how to play the new hi-tech games, and teach them to play classics like *Pac Man* and *Space Invaders*. You'll be surprised how fun a little friendly competition can be!

Give your children scriptures to stand on that address every emotion they are experiencing. If they are fearful, tell them "God didn't give us a spirit of fear but of power, love and a sound mind" (2 Timothy 1:7). Confess that scripture over them each day. Say it together as you drive them to school each morning or pick them up from their extracurricular activities. Get that Word on the inside of them.

If they are brokenhearted, let them know that He heals the brokenhearted and binds up their wounds (Psalm 147:3; Luke 4:18). It's good to be honest and vulnerable with your children. Let them know that the divorce hurt you, too. Let them see you cry. Tell them that you are going to say that scripture with them every day until it becomes a reality in all of your lives.

I know it's difficult to see your children hurting. Remember, God loves them even more than you do. You can trust Him to care for them. If you haven't already done so, entrust the welfare of your children to God. He knows what they need and what they've been through.

Of course there will be some specific issues that are bound to come up as you blend your two households, and the better prepared you are going into the marriage, the better your children will adjust. Following are three areas you'll need to combat early on.

1. The idea that "It's all my fault."

When divorce happens, it's quite common for children to blame themselves for the downfall of their family. They think it's their fault that Mom and Dad split up. They may never tell you how they're feeling, but be aware that feelings of guilt may be present. Let your children know that they didn't cause the divorce. Reassure them that just because you and your ex-spouse are no longer together, you will never leave them or stop loving them.

2. Sibling rivalry.

When each spouse brings children from a previous marriage into a new household, there may be some "jockeying for position" within the new family structure. It becomes a juggling act to keep everyone happy.

While giving your own children extra attention to reassure them of your unconditional love, you must be careful not to show favoritism since your "new children" are wondering if you will love them, too. Don't be alarmed when the, "You love your kids more than us," remarks are hurled in anger. Approach this issue like you would anything else—with prayer, love and tenderness. Try and spend a little "alone time" with each child every day, and encourage your spouse to do the same. This is very important early in the marriage.

3. "You're not the boss of me!"

It's not uncommon for children to resent the "new parent." However, do your best to see the situation from their perspective. To them, you may seem like the enemy. They may still have false hopes that their "real parents" will get back together. Depending on their age and maturity level, your spouse's children may reject and rebel against you. Be ready for this. Don't take offense. Offer unconditional love, but don't allow them to run over you or disrupt the entire household.
Discipline in love, and know your boundaries. If they already have a wonderful mother, don't try to replace her. If they have a wonderful dad, let them know that you aren't trying to take his place. Continue offering love, even if it's not returned. Don't get angry or lash out, even if you feel justified. Let Christ shine through you, and determine to be the peacemaker in the family. God will help you. Remember, no matter how awful it seems at times, nothing is too big for God!

*   *   *   *   *

It's difficult enough blending two people who have never before been married; however, it seems downright overwhelming to do so when you've been around the block before and have children to boot! Blending families successfully requires diligence, sacrifice and compromise, but the end result is worth it. Make the determination to do whatever it takes to make things work in your new family. Before you know it, the dust will have settled and you'll discover that you're part of something wonderful!

Blended families are common in today's society; but it takes more than wishful thinking to make them successful. With diligence, determination, creativity and prayer, you can resolve differences and establish and strengthen family ties.

Try one or more of the activities listed in this chapter. In addition, be sure to pray over your new family several times daily and do your best to approach every challenging situation in God's strength instead of your own.

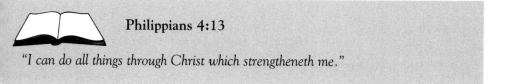

Philippians 4:13

"I can do all things through Christ which strengtheneth me."

30

TABLE FOR ONE

Coping With the Death of a Spouse

M illions of people every year lose a spouse every year due to a terminal illness or accident. Even when death is expected, it's still a devastating experience for those left behind. Nothing can prepare you for the loss of someone dear to you.

Death brings sadness, and there should be a time for grieving. The loss of your spouse will leave a void in your heart and life. You may be unable to perform routine tasks or find the energy or the will to get out of bed in the morning. Legalities, financial matters and other issues seem unimportant at the moment. In addition, your emotions may be going haywire, ranging from depression, loneliness and anger to despair and shock. Although what you are feeling is natural, you cannot allow your life to end with the passing of your loved one.

If the person who died was born again, you have reason to rejoice because he or she is in heaven. That's why the funeral service for a born-again believer is often referred to as a "home-going." Luke 10:20 says to, "...*rejoice because your names are written in heaven.*" And in 1 Thessalonians 4:13-14, the Apostle Paul says, "...*I would not have you ignorant, brethren, about those who fall asleep [in death] that you may not grieve [for them] as the rest do who have no hope [beyond the grave]. For since we believe that Jesus died and rose again, even so God will bring with Him through Jesus those who have fallen asleep [in death]* (AMP). Born-again Christians have reservations there. You pass through this earth with heaven as the ultimate goal!

However, if the person who died did not acknowledge Jesus as his or her personal Savior, you must realize there is nothing you can do for them now. They made a decision, and God will honor it, regardless of the fact that they chose poorly. The best thing you can do is to make sure that *you* are born again. If you don't know Jesus as your personal Savior, you can take care of that right now. Turn to Appendix A in the back of this book, read what it says, and pray the prayer of salvation. Then return to this chapter.

Death Has Lost Its Sting

For Christians, death isn't the end; it's only the beginning. That's why you shouldn't mourn like an unbeliever. You have a great hope, and Jesus Christ is the realization of that hope! (Colossians 1:5, 27; 1 Corinthians 15:57). First Corinthians 15:54-55 tells us that the grave no longer has the victory over us; on the contrary, Jesus defeated death's sting with His resurrection!

It is normal and healthy to grieve for a season, but don't allow death's sting to keep you in a continual state of mourning. There are people who never recover from the cycle of grief. Their walls are covered with pictures of their deceased loved one, and they keep adding to the collection. Year after year they continue to grieve and are never fully able to get on with their lives. Some even feel that their loved one is "watching over them" or visits them to tell them things. If this happens, a spirit of grief has attached itself to the mourner, and they need prayer and deliverance.

The Stages of Grief

At some point in your life, you will face the loss of someone or something precious to you. Although the grief you feel may seem unbearable, understand that it is actually a process of healing that occurs over time.

Stage 1: *Denial and isolation.* At first you may be in a state of shock and try to deny what has happened or withdraw from others.

Stage 2: *Anger.* You may be furious at the deceased for leaving you or blame God for letting it happen. In addition, your feelings of anger could be self-directed. You may be angry at yourself for letting the incident happen, although there was nothing you could have done to prevent it.

Stage 3: *Bargaining.* You begin to bargain with God, saying things like, "If I do this orthat, will you bring [him or her] back?"

> **Stage 4: *Depression.*** You may feel numb, lonely, sad, anxious, guilty (for being alive) and unmotivated. It's difficult to perform ordinary tasks or find pleasure in activities you used to enjoy. You may continue to isolate yourself from others.
>
> **Step 5: *Acceptance.*** This stage occurs when your feelings of anger and sadness have tapered off. You understand and accept the reality of your loss and begin to move forward by resuming your interest in life.
>
> Sometimes people "get stuck" in one of the first four stages; however, with time, they are able to progress to the last stage and move on with their lives. Denying, minimizing or suppressing a person's right to grieve only causes more stress to their mind and body, and prolongs the healing process.
>
> The best thing to do during this time is to take good care of yourself (or the person who is grieving) by eating nutritious meals, exercising, drinking plenty of fluids and getting enough rest. A close circle of family and friends can also assist in overcoming feelings of loss.

For some people, tradition binds them to wear black and mourn for a year. In fact, they'll wear black every day. They wear black like a badge that declares how sad they are. Sorrow can effectively paralyze you from moving beyond your loss, taking two lives instead of one. There are a few things you can do, however, to help yourself get through this time.

1. Don't bottle up your feelings.
2. Don't avoid other people.
3. Establish a daily routine to keep yourself going.
4. Take a college course, art class, piano lessons or volunteer at your church or local charity.
5. Find someone who understands what you're going through to be your sounding board from time to time.
6. Begin an exercise program. Exercise produces endorphins, which counteract depression.
7. Determine the things your mate handled that you must now take care of, such as paying bills or driving. Ask for help in those areas

if you're unsure of how to proceed.

8. Worship the Lord even if you don't feel like it. The joy of the Lord is your strength (Nehemiah 8:10).
9. Join a Bible study group or a group of like-minded people.
10. When you start to feel down, encourage someone else with a card, flowers or freshly baked cookies.

Practically Speaking...

In the midst of your grief and shock, you may feel overwhelmed by funeral expenses—especially if the death was sudden. In some cases, your loved one may have purchased funeral insurance and made decisions concerning his or her funeral long before their departure. Regardless of whether they were prepared to die or not, there are still some decisions you will have to make. If you're in this situation, don't be alarmed. Ask God for wisdom, and He will give it to you (James 1:5).

The average funeral costs approximately $6,000 to $10,000. Incorporate fees for flowers, obituary notices, burial liners or vaults and special transportation, and you've easily added another $1,000 to the bill.

An in-ground burial costs more than a mausoleum-crypt space. Caskets are by far the most expensive item in a funeral. They range anywhere from $2,000 to $15,000, depending on their composition. Don't be talked into buying the most expensive style. If you have insurance with the funeral home, the cost of the casket and other preferred details have already been selected and paid for; however, the preparation for the burial site is not covered in funeral policies. You will have to pay for that.

The loss of your spouse, although tragic and painful, is not the end of the world.

Funeral homes are required by law to provide you with a price list that will help you understand your options and the expenses of each plan. Every funeral home should have separate price lists for general services, caskets, cremation and other burial containers. Some of the options you'll want to review are transportation of the body to the funeral home and burial site, embalming and dressing of the body, music at the service, the use of the facilities for the viewing, wake or visitation, and so on.

Larger cities often require police escorts to the burial site, which is an extra expense. Headstones are an additional expense as well. If your mate was a U.S. Veteran, the local Veteran's Association will place a granite foot-marker at the grave if a headstone has not already been placed there. The Veteran's Association will also provide you with an American flag and a bugler to play "Taps." Another option you may wish to consider is burial in Arlington National Cemetery in Washington, D.C. For more information, visit www.dchomepage.net or call (703) 607-8052.

Only by reviewing all the options can you accurately determine the total cost. Don't be afraid to ask questions. If you aren't able to go to the funeral home to make the arrangements, ask the funeral director to mail you the price lists. If the funeral director refuses to mail the lists, ask for the prices to be quoted to you over the phone. Funeral homes are required to do so by law.

Remember, the amount of money you spend on a funeral and burial has *nothing* to do with your feelings for the deceased. Don't let your emotions cause you to make bad financial decisions. It's a good idea to take someone with you who might be less emotional.

Photo Memories

Many funeral directors request photographs of your loved one to be displayed during the viewing. If they don't, you may consider putting together a photo collage yourself. This allows family and friends to recall fond memories of the deceased's life. The collage doesn't have to be fancy—any snapshot from vacations, holidays or birthdays neatly pinned to a small bulletin board will work

---

Ask for Help

After the funeral is over and all of the well-wishers have gone home, the reality of the event settles in. You're probably wondering, "What do I do now?" That's a normal reaction. The answer to that question begins with turning to God. Let Him love on you a while. Read and reflect on Isaiah 54:4-5, Psalm 10:14, Psalm 68:5 and 146:9. Allow God to bring you through the healing process. He promises to never leave you nor forsake you (Hebrews 13:5). That means you don't have to feel Him or see Him to know He is there.

In addition, there are people and organizations that understand what you are feeling and the adjustments you have to make. The American Association of Retired People (AARP) has a program called "Grief and Loss" that offers a wide variety of free resources and information to help adults of all ages deal with loss and death. Call 1-800-424-3410 to see if that program is offered in your area. You may also wish to consider using the grief counseling program or support in area hospices or churches. Get information about these classes, or ask a friend to do it for you. Then be sure to attend one or more of these sessions.

The worst thing you can do at this time is hide your grief or suffer in silence. You'll find that friends and family want to help but may not know what to do. Tell them what you need. Don't be ashamed or embarrassed. Above all, don't isolate and withdraw yourself from others. Reach out and allow people to help you figure out your budget, pay the bills or drive to the market.

> *The worst thing you can do is hide your grief or suffer in silence.*

You may also need help getting your affairs in order. For instance, you will need to contact your spouse's employment (if your spouse was working at the time of death) to apply for a continuation of benefits. If you are widowed, you may be able to receive Social Security Survivor benefits, based on your spouse's earnings, as early as age 60. Check with your local Social Security office to find out the specifics of your situation.

Then there's the matter of the estate, the pile of legal documents and the remaining medical bills sitting on your desk. Again, ask for help. Don't be too proud to admit you're a little out of practice when it comes to the finances of the home. If your spouse always took care of those matters, it's understandable. No one will think less of you for seeking advice and assistance.

Moving On

Often the death of a spouse makes it difficult to keep things running smoothly—especially if you have children. If this is the case with you, be honest with your children about what has happened to your mate. Answer their questions about death honestly and reassure them of your love. Assuage any fears they may have by telling them that God will look after everyone. Be perceptive! Children often develop a fear of abandonment—they think that if one parent left, the other will do the same. Do your best to reassure them that you aren't going any-where, and be sure to spend quality time with them daily.

By far, this is one of the most stressful times you and your family will ever experience, but there are a few things you can do to help yourself through it.

1. Avoid making any big decisions until you're emotionally ready.
2. Prioritize your life.
3. Eat nutritious meals even if you don't feel like it.
4. Get up. Practice doing a few stretches every morning.
5. Read at least one chapter or more from the Word of God before facing the day.
6. Relax. Consider taking a trip or two, if your finances allow.
7. Keep in touch with family and friends.
8. Listen to praise and worship music.
9. Adopt a pet if your living situation allows it. They make great companions.
10. Don't try to solve every problem all at once. Take baby steps instead.
11. Try to get out of the house at least once every day. Don't become a hermit.
12. Keep a journal and record memories, feelings and encouraging scriptures.
13. Don't feel guilty for enjoying life. Your loved one wouldn't want you to be sad forever.
14. Set small goals and reward yourself each time you achieve one.

There are other steps you can take, in addition to the ones listed above, that will help you to move on. First, let yourself cry. This may be especially hard for a man. Follow Jesus' example; He wept (John 11:35). Allow your emotions to follow their natural course. It's unhealthy to keep your feelings bottled up. Second, plant a tree or flower garden, or write a poem or song in memory of your loved one. Help others in need. Sometimes taking action will help you to heal.

Third, and most important, trust God. Find comfort in His Word. In fact, it's a good idea to memorize a passage of scripture every week. When you're feeling lonely or sad, the Word will rise up inside of you and you'll be able to say, "Jesus will never leave me or for-sake me. He is always with me. He is my help in time of need, a Friend who is closer than a brother. He is leading me down the path toward a good life. He is perfecting everything that concerns me. Because of that, I can do all things

> *Don't feel guilty for enjoying your life. Your spouse wouldn't want you to be sad forever.*

through Christ Jesus who gives me strength" (Matthew 28:20, John 14:18, 27; Proverbs 18:24; Ephesians 2:10 AMP; Psalm 138:8; Philippians 4:13)!

* * * * *

It is normal and healthy to grieve for a season, but don't allow the death of a loved one to keep you in a continual state of mourning.

The loss of your spouse, although tragic and painful, is not the end of the world. Allow yourself to mourn their loss, but be sure to put it in perspective. Remember, Jesus is there for you whenever you call, ready and willing to help you and your family through this time. Before you know it, the hurt will have disappeared, and you'll be left whole—spirit, soul and body (John 14:27).

Although the loss of a loved one may seem unbearable, grief is actually a process of healing that occurs over time.

Allow the grieving process to follow its course, but don't remain stuck in that cycle. Use the suggestions listed in this chapter to assist you in coping with your loss. Don't be afraid to ask for help. Most importantly, find comfort and peace in God and the unconditional support of others.

Psalm 30:5

"…*weeping may endure for a night, but joy cometh in the morning.*"

31

EXPANDING YOUR TENT
Caring for Extended Family Members

Caring for an elderly relative has now become a commonplace practice for most families. The reasons for taking on this responsibility vary. Often it is easier to care for an ailing or elderly parent or relative at home than to pay the cost of a hospice, retirement home or assisted living facility. Cultural traditions may also play a role in caring for an extended family member.

Maybe you're in this situation or heading down that path, wondering how you're going to care for your growing children *and* aging relative at the same time. You may be secretly asking yourself, "Why should I bring these added frustrations and increased demands into my life?"

There is no simple answer to that question; however, the Bible does have something to say about this topic. 1 Timothy 5:8 says, *"But if any provide not for his own, and specially for those of his own house, he hath denied the faith, and is worse than an infidel."* And James 1:27 (AMP) says, *"External religious worship [religion as it is expressed in outward acts] that is pure and unblemished in the sight of God the Father is this: to visit and help and care for the orphans and widows in their affliction and need, and to keep oneself unspotted and uncontaminated from the world."*

You are God's arms and legs in this world. It is through *you* that others learn about and experience His love and caring. The Bible makes it clear that you should care for orphans, widows and family members in need. It doesn't say that you *only* have to look after them if it fits into your schedule or if you have the resources to do so.

The Book of Ruth illustrates a wonderful example of one relative caring for another. After Ruth's husband and father-in-law had died, her mother-in-law, Naomi, encouraged her to return to her family. Ruth, however, refused to leave.

Ruth 1:16-17, NKJV

Entreat me not to leave you, Or to turn back from following after you; For wherever you go, I will go; And wherever you lodge, I will lodge; Your people shall be my people, And your God, my God. Where you die, I will die, And there will I be buried. The Lord do so to me, and more also, If anything but death parts you and me.

After the two women returned to Naomi's homeland, Ruth provided for her by going to the fields to pick up what was left over from the harvest (Ruth 2:2). Ruth sacrificed her own plans and desires to care for her elderly mother-in-law. God did not forget Ruth's kindness. He later provided Ruth with a husband, Boaz, and a son, Obed, the grandfather of King David (Ruth 4:13).

> *You are God's arms and legs in this world. It is through you that others learn about and experience His love and caring.*

Doing things God's way has its rewards. Of course, that doesn't mean the journey isn't difficult at times. Caring for an elderly loved one or an aging parent can be challenging, heartbreaking, frustrating and draining. In the same way that He rewarded Ruth for caring for her mother-in-law, God will also reward you. He will be your strength when you think you can't go another day (Isaiah 41:10). He will be your comfort in times of trouble (Isaiah 66:13). He will provide you with wisdom when you don't know what to do (Proverbs 2:7).

In addition to experiencing the rewards of obedience to God for caring for your aging loved ones, there are practical and emotional reasons why you should do so.

1. You feel very close to your elderly parents or relative.
2. There are no finances to place him or her in a nursing facility.
3. You feel obligated to care for them because at one time they cared for you.
4. You are afraid that someone else would not care for them with the same respect and attention you give.
5. The elderly relative is unable to care for him or herself.

Once you've decided that you are going to take responsibility for your aging loved one, you must answer a few questions: Will you care for this person in your home? Will he or she require home health care? Do you have the resources to pay for a long-term health care situation? Do you have the support of your immediate family? Are there other family members who can help you?

As you seek the Lord for His direction, be confident in the fact that He will show you what to do. Once you receive your answer, proceed in peace. Leave your worries and concerns in your prayer closet.

Home Is Where the Heart Is

Most of the elderly prefer to stay in a homelike environment if at all possible, so opening your home to an aging loved one is a wonderful thing to do. However, you'll need to make some practical preparations to accommodate your new resident, depending on their health, mobility and mental status.

Here are a few things to consider:

- Make sure there is a clear path to each room, without slippery floors, rugs to trip over, or raised room dividers.
- Place guardrails on the bed and safety gates at the top and bottom of the staircase, if necessary.
- Purchase light-sensitive night lights and place in your loved one's room, bathroom or hallway to help them find their way around at night.
- Place smoke detectors on each floor and periodically check them to ensure they're operating properly.
- Provide a specially equipped telephone with speed dialing, a large digital display for easy reading and a ring and voice/volume enhancer.
- Put rails on the shower/tub and near the commode. You may also wish to purchase a shower chair and shower head that can be removed from the wall to make bathing easier.
- Ask your loved one's doctor about diet, medicines, limitations and daily exercise routines.
- Install a wheelchair ramp to your home if necessary.

Assess the skill level of your loved one, then develop a daily care routine and follow it. Once you get into a pattern, your care giving will be much easier. For example, if your aging mother has trouble brushing her teeth and hair, work those personal hygiene activities into your morning routine so that she

The minute you start to feel overwhelmed, frustrated, irritable or depressed, it's a signal that you should back up and reassess the situation.

will have clean teeth and nice hair every morning before you leave for work or by a specific time each morning. If your elderly father can no longer fasten tiny buttons, buy him sweaters that zip, shoes that slip on and pants that fasten with Velcro.

It's also a good idea to keep a folder of important information, and add to it as you go. In this way, anyone who may have to take over while you're away will have an extensive "cheat sheet" full of important health information and contact numbers. This can include:

1. Morning and evening schedules.
2. Doctors names, areas of expertise, contact numbers and directions to their offices.
3. Names and numbers of others who can help.
4. Names and contact information for lawyers and financial advisors.
5. A list of where certain things are kept, such as the thermometer, heating pad or games.
6. A detailed list of medications with a schedule and dosage chart.
7. Emergency numbers and name of the closest hospital.
8. A detailed list of strengthening exercises that should be performed daily.
9. A schedule that shows when physical therapy, speech therapy or occupational therapy are to be given.
10. A list of dietary restrictions, favorite foods, food allergies and eating schedule.
11. A brief medical history (especially if the care-receiver has suffered a recent or a prolonged illness)

If your loved one is in need of daily medical attention, speak with a social worker at your local hospital and find out if your loved one's insurance will pay for home health care. If so, ask how long, and how much they are willing to pay. This social worker can also direct you to several home health care agencies.

Take your time and interview a few of the workers from each service. After all, you want to put your loved one in the hands of someone competent and caring. During your interview, notice the person's appearance: Is he or she clean and neat? Do they seem well organized? Were they on time for your meeting? Be sure to ask questions about past work history, the kinds of patients they have cared for, and why he or she chose home health care as their profession. If possible, ask God to lead you to a Christian agency, but be sure to ask the same questions.

Do You Have What It Takes?

It's a good idea to assess your skills and abilities *before* assuming the role of a caregiver. Take a moment to ask yourself these questions:

- What care-giving tasks can I do?
- Can other family members or friends handle some of these tasks?
- Are there any needs that can be met by utilizing services in the community?
- Can I perform basic First-Aid procedures? Do I need CPR certification?
- What resources are available to me?

Develop a care-giving strategy and attack your shortcomings with wisdom and determination. Do research on the Internet. Call friends or family who are already handling this responsibility. See if your community has a Division of Aging that may provide assistance with homemaking, outside chores or transportation. You can also contact other agencies such as The National Association for Home Care (*www.nahc.org*); the AARP Caregivers Circle (*www.aarp.org*); and the National Association of Professional Geriatric Care Managers (*www.caremanager.org*).

There is a wealth of information and assistance that you can tap into. Don't try to do it all by yourself, or you'll get frustrated and feel overwhelmed. Those in a care-giving situation often feel isolated and very alone. Too many caregivers think they are failures if they can't successfully juggle their usual responsibilities, an outside job and the additional strain of another person in the household.

Take Care of Yourself

The minute you start to feel overwhelmed, frustrated, irritable or depressed, it's a signal that you should back up and reassess the situation. Why do you feel that way? You may need some extra help with your loved one in certain areas. If you can't find someone to step in and help, let some of your other responsibilities take the back seat for a while. Have you scheduled any days off for yourself? Are you enjoying life, or allowing it to pass you by?

There is a wealth of information and assistance that you can tap into.

It's healthy for you to go out and be with friends. Laughter brings perspective to your emotions and having fun rejuvenates your mind. Make sure you set aside time each week to do the things you enjoy. Don't live like a hermit! Yes, circumstances have changed, but that doesn't mean that *your* life ceases to exist!

If you're feeling overwhelmed and depressed, check out what your emotions are saying. If you have neglected your daily time with God, do your best to get back in His presence. In your time alone with Him, you will find the wisdom and the strength needed to continue your work.

Here are a few things you can do to help yourself:

1. Take a break from continual care. Try a mini-vacation or day off.
2. Let others help you. Take them up on their offers to "babysit" while you run errands, go to dinner, or spend time with friends.
3. Take advantage of outside services, especially if they are free or inexpensive.
4. Treasure the special moments you share in your household.
5. Don't misread your emotions. Hear what your body is telling you. If you're tired, rest. If you're overwhelmed, get help. If you feel isolated, take time off.
6. Praise the Lord in the midst of difficult moments or days.

Consider Other Options

If you are absolutely unable to care for an aging relative in your home, do the next best thing by obtaining all the facts and exploring all of the options to determine the best course of action. Following are four choices that might prove helpful to your family's situation.

1. Adult Day Services.

These are places where older people can receive supervision, socialization, recreation, meals, limited health care and counseling. Fees are usually based on the elderly person's ability to pay, which keeps the services affordable.

This can be a good thing for you, too. For example, if you wish to go

Christmas shopping while your children are in school, you could arrange for your elderly loved one to spend the day at an Adult Day Services facility. It will provide a needed break for both you and your loved one.

2. Hospice Care.

A hospice is generally reserved for those with a life expectancy of six months or less. They usually provide at-home health care, pain management and social services. In most cases, Medicare, Medicaid or other insurance carriers will cover the expenses. Some hospices have state funding for individuals without health insurance. If you need help, ask.

The Bible makes it clear that you should care for orphans, widows and family members in need.

3. Assisted Living.

This option is great for elderly people who are still able (and prefer) to live alone but need the help of others to accomplish various tasks. For instance, if your 90-year-old mother is healthy enough to live alone, but she no longer drives, then you can hire a home care aide to go grocery shopping for her.

An aide will help with laundry, cooking, running errands, minor home repair and shopping. In some cases, they will assist with the daily bathing and dressing ritual. These workers are usually paid on an hourly basis. This is an especially good option if you live in a different city than your aging loved one, and he or she does not want to relocate.

4. Nursing Homes.

Nursing homes have received a bad reputation over the years, with news stories and undercover exposés discussing the horrors of abuse and neglect. There are some good facilities out there—you just have to look for them.

When beginning your search, involve your loved one in the decision-making process. That way, he or she won't resist the change in lifestyle or feel a loss of control. Begin by making a list of nursing homes near family and friends. Then visit those facilities on several different occasions to get an accurate picture of each one.

While there, speak with the residents of the nursing home. They will give you the "inside scoop." Also talk to employees such as nursing assistants, who give about 90 percent of the care. Find out if there is a high employee turnover rate and if so, the reasons for it. Try to eat a few meals at each facility and observe craft or activity time. Do the residents get assistance eating if they need it? Does someone help them with the activities? Here are some other things to consider:

- Does the staff treat each resident with dignity?
- Do the nurses and aides respond promptly to the residents' calls for help?
- Does the nursing home provide homelike surroundings? Pets? Home décor?
- Are organized outings offered?
- Does the home provide physically and mentally challenging activities?
- Is there a strong smell of urine or feces in the halls or rooms?
- Is there enough staff on call to handle the number of residents?
- Are restraints used on residents? If so, what types?
- Are the residents well groomed and properly dressed?
- Is the atmosphere happy or depressing?

God will give you the wisdom to make the best decision possible.

Keep Your Eyes Open

After your loved one is settled in a nursing home, be on the alert for the following signs. They could be an indication of abuse or neglect.

1. Personality changes
2. Continual crying or refusal to talk
3. Weight loss
4. An unkempt appearance and poor personal hygiene
5. Dirty living quarters
6. Confusion
7. Sleeping all the time due to depression or sedation

If you suspect abuse or neglect, immediately report the facility to your local authorities.

Ask each facility that you're interested in to provide you with past state surveys. Review their score. It's also a good idea to speak with doctors, pastors and social workers in the community who might be able to recommend a particular facility or know which ones are better than others. Be an investigative reporter, gathering all of the facts before making a final decision.

For more information about choosing a good nursing home, visit the National Citizens' Coalition for Nursing Home Reform Web site at *www.nccnhr.org* or the American Association of Homes and Services for the Aging (AAHSA) at *www.aahsa.org/public/consumer.htm online.*

If you're concerned about the cost of putting your loved one into a nursing home, find out which nursing facilities are certified for Medicare and Medicaid. While Medicare does not pay for long-term nursing home stays, Medicaid will pay for those who have incomes that qualify. About 70 percent of all nursing home residents receive assistance from Medicaid.

Lastly, don't feel guilty about moving your loved one into a nursing home. Believe it or not, some elderly people are actually happier being around those their own age. They may feel more independent since they don't have to rely on you or any other family member for their care.

*   *   *   *   *

Aging is a natural process. As you age, you become more and more like a child, having to depend on others for your well-being because you lack the physical strength to do it yourself. But just because your body is winding down doesn't mean that your mind is doing the same thing! On the contrary, many elderly people are as sharp as ever; they only require assistance when it comes to physical activity.

If you are absolutely unable to care for an aging relative in your home, do the next best thing by obtaining all the facts and exploring all of the options to determine the best course of action.

Of course it's ideal for family members to care for their own; however, this is not always possible. Before taking on any new responsibilities or placing your loved one into the care of another, take a moment to seek God first. He will give you the wisdom to make the best decision possible. In addition, trust and rely on Him through the transition period. Remember, He loves your aging relative even more than you do, and He will surround them with peace, love and satisfaction.

Taking care of an elderly loved one is scriptural and of great benefit to all concerned.

Research the different options available to you regarding the care of an elderly loved one. Discuss your findings with your elderly loved one, spouse, immediate family or siblings and agree on the best course of action. Above all, pray for God's wisdom and guidance before making a final decision.

Leviticus 19:32, NIV

"Rise in the presence of the aged, show respect for the elderly and revere your God. I am the Lord."

Part VI

Life on the Edge

32

DOMESTIC VIOLENCE

Over the years, I have officiated a number of funerals for women who were victims of abuse. Some were members of my church. Burying them wasn't easy, especially when I knew that some of these women had left children behind.

As a pastor, it hurts me to have to officiate those services. Part of me is remorseful because of the nature of these women's deaths, while the other part is angry with the husbands or boyfriends—angry at their inability or unwillingness to handle their anger, stress or frustration in more constructive ways. Truthfully, as a person, you want to retaliate on behalf of the women, because they did not deserve to die and leave their children motherless.

Many men have told me, "I don't know why I hit my wife. I just do it," "She deserved it," or "I know it's wrong, but I can't help myself." Lame, cowardly excuses like these bother me. The man who claims ignorance or lack of self-control is the very same man who can control his temper just fine when there are other people in the room. Everyone has the ability to control his or her anger; it's a matter of choice. There's simply no excuse good enough to justify abuse of any kind. It's that simple.

I have seen the damage of domestic violence firsthand. I've counseled wives who came into my office with large, visible bruises and broken bones. They were so emotionally and psychologically damaged that they were at the point of losing their minds. It's in times like those that I wonder why some people, especially ministers, counsel women in abusive relationships to stay with their husbands and "allow God to work it out." That's easy for them to say when they're not the ones getting beaten with a baseball bat or burned with an iron. They don't have to walk on eggshells every minute in fear that their spouse will kill them or the children if they say or do the "wrong" thing or attempt to leave the situation. And these people certainly don't go to bed fearing that they will be raped.

Unfortunately, some individuals can be extremely insensitive to what others are going through. That doesn't mean pacify or hold a pity party for anyone. But you must be sensitive to the needs and hardships of others. That's called compassion—love in action. As pastors, Taffi's and my job is to give you practical, biblical solutions to the challenges you face in life. We may not tell you what you *want* to hear, but we will give you the answers you *need* in order for you to experience God's best in your life.

> *Abuse is the maltreatment of any person within a family or a close personal relationship.*

In Harm's Way

Abuse is the maltreatment of any person within a family or a close personal relationship. This can include physical, verbal and sexual assault or threats of assault or death. Although the majority of abuse occurs against women, it is *not* gender, age or race-specific; *anyone* can be a victim. In addition, most violence against individuals is done by someone they know and trust, such as a spouse, parent, fiancé, friend or other relative.

There are a variety of reasons why one person may abuse another. The root issue is that most abusers have low self-esteem and feel powerless and ineffective in the world. Although they may appear successful, he or she may feel inadequate inside. Here are several other common root causes of which you should be aware.

1. A means to gain control.

An abusive spouse may use violence to gain control and exercise power over his or her mate. They want to make sure he or she knows who is "the boss." Some men think that beating their wives is a sign of true manhood, but it's not. Only cowards hit women. Real men use their hands to love, not abuse.

2. Lack of respect for women.

Women are human beings endowed with the same mental, emotional and spiritual abilities as men; the only real difference is in their needs, the way in which they process information and the genetic makeup of their bodies. However, due to ignorance or erroneous teaching, abusers tend to view women as property, sexual objects or subservient individuals. They lack respect for the opposite sex as a whole; as a result, they abuse what they do not understand or are unable to appreciate.

3. Substance abuse and addiction.

The use of narcotics and alcohol by the abuser can play a major role in domestic violence. Alcohol and illegal drugs lower inhibitions, amplify emotions and raise the tolerance for pain so that the abuser can do a great deal of physical harm not only to the victim, but to him or herself as well.

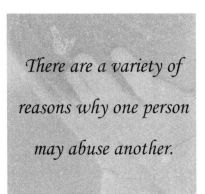

There are a variety of reasons why one person may abuse another.

4. A history of abusive behavior.

Generally men who beat their wives were raised in homes where domestic violence was a common occurrence. Rather than learning the importance of affection in relationships, they witnessed the violent outbursts of their fathers or other male role models. In their minds, abuse and "love" walk hand in hand. Because no one puts a stop to it, this cycle of violence is perpetuated from one generation to the next.

Breaking a Generational Curse

Many families have certain behaviors that are unknowingly passed down from one generation to the next. Usually these actions are detrimental to the individual and family unit. They are most commonly referred to as a *generational curse*. This can include things such as alcoholism, abuse, obesity, promiscuity and so on.

How do you stop the cycle? First, make a quality decision to live by biblical principles. Proverbs 23:7 says, *"For as [a man] thinketh in his heart, so is he…."* Second, you must renew your mind.

This is done by aligning your thoughts with God's Word through the daily study and application of scriptures to your life (Romans 12:2). Eventually you will change the way you think, ultimately transforming the way you live.

You may also want to consider daily confessions of God's Word over your marriage. As you speak aloud what the Bible has to say about healthy marriages, the power of generational curses will break. Here is a sample confession to get you started:

> *"Father, in the name of Jesus, I declare that I am a loving husband (wife). I love my spouse even as Christ loves the church. I submit myself first to You and then to my spouse. I will not be bitter and aggressive. I will live above reproach. I am temperate and self-controlled. I am disciplined, hospitable and show love at all times"* (Ephesians 5:21-25; Colossians 3:18-19; 1 Timothy 3:1-3, AMP).

Words are like seeds. Once planted, they will eventually produce a harvest (Proverbs 18:21).

Abuse is *never* the victim's fault. The psychological and emotional problems of the abuser do not justify his or her explosive reactions. No one asks for, or enjoys, being physically, verbally or sexually assaulted by someone who claims to love them. If you or someone you know have had the blame for violent outbursts placed on your shoulders, do not believe or accept it! It's simply *not* your fault.

The Cycle of Violence

Generally, domestic violence does not occur on a continual basis, but in a cycle that is made up of three phases: (1) *tension-building*; (2) *acute battering incident* (in which verbal, sexual and other physical assault may occur); and (3) the *"honeymoon"* stage.

In the first phase, tension builds

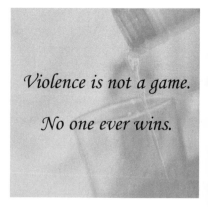

Violence is not a game.

No one ever wins.

between the husband and wife. Anything can contribute to an increase in tension, such as financial problems, disciplinary disputes regarding the children, in-law challenges or work-related issues. As a result, one or both partners yell, argue and complain frequently. Over a period of time, the verbal, emotional and physical abuse increases and escalates in severity. The abused spouse tries to cope with the circumstances and attempts to control the abuse by trying to avoid arguments, placating their spouse or "giving in" to any demands. Unfortunately, these coping mechanisms do little, if anything, to stop the impending acute battering incident.

Once the tension become unbearable, the second phase occurs. The "trigger" for moving into this phase is usually based on the internal emotional condition of the abuser, or an external issue, such as a problem at work, a flat tire, broken dish, wrinkled shirt, and so on. The trigger will vary for each incident. In some cases, the victim will provoke the abuser in order to "get it over with." At this point, the abusive spouse takes out his or her frustration by punching, slapping, kicking, spitting, pushing, tripping or raping their spouse. He or she may use lamps, pots and pans and knives as weapons, therefore turning the home into a war zone.

This reminds me of an aunt of mine. Several years ago, she and her husband had been arguing earlier in the day when they eventually had a shootout! It was like a scene from a movie. There were several old cars parked in front of their home: my aunt was behind one, he was behind another. Both were shooting at each other. She'd shoot a couple of times and duck, then he'd do the same. This lasted until my uncle ran out of bullets. He yelled out, "Hey, I ran out of bullets," and she said, "I'm gonna kill you now!" Thank God no one was hurt.

Although my aunt's story is somewhat humorous, many couples are experiencing war-like situations at home. Perhaps you can relate to this. From the outside, things may look okay, but as soon as the front door closes, everything changes. If you are out running errands or working, you may not even want to go home, because you know what awaits you there.

Sadly, many victims are beaten to the point of losing consciousness, hospitalization and even death. Often neighbors and relatives hesitate to get involved out of fear for their own safety or the mentality that, "It's not my business." There is no escape once the acute battering incident has begun; the control rests entirely in the hands of the abuser. When he or she has released their frustration, the couple moves into phase three.

The Cycle of Violence

Phase 1:
Tension-Building

Abuser gets angry; increase in aggressive behavior (usually toward objects); breakdown in communication; increase in verbal and minor physical abuse; abuser places unrealistic/greater demands on the victim; abuser attempts to isolate partner from family/friends; victim tries to appease abuser; victim feels as if he/she is walking on eggshells; frequent arguments; abuser expresses feelings of hostility, tension and dissatisfaction.

Phase 3:
The "Honeymoon"

The abuser: acts like the abuse did not happen; is apologetic (gives hope for change); promises not to hit the victim again; may blame the victim for the onset of violence; promise to get help; give gifts; become emotionally close to the victim; becomes generous, loving and helpful; expresses a genuine interest in the welfare of the victim; begs for forgiveness

Phase 2:
Acute Battering Incident

Severe physical abuse directed toward the victim: punching, biting, tripping, kicking, pinching, shoving, pushing, choking, slapping, hitting, use of objects/weapons; sexual abuse/spousal rape; verbal/emotional abuse; threats to life of victim/children.

The "honeymoon" period is the calm after the storm. The abusive spouse realizes he or she went too far and begins to show loving behavior through apologies, kind words, terms of endearment and gifts. They promise that the abuse won't happen again and claim to have learned their lesson. At this point in time the couple become closer emotionally. This, coupled with the low self-esteem, shame, fear and isolation that comes from going through the cycle repeatedly, makes it difficult for the victim to leave. In other words, he or she develops what many people call *Battered [Women's] Syndrome*, or a "learned helplessness."

Love is a force that conquers all.

Ironically, although the abuser apologizes to his or her mate, they may still place the blame elsewhere. For example, they may say, "Honey, I love you. I don't mean to hit you. It's just that you make me angry sometimes," or "I don't mean to hurt you; it's just that there's this thing going on at work that's really stressing me out." Regardless of how it is phrased, the purpose of these statements is to make the victim feel responsible for the abuse. Remember, *it's not the victim's fault.*

After the honeymoon phase is over, the cycle begins again. Tension will build and something else will trigger the abusive spouse's frustration again and again.

Why Stay?

All too often people are quick to blame the victim for staying in an abusive relationship. They believe he or she likes or needs the abuse, "loves the abuser too much," or has a self-esteem problem. However, there are a variety of reasons why victims stay in these relationships. They generally:

1. Fear the abuser will become more violent
2. Fear their life or the lives of their children will be in jeopardy
3. Rationalize that the abuse is due to external problems such as alcohol, drugs and work-related stress
4. Hope for better times, since the abuser does not hit all the time
5. Lack support from family, friends, clergy and police (may be dissuaded from filing charges against the abuser)
6. Know the difficulties of single parenting
7. Know that the abusive spouse controls finances and other necessary resources

8. Do not know about or have access to help and safety
9. Fear not being able to make it on their own
10. Fear losing custody of the children
11. Distrust the legal system and lack adequate police protection
12. Have the mindset that their identity and worth is contingent on being married and it's their responsibility to make the relationship work

This list is not all-encompassing; every situation is different. As the abused, the best thing you can do is to be honest with yourself. If your life or the lives of your children are in danger, the best thing to do is leave the situation. You should not have to sleep with one eye open simply because someone told you you had to stay out of obligation to your spouse. Of course marriage is an obligation; however, God does *not* sanction violence.

Keep in mind that no one can make up your mind for you. You must follow *your* own conviction—not anyone else's. And don't blame anyone for the choice you make. The truth is, your decision will cost you either way. Leaving your spouse may prove more stressful because you will have to try to make it on your own, while staying may threaten your existence. Change is never easy. Trust God and allow Him to direct you. Whatever you decide, remember, there *is* help available for you.

Where to Go for Help

Domestic violence can have long-term effects on the victim and their children. This may include the risk of permanent physical, emotional and mental damage, and even death. Children of domestic violence generally mature into victims or abusers themselves, beginning as early as their teen years.

Perhaps you want out but don't know what to do. There is a wealth of information available to victims of domestic violence. Two great resources are the National Coalition Against Domestic Violence (NCADV), *www.ncdav.org*, and the National Women's Health Information Center (NWHIC), *www.4woman.gov* or 1-800-799-SAFE. Both organizations offer a great deal of information regarding abuse, support groups, shelters and the rights of victims.

Whether you realize it or not, you have rights. You have a right to legal protection against your spouse and the right to receive shelter and other types of assistance. A simple phone call to any toll-free, 24-hour domestic violence hotline can open the door for help. Check your telephone book or the Internet for the names and telephone numbers of organizations in your area.

Keep in mind that many shelters do not publish their street addresses. When an individual calls for assistance, a representative from the shelter will meet him or her in an agreed-upon location for pickup. This protects the victim from the abuser and helps him or her to feel a little more secure about requesting help. Many shelters also provide daycare services for working mothers or mothers seeking employment and short-term (limited) financial assistance as well as help with errands, apartment and job hunting, legalities, and so on.

Create an Emergency Plan

You may find yourself in a situation where you must get out of your home in a moment's notice and are only able to leave with the clothes on your back. In that case, it's always a good idea to head for the nearest public telephone so you can call the local authorities. They, in turn, will assist you in contacting a shelter. However, it's always best to develop a plan of action for leaving *before* you find yourself in that position. Here is a list of things to do to make things easier.

- **Memorize** the telephone numbers of your local domestic violence hotline or shelter.

- **Arrange to stay temporarily** with a friend, coworker or relative, if possible.

- **Keep a set of spare keys,** important documents and a small amount of cash in an easily accessible place.

In addition:

- **Set aside money in small amounts** (to avoid suspicion). Open an account in a bank or credit union that is in a separate location from where you and your spouse cur-rently handle financial transactions. This will prevent your spouse from contacting your current bank to get information. Although the tellers are not allowed to give out information about accounts, they may be tricked or intimidated into giving information to an inquiring spouse.

- **Open a post office box** and have personal mail and bank information sent there.

- **If possible, remove your name from any joint credit cards or loans.** This will protect you financially in case your spouse decides to retaliate by filing for bankruptcy or maxing credit card limits.

- **Open a safe deposit box** to store new bank account information.

- **Begin looking for an affordable apartment.** If your finances allow you may wish to consider features such as a home security system, apartment complex security gates, second or third-story apartment and 24-hour security personnel. If your resources are limited, invest in a deadbolt or ensure that the doors have secure locks.

- **Map out a public transportation route** or alternate methods of transportation.

Do yourself a favor and get help before it's too late! Your life is too precious to be taken away from you in tragedy. Remember that you are special to God. No matter what you're going through, no matter what has been said, never forget that God is with you and you aren't alone. He'll never leave you.

Notice the Red Flags

The key to enjoying God's best in life is to be honest with yourself concerning your situation. If you're reading this chapter, it could be that you are in an abusive relationship but you're either not convinced or don't want to admit it. You may think that everything in your relationship is okay since you aren't being hit or sexually assaulted. Keep in mind, however, that abuse is not always physical. Verbal abuse can be equally as damaging as physical violence.

Here are several questions to ask yourself to help you determine whether or not you are in an abusive relationship. Think of them as "red flags." Does my partner…

- Purposefully embarrass me in front of others?
- Belittle my accomplishments and goals?
- Make me feel incompetent or unable to make wise decisions on my own?
- Threaten to harm me in any way?
- Make me feel like I'm worthless without him or her?
- Treat me roughly by grabbing, choking, pushing, slapping, hitting, biting, kicking, pinching or tripping me?
- Investigate everything I do because he or she distrusts me and thinks I'm being unfaithful? Is he or she unreasonably jealous or possessive?
- Keep me from doing things I enjoy?
- Punch walls or throw or break objects when angry?
- Try to intimidate me physically?
- Forbid me to associate with friends and family?
- Make me feel like he or she is controlling my life?
- Blame me for how they act toward me?
- Is he pleasant and charming in front of others, but domineering and abusive behind closed doors (like a Dr. Jekyll and Mr. Hyde)?
- Force me to perform sexually when I don't want to?
- Make me feel afraid whenever he or she is around?

In addition, you may also want to take a moment to evaluate yourself. Consider the following. Do you:

- Experience frequent bouts of depression?
- Visit hospitals or clinics frequently?
- Remain isolated from family and friends?
- Have noticeable bruises, teeth or burn marks, or broken bones?
- Make excuses for your injuries or cover them up with clothing and makeup?
- Refuse to seek medical attention for fear of angering your spouse and making the situation worse?
- Make excuses for your spouse's violent outbursts?
- Miss work due to the nature of your injuries?
- Use drugs or alcohol? Is this uncharacteristic for you?

- Talk of suicide or have you attempted suicide?

These red flags are clear warning signs that danger and possible fatality may be imminent. Find a way to contact your local authorities and seek medical attention. Don't be deceived into thinking the problem will go away by itself.

A Word to the Abuser

If you have been abusive to your spouse, child, relative, or friend, stop it today! Violence is not a game. No one ever wins. If you value something, then you will cherish and preserve it. There are better ways to relieve stress and frustration than to hurt someone. Listen to the other person when he or she tells you that your words and actions hurt them. Do not confuse fear with submission and control with masculinity.

Admit your abusive behavior to yourself and others. Seek professional help. You need anger-management, problem-solving and communication-building skills. Admitting you need assistance is the first step to change. There are many people who are willing to help you make the necessary adjustments so you can become a healthy individual and allow you and your family to reconcile.

In addition, admit your wrongdoing to God and ask for His forgiveness and help. By sincerely repenting, or making a 180° turn away from your negative actions to God, you position yourself to receive more of His power and ability in you, enabling you to overcome generational curses, a negative or erroneous mind-set, and your abusive behavior.

*   *   *   *   *

Taffi and I want you to know that domestic violence doesn't have to dominate your life, regardless of whether you are the abuser or the victim. Whatever your situation, allow the love of God to have its place in your heart. Love is a force that conquers all. It's what successful families are made of!

Domestic violence is a serious issue that affects thousands of families across the nation and around the world. Knowledge, understanding, compassion and a decision to change play key roles in the victim getting out of this kind of life-threatening situation.

Assess your situation and determine the best course of action for you (and your children). Seek the help you need and don't allow anyone to make you feel bad about the choice you have made.

Psalm 91:15-16

"He shall call upon me, and I will answer him; I will be with him in trouble; I will deliver him, and honor him. With long life will I satisfy him, and show him my salvation."

33

SUBSTANCE ABUSE

Habits and addictions do not develop overnight, but gradually. Likewise, breaking them takes time. A *process* is involved. Sometimes that process can be sweatless, and other times, it can be very tough. This chapter is about the process of overcoming substance abuse. You or someone you know may be struggling in this area. Perhaps you have tried to "kick" certain addictions on your own but were unsuccessful. It may seem that for every step you take toward becoming "clean," you take three or four steps backward. It appears that you are experiencing one setback after another.

Results…everyone wants them. But how many people are really willing to pay the price? Results don't come cheap. It takes hard work and a determined effort to achieve what you want. But it doesn't do you any good to know that you have an addiction and need to get rid of it. That's like me telling you that there is a million dollars in the bank under your name, but I don't give you the specifics on how you can withdraw it. Taffi and I want to give you the practical steps you need to live clean and sober once and for all. That's the result we're striving for. As you read on, keep this formula in mind:

Information + application = manifestation

What Is It?

Substance abuse is defined as "the overindulgence in, and dependence on, an addictive substance, especially alcohol or a narcotic drug." It is also called *chemical abuse*.

Believe it or not, many married couples have to deal with the issue of chemical abuse. One or both spouses may suffer with an addiction. In addition, parents may have to deal with children and teenagers who are addicted to drugs and alcohol.

Some estimate that the highest illicit use of drugs and alcohol is found among youth ages 18 to 20 years old. They also estimate that marijuana, a "gateway drug," is the most commonly used substance among young people. In addition, research has shown that millions of teens are binge drinkers, consuming at least five or more drinks in a specific period of time. Many motor vehicle accidents and fatalities are caused by teens driving under the influence.

Decide today to change the way you think so you can transform the way you live.

There are several well-known organizations that have taken a proactive stance regarding chemical abuse. With the belief that prevention is the best medicine, the "Say No to Drugs," Mothers Against Drunk Driving (MADD), Students Against Drunk Driving (SADD) and Drug Abuse Resistance Education (D.A.R.E.) programs have helped to raise awareness in communities worldwide.

The sad truth is that in spite of the initiative taken by these organizations, substance abuse is still a common occurrence. It would be foolish to think that the problem is under control. However, you can determine whether or not *your* home is affected by it. By increasing your knowledge base and learning what substance abuse is, how it develops, its effects on the body and how to break out of an addiction, you stand a better chance of keeping your family out of harm's way.

Know Your Chemicals

Addictive substances come in a variety of shapes, sizes and colors. There are five basic categories: opiates, stimulants, depressants, cannabis and hallucinogens. The following information lists examples of each type of drug, the names by which they are commonly referred to and their effects on the body.

1. Opiates.

These include Heroin, Opium, Morphine, Codeine, Oxycodone (Percodan), Hydrocodone (Vicodin), Meperidine (Demerol), Methadone and many others. Of course, these are only clinical names. You may be more familiar with terms such as, *Smack, Junk* and *Hard Stuff.*

Opiates are sedatives that give you a "good feeling" at first. They slow your reflexes and breathing, as well as make your skin cold and speech raspy. Increased use of narcotics will build a tolerance to the point where you require more of the drug to achieve the same high the next time you use.

2. Central Nervous System Stimulants.

As the name implies, these substances affect the central nervous system (CNS). They include Amphetamines, Cocaine, Methamphetamine, Methylphenidate (Ritalin), nicotine and caffeine. Their street names are *Crank, Speed, Uppers, Blow, Coke, Snow, Free-base, Stardust, Crystal, Meth, Pep Pills* and *Bennies*. Also included in this list is nicotine, the active ingredient in tobacco, and Methylene-DioxyMethAmphetamine (MDMA), more commonly referred to as *Ecstasy, E, XTC, Love Drug* and *Scooby Snacks*.

Some of these stimulants are psychologically addictive and produce *euphoria* (the feeling of invincibility or that there are no problems). You feel like Superman because they dull pain. They increase respiration and heart rate and elevate body temperature. Hyperactivity, nervousness and talkativeness are other common effects. Oftentimes, stimulants replace euphoric feelings with panic, confusion and aggression.

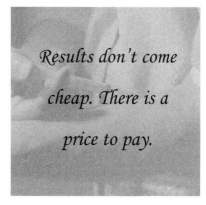

Results don't come cheap. There is a price to pay.

The psychological effects are numerous. MDMA is also known to produce hallucinations.

Caffeine, which is found in many over-the-counter drugs (such as NoDoz, Midol and Excedrin), coffee, tea, soft drinks, yogurt, chocolate and candy, can be very addictive. It is believed that although a dosage of 50-100 mg. of caffeine (the amount of one cup of coffee) will increase mental clarity and energy, abuse of this stimulant will lead to caffeine intoxication. Symptoms of this abuse are irritability, tremors, heartburn, fatigue and poor concentration.

Nicotine is colorless, has a strong acidic taste and is highly poisonous in its natural form—approximately 50 mg. can kill a person in minutes. When placed in cigarettes, cigars, pipe tobacco and chewing tobacco (approximately 10 mg.), it is combined with several other chemicals known to cause cancer and irritate the eyes, nose and throat. In addition, it is highly addictive. Short-term effects produce feelings of relaxation. Long-term effects include cancer, emphysema, asthma, chronic bronchitis and coronary heart disease.

3. Central Nervous System Depressants.

These drugs include alcohol and barbiturates such as Phenobarbital, Amobarbital, Pentobarbital and Secobarbital. Their more familiar street names are *Reds, Yellows, Blues, Pink Ladies, Ludes, Barbs, Downers* and *King Kong Pills*.

Other depressants include Methaqualone, Lithium Carbonate, Lithium Citrate and Benzodiazepine, also known as "Benzos." Heroin, speed and ecstasy addicts tend to use Benzos as sleep aids or as a cure for insomnia when they're trying to kick their habit.

CNS depressants slow the brain's normal operation, to include slurred speech, lack of coordination, decreased attention span, impaired judgment, mood swings, double vision, dizziness, drowsiness, lowered body temperature and aggressive or suicidal behavior.

4. Cannabis.

Cannabis is the plant that produces hashish and marijuana. These drugs are often referred to as *Hash, Pot, Weed, Joint, Ganja, Dubie (Doobie), Mary Jane, Reefer, Roach* and *Hemp*. Many in the medical profession believe marijuana to be a "gateway drug" to more addictive and damaging substances such as cocaine and heroin.

It is believed that the effects of these substances are most intense during the first hour. The short-term effects may include hunger, talkativeness and laughing more than usual. Eyes become reddened, coordination is reduced and attention span decreases.

The risks associated with continual use of cannabis are chronic bronchitis, possible birth defects and stillbirth, chronic respiratory problems and lung, mouth or throat cancer. Overdose can lead to a coma, nausea, paranoia and anxiety attacks.

5. Hallucinogens.

These substances include Lysergic Acid Diethylamide (LSD), Peyote, Psilocybin, Ketamine, Gamma-hydroxybutyric acid (GHB) and Phenyl Cyclohexyl Piperidine (PCP). Some street names for LSD are *Acid, Blotter, Lucy in the Sky With Diamonds* and *Sugar Cube*. The names for PCP are *Angel Dust, Dust, Super Weed, Elephant* and *Rocket Fuel*.

The effects produced by hallucinogenic drugs include, but are not limited to, anxiety, disorientation, increased pain threshold, hallucinations, depression, schizophrenic behavior, altered body sensations, synesthesia (sensory crossover) and paranoia (especially with PCP).

Gamma-hydroxybutyric acid (GHB), with its street names *Designer Drugs*, *Liquid Ecstasy* and *Easy Lay*, is a date-rape drug. It causes a state of relaxation within 10 to 20 minutes, and can last up to four hours. Combining this drug with alcohol can result in nausea, difficulty breathing, loss of consciousness, liver failure and vomiting.

What I've shared with you thus far is only a small amount of information. I encourage you to increase your awareness by browsing the Internet, visiting libraries and bookstores, and meeting with substance abuse counselors. What you learn may ultimately save your life or the lives of others.

Inhalants

Inhalants include a variety of breathable chemicals, such as aerosol sprays, glues, correction fluid and household cleaners, that produce mind-altering results like:

- Light-headedness or sensations of spinning, moving and floating
- Mild hallucinations
- Dizziness or drowsiness
- Euphoria
- Nausea
- Symptoms similar to alcohol intoxication (slurred speech, slowed reflexes, poor judgment, confusion, dis orientation)

Usually inhalants are sprayed or placed into a small plastic bag. The bag is then held over the nose and mouth, and the contents inhaled. Others may be inhaled directly from their containers or soaked onto a piece of cloth.

Because inhalants pass directly into the bloodstream through their lungs, the effects can be felt immediately. However, their duration depends on the substance used; some last a few seconds, others for hours. Abusers can suffer from high-blood pressure, severe nausea and vomiting, damage to the central nervous system, liver, kidneys, lungs and bone marrow. In addition, there is a significant risk of death due to respiratory failure, suffocation and heart failure.

Stages of Substance Abuse

As I have stated previously, habits and addictions are not developed overnight. No one becomes an addict with the first sip of beer or the first puff of marijuana. Substance abuse usually occurs in stages: (1) experimental use; (2) social use; (3) chemical dependency; and (4) chronic chemical dependency.

Stage One: Experimental use.

In the beginning, you experience the "good feelings" certain substances can produce. Usually, your first high makes you feel like you're on top of the world. You lose your inhibitions and feel free to do anything. During this phase, you drink or get high on a very limited basis, such as weekend parties.

Stage Two: Social use.

During this stage, you *plan* the use of certain substances. You *purposefully* seek a "buzz" from liquor or a high from using drugs. Tolerance develops—you require more of the drug to achieve the same results as before. For example, whereas a few puffs of marijuana or a glass of wine would get you high or drunk, you now need to drink or smoke more to get the same effect. Certain boundaries or rules are put in place, such as: "I won't drink at work or in the morning," "I don't drink before 6:00 p.m." or "I don't drink around family."

Stage Three: Chemical dependency.

Addiction develops. You no longer have to be with others to get high or drunk. Sometimes you lose control and get drunk when you really didn't plan to. You cross the boundaries and break the rules you have established.

At this point, you have become so chemically dependent that your lifestyle changes. You rearrange your routine to accommodate the habitual use of drugs. Often, you experience blackouts and memory lapses. Your relationships with friends and family suffer. Consequently, you deal with feelings of sadness, depression, anger, irritability, anxiety and guilt. Eventually denial grows. You refuse to accept that you have a problem. Addiction is now your way of coping with circumstances at home or at work.

Stage Four: Chronic chemical dependency.

During this stage, the abuser uses drugs to feel normal and avoid withdrawal symptoms. Isn't that ironic? You use a substance to escape reality, only to depend on it later for a sense of normalcy and to keep your body functioning.

A chronic user makes getting high a priority over everything and everyone. They may violate their morals and values just to get a "fix." Sometimes individuals will steal or even prostitute themselves for drugs. They become paranoid, fearful and sometimes suicidal.

Some experts say that once a person reaches the chronic stage of substance abuse, he will remain chemically dependent for the rest of his life. In their view, chronic substance abuse is a permanent disease from which you never completely recover, even if you stop using drugs and the disease has gone into remission. "Once an addict, always an addict."

Be Consistent

As a Christian, I see things differently. There is no such thing as an irreversible disease. I don't care how addicted you or someone you know may be to alcohol or drugs, you *can* break free. I know people who have overcome substance abuse. Some of them are members of my congregation. There is a cure! With God, *all things* are possible.

Consistency is the key to breakthrough. When you're consistent about living drug-free, you develop a determination, or a "doggedness" that says, "In the name of Jesus, I'm not going to let this addiction hold me back any more. I take authority over it, and I'm not going to quit until I'm completely clean!" You see, people with a tenacious determination obtain positive, long-lasting results and experience breakthrough in every area of life.

Living drug and alcohol free is possible. It simply takes a consistent effort and a *quality decision* on your part to be free. If you truly desire to overcome your bad habits and addictions, make up your mind to do so and think the way that God thinks. In other words, renew your mind through the daily reading, study and application of God's Word to your situation (Romans 12:2).

Your greatest battle against drug abuse will be fought in the arena of your

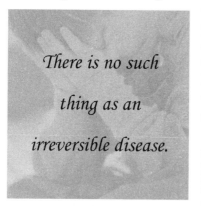

There is no such thing as an irreversible disease.

mind. Sure, you can stop cold turkey for a couple of weeks, months or even years. But if the devil can make you *think*, just for a moment, that you'll *never* be free, you never will. You'll live in continual fear of relapse. Before long, you'll be using again. Keep in mind that you are what you think (Proverbs 23:7).

Renewing the mind involves realizing the damage that drug and alcohol abuse can cause. Not only are you affecting your life, but the lives of others as well. Along with the physical, psychological and emotional effects substance abuse has, think of the damage it can have on your marriage—separation, divorce or losing custody of children.

During my counseling sessions over the years, I have always given people the biblical solution to breaking addictions. The Bible refers to addictions as *lasciviousness* (Ephesians 4:19). *Lasciviousness* is simply "unrestrained behavior." When your mind is not renewed to God's Word, you begin dwelling on negative thoughts.

For example, you may develop an intense curiosity to experience alcohol or drugs for yourself. Eventually, those thoughts will lead to action. The more you indulge in drinking or drug use, the more that behavior becomes second nature to you. Think back to the stages of substance abuse. The experimental use of drugs can eventually lead to chronic chemical dependence. This describes the gradual development of lasciviousness.

The Word of God says that lasciviousness is a "work of the flesh" (Galatians 5:19). In simple terms, it is a product of sinful human nature. Your flesh, or soul (the place where your mind, will and emotions reside), is at its *strongest* when it is dominating your spirit (see chapter 30). Therefore, it stands to reason that your flesh is at its *weakest* when your spirit dominates. That's why Galatians 5:16 says if you walk (live) by your spirit, you won't fulfill the desires of your flesh.

Go For Help

Following are several Internet Web sites that contain information and links to help you become more knowledgeable about substance abuse and find help centers in your area.

- **National Council on Alcoholism and Drug Dependence, Inc.**
  1-800-NCA-CALL
  www.ncadd.org

- **Mothers Against Drunk Driving (MADD)**
  1-800-GET-MADD (1-800-438-6233)
  www3.madd.org

- **Students Against Drunk Driving**
  www.saddonline.com

- **Phoenix House**
  www.phoenixhouse.org

- **Substance Abuse and Mental Health Services Administration**
  (SAMHSA) *www.samhsa.gov*

Defend Your Decision

I used to be addicted to apple pies; I couldn't resist them! Now I know that doesn't sound as harmful as a chemical addiction, but it was an addiction just the same. I used to eat whole pies by myself and would get upset if you tried to eat a piece.

For awhile, it seemed that the harder I tried to cut back on eating apples pies, the harder it was to maintain my decision to eat in moderation. But the more I trained and forced myself to stay within the boundaries I had set concerning healthy eating, the more disciplined I became. Today, I don't have a problem with bad eating habits. I can eat a slice of apple pie every once in a while and leave it at that. I'm not addicted to food. *I'm* in control—not my cravings.

Set boundaries around your decision to quit using alcohol and drugs and stick to them. Allow the Word of God to define those boundaries. For example, 1 Peter 5:8 encourages you to *"Be sober [and] be vigilant...."* In other words, be alert, awake and watchful. When you're not, you open the door for addiction to creep into your life to tempt, harass and pressure you to give in (Ephesians 4:27). When you commit to your decision to resist the temptation to get high or drunk, it won't be long before you become proficient at resistance.

I encourage you to always be on guard. Sometimes that means speaking to yourself. "No, I won't give in. That drug is bad for me. I am stronger than this temptation, and I choose the things of the spirit over the things of the flesh." Positive affirmations such as these are what the Bible calls your *profession,* or *confession,* of faith (Hebrews 10:23). Confessions are God's way of helping you to align your thoughts and words with His thoughts and words. Proverbs 18:21 says that you can either speak life or death to your situation. God wants you to speak life over yourself daily. So don't go to an Alcoholics Anonymous or Narcotics Anonymous session and say, "Hello, my name is John Smith and I'm an alcoholic." Don't confess what you *are*—you already know you have a problem! Instead, speak as if you've already been set free and delivered from alcoholism. Speak what you *believe.* See yourself as the Word of God describes you.

I encourage you to study the Bible, particularly the scriptures that I've mentioned as well as others that speak of freedom from bondage and sin (John 8:31-32; 1 Corinthians 10:13; Galatians 5:1; James 4:7). Confess those scripture at least 10 to 20 times a day.

Like I said before, results don't come cheap; you must work for them. Remember, you're fighting a war for control over your life. Confessing the Word daily is a means of building a defense system against the flesh so you can overcome substance abuse. Speaking God's Word builds your confidence in His ability to empower you to live drug-free.

*   *   *   *   *

Decide today that you will change the way you *think* so you can change the way you *live.* Change may mean enrolling in a detoxification program or joining a support group. The point is to get help. There are many private and civic organizations that can help you kick that habit. Don't try to quit by yourself; get help from others. But always remember to allow God to direct your steps toward clean living.

A dependency on alcohol or other chemical substances affects every area of a person's life—physical, mental, emotional, relational and spiritual. However, here is a way out through the Word of God and support from others.

List the areas of your life where you've compromised godliness. Take the top two areas and spend the next 30 days focusing on making those areas line up with God's Word. If you suspect that chemical dependency is an issue for you, seek help from family, friends, a clinic, a local church or a support group in your area.

Ephesians 5:18

"And be not drunk with wine, wherein is excess; but be filled with the Spirit...."

34

DEPRESSION AND SUICIDE

Depression and suicide are epidemics that touch the lives of thousands of people every year; yet in all my years of ministry, I have never heard a sermon specifically on either topic. Because of this, there are many questions that remain unanswered, such as, "Is suicide the same thing as murder?" "If someone takes his or her own life, will they go to heaven?" "Is depression a sin?"

People who have committed suicide were so severely tormented by negative thoughts that they became mentally and emotionally unbalanced. The line between right and wrong became blurred, making it difficult for that individual to distinguish between what was sin and what was not. At that point, only God can judge the state of a person's mind and abilities. He is a righteous Judge, and only when the person stands before Him, will He announce the verdict.

If you are presently battling depression and thoughts of suicide, you *are not* in that category. You are still able to recognize the value of life and the difference between right and wrong, although you are being tormented and challenged. You can still make the decision to fight for your life. You are the one this chapter is for.

Are You Blue?

Suicide is the "act of taking one's own life voluntarily and intentionally." It is perhaps the most selfish act a person can commit because of its devastating effects—emotional and mental—on those left behind. When a person chooses to take his or her life, they have ignored the strongest instinct of human nature: self-preservation. While most people overcome depression and suicidal tendencies through the realization that their crisis is temporary and death is permanent, others view the situation as inescapable and suppress their self-preservation instinct by remaining in a saddened state and commit suicide.

Depression is the primary reason behind suicide and affects millions of people each year. Symptoms can persist for weeks, months or years and may include prolonged sadness or unexplained crying spells. Often there are changes in appetite and sleep patterns as well as increased levels of irritability, anger, worry, general anxiety and agitation. Pessimism, indifference and lethargy, feelings of guilt, worthlessness and failure, an inability to concentrate, and reccurring thoughts of death or suicide are other common symptoms.

Although stressors such as feelings of loneliness or helplessness, financial difficulties, marital challenges, illness or the loss of a loved one can trigger depression, there are also biological causes like chemical imbalances (Bipolar Disorder) and hormonal changes (menopause). Medication and counseling are often used to treat such cases.

Now don't misunderstand me. I know it can be a very difficult thing for anyone to feel as though no one loves them, that there's no way out of a bad situation or they don't have anyone to confide in. However, there *is* a solution. Regardless of the challenges you may be experiencing, you *can* live on.

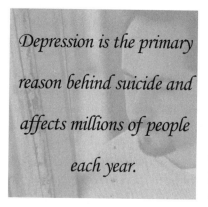

Depression is the primary reason behind suicide and affects millions of people each year.

Several years ago I experienced the loss of my father as well as the loss of several close friends. It was a very rough time for me. What made it even *more* difficult was the fact that the officiating minister at one funeral encouraged the congregation to hold on to their grief because it was a part of who they really were. That was a terrible thing to say! All it did was keep us in the destructive cycle of grief. Yes, it is natural to mourn the loss of someone dear to you; but it shouldn't be a lifestyle. That only prolongs the sense of loss and ushers in a deep depression.

Some time later, a friend of mine cried in my arms over the loss of his father. I tried to comfort him because I knew what he was going through. However, I quickly began to relive the sadness of my father going home to be with the Lord. I couldn't get past it. All I could do was grieve, day after day, week after week. Often when people get "stuck" like that, they no longer think about the faithfulness of God or how much He cares for them. Instead, they begin asking, "Why did God let this happen?" Their faith and hope in Him transform into doubt and anger.

"Why, God?"

God is not to blame for the difficulties you are facing; He's trying to get you out of them. Before blaming God, the first thing you should do is to evaluate yourself. Was it a shortcoming on your part that prevented you from experiencing success in a certain area? For example, it's not God's fault that your marriage is rocky. Have you done all you know to do by applying biblical principles and enhancing your level of sensitivity and communication and problem-solving skills? If your finances are a mess, are you overspending? Are you tithing? Do you stick to your budget?

Once you've analyzed yourself, then try to objectively analyze the situation. Is there something you and your spouse could have done better? How can you work together to resolve the issues? Have you asked anyone for help? Every problem has a source. When you discover the point of origin, you can then think of practical solutions. In addition, don't base your decisions on emotion. Emotions are temporary; they change all the time. Use the Word of God as your guide for successful decision-making. It is unbiased truth.

Your heavenly Father loves you and longs for you to come to Him for help in every situation you face in life. In Hebrews 13:5 He said, "...*I will never leave thee, nor forsake thee.*" He's closer to you than the air you breathe. Just say, "Lord, I don't understand this, but I know that You love me. Help me now."

God is waiting on *you* to employ Him and all of His resources to bring about your success. It's never too late. As long as there is breath in your body you can still be victorious.

In my attempt to deal with the question of "Why?" I sought the Lord. I knew in my heart that this perpetual grieving was not the will of God for my life. After spending time in prayer and meditating on the Scriptures, I eventually realized that I was not only dealing with grief, but also with fear. It was the fear of not knowing how to go on.

During the course of a day, week, month or year, most people never contemplate death. Of course they *know* that at some point everyone dies, but they don't dwell on that. In addition, the average person normally doesn't have a contingency plan for his or her life—what to do when a loved one leaves, either vol-

It's at this juncture in life that most people start asking the most infamous questions of all: "What am I here for?" "Why was I born?"

untarily or involuntarily. As a result, when tragedy strikes, they're devastated. Grief and fear take over, and questions rise to the surface: *What am I going to do? Who can I turn to?*

Grief and fear are directly related to each other. For example, you can grieve, or have regret, over a bad decision that you've made. If that grief isn't put in check, you will begin to fear that you will never make a right decision. You may also think that you are a failure and everything you attempt to do winds up as a disaster. Before you know it, fear has you paralyzed. You don't know how to break out, what to do or which way to turn. You begin believing the negative thoughts that tell you you are a failure. Suddenly, everything seems hopeless.

It's at this juncture in life that most people start asking the most infamous questions of all: "What am I here for?" "Why was I born?"

The Choice Is Yours

Those questions will bring you to a crossroads in your life. This is where you'll decide whether or not there really is a God. You may do some research by visiting churches, speaking to ministers or other people of faith or studying relevant books. But this doesn't necessarily mean that you'll become a Christian. On the contrary, you may choose to embrace all religions equally or reject them. You may decide to place your belief in something other than Christianity, or in nothing at all. The choice is yours. However, there is a price to pay for making the "wrong" decision: eternity in hell, and even hell on earth.

If you have accepted Jesus Christ into your heart as your Lord and Savior, then you are not only guaranteed eternal life with God in Heaven, you are also endowed with the ability to experience heaven on earth.

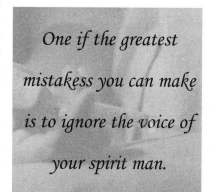

One if the greatest mistakess you can make is to ignore the voice of your spirit man.

Without Jesus as your life's anchor, you will continue to be tormented by feelings of hopelessness, fear and frustration whenever challenges arise. If not dealt with, there's a good chance that eventually those feelings will begin to overwhelm you until one day you'll begin to believe that your existence is futile. That's when you may decide that suicide is the only way out.

Fear makes it seem as though you are stuck in a rut when you're really not. There is a way out of every situation you face in life. The Bible is your instruction manual. When you apply its principles to your life, you are always able to see the light at the end of the tunnel. Why? Because you know that God gives strength to the weary (Isaiah 40:29) and wisdom to those who ask (James 1:5). However, if you are born again and choose to take your own life, you will have failed to carry out God's plans for you. If you are not born again, when you die, you will spend eternity in hell because you chose to remain spiritually separated from God before terminating your life.

I know that sounds harsh, but it's the truth. You may not want to believe that there is a hell because "God loves everyone and He would never send a person to a place like that." Yes, He does love everyone and doesn't want *anyone* to go to hell (John 3:16); however, *He* doesn't send anyone there—they send themselves. People exercise their free will and choose to go to hell when they fail to make Jesus Christ their Lord and Savior.

Your spirit, when properly nourished on the everlasting truth of God's Word, will be empowered to withstand the storms of life.

Many people believe there is a heaven, but they don't believe there is a hell. They fail to realize that not only is God real (Genesis 1:1), heaven and hell are real too (Ecclesiastes 5:2; Luke 16:23). There are angels and demons that exist in the spiritual realm. And believe it or not, Satan is also real (Luke 10:18). As a matter of fact, he's the one encouraging people to take their lives. In John 10:10 Jesus calls him a thief who comes only to kill, steal and destroy.

Satan's tactics haven't changed since the day he disguised himself as a serpent in the Garden of Eden (Genesis 3:1-6). Just as he did with Eve, his goal is to infiltrate your mind and place repetitive, negative thoughts within you. These thoughts are designed to cause you to panic and convince you to take your life based on what things feel or seem like:

"I don't think I can make it without him or her."

"It seems like I'm never going to get out of all this debt."

"It feels like I'm in this world all by myself."

"I don't think anybody really loves me."

"I don't think anyone cares if I live or die"

"It seems as though I'm a total failure."

"It seems that the only way to peace is death."

When you recognize where the opposition is coming from, you can fight aggressively and win the battle.

Your Tank Is Empty

In chapter 31 I discussed, in detail, the three parts of a person: spirit, soul and body. I want to focus on your spirit.

Your spirit man has a voice that you know as your conscience. Some may call it intuition or a "hunch" or "gut feeling." Regardless of the term used to describe it, it's a deep knowing that's trying to communicate itself to your mind. If you follow your conscience, you can live a life free from mistakes. It sounds like a dream, but it's a fact.

Just about everyone knows of a time in their lives when they wished they had followed their inner voice. If they had, they never would have made certain decisions. For example, your gut (spirit man) said, "Don't marry this person. Cancel the wedding." But the voice of reason (your mind) said, "You've already sent the invitations out and those deposits are non-refundable." So you marry anyway, and not too long into the marriage, the true character of your spouse is revealed. You may even find yourself in an abusive situation. The Holy Spirit tried to tell your spirit man what to do. You had a hunch, but you didn't pay attention to it.

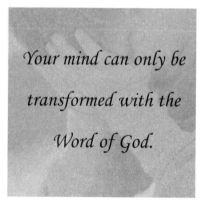

Your mind can only be transformed with the Word of God.

One of the greatest mistakes you can make is to ignore the voice of your spirit man. Many people have allowed their intellect to reign supreme in their lives while their consciences have been suppressed. As a result, they continually make mistakes because their spirit, which should be guiding them, is not permitted to do its job. That, coupled with a "Word deficiency," causes the spirit to become empty. The soul—the place where your mind, will and emotions reside—now controls their lives.

Let me sum this up for you: the root of all emotional torment stems from an empty spirit.

Your spirit is empty because you have suppressed it and not filled it with the truth of God's Word. There is no ammunition to combat the negative thoughts filtering through your mind. Therefore, you entertain and become consumed by the problem more than the solution.

Your mind can only be transformed with the Word of God. When you read the Bible, those scriptures feed your spirit and make it strong. When your spirit is strong, it battles against and defeats negative or destructive thoughts.

On the other hand, when your spirit is empty, the voice of the soul is over-whelming. Your emotions go haywire. Every thought is of gloom and despair. Each challenge seems like a dead end, and you find yourself in a state of depression. That's the time you're most vulnerable to the idea that your life is no longer precious. This is where a demonic spirit of suicide comes in to entice you; and you, desiring for life and people to be fair, allow yourself to be deceived.

Suicide Watch

Have you noticed a change in your loved one, friend or co-worker? At first you thought they might be slightly depressed or upset about something, but they're just not snapping out of it.

- If you suspect they might be contemplating suicide, here are some signs to look for.
- Giving away prized possessions
- Trouble eating, sleeping or concentrating
- Is preoccupied with death and dying
- Loss of interest in hobbies, work, school or other social activities
- Getting their "house in order"
- A lack of interest in the future
- Says such things as, "You'd be better off without me" or Maybe I won't be around anymore."
- Loss of interest in personal hygiene
- Daring or risk-taking behavior
- Drastic personality changes (withdrawal or aggression)

Following are guidelines that will assist you in reaching out to a suicidal individual.

- Trust your instincts. Take their threats seriously.
- Show that you are concerned and want to help. Talk with them.
- Ask them direct questions. The more thought out their plan is, the greater the immediate risk.
- Don't be judgmental.

- Get professional help even if the person tells you not to.
- Do not leave the person alone.
- Do not promise not to tell anyone.

Symptoms of an empty spirit are depression, insecurity, confusion, irritability, frustration, rejection, loneliness and suicidal tendencies—the very same symptoms of depression. I know these emotions are strong, and I am in no way attempting to minimize them. Just keep in mind that when your spirit is at its weakest, your soul is at its strongest.

When faced with a challenging situation, get in the presence of God. It's not a hard thing to do. You can do this just by raising your hands and yelling, "Help!" God's presence destroys anything that would hinder you from experiencing His best in your life daily. In Exodus 33:14, God said, *"My presence shall go with thee, and I will give thee rest."* The power and peace His presence brings will go with you wherever you go. It is the force that nurtures and strengthens your spirit, causing it to *dominate* your soul.

For More Information

The following agencies can assist you in obtaining more information about depression and suicide. In case of an emergency, call your local authorities or 1-800-SUICIDE to reach a crisis center in your area.

- **National Mental Health Association**
  www.nmha.org or 800-969-NMHA
- **American Association of Suicidology**
  www.suicidology.org or 202-237-2280
- **Suicide Prevention Advocacy Network**
  www.spanusa.org or 1-888-649-1366

A New Beginning

God desires for you to live and be led by your spirit, not your mind, will and emotions. Why? Your spirit, when properly nourished on the everlasting truth of God's Word, will be empowered to withstand the storms of life. It will remain constant because it is established on a firm foundation. Your soul, on the other hand, can play tricks on you. It changes with the direction of the wind. Don't allow the inconstant portion of who you are to make decisions for you. Instead, take control of your thoughts and emotions and be led by your inner man.

Throughout the course of your life, you will encounter a number of situations that will make you want to give up, cave in and quit. Keep in mind, however, that quitting is not an option. If you are contemplating suicide or have contemplated it at some point in your life, take heart. All is not lost. I believe that as you realize what is happening and take steps to fill your spirit, you will climb out of the despair that has enveloped you.

* * * * *

Depression and suicide are not solutions to a problem, but rather the result of an empty spirit and untamed emotions. Begin to see yourself and your future through God's eyes. You are a priceless treasure to Him, and He has a great plan for your life. Let Him love you and show you how to live life to the fullest.

Depression and suicidal tendencies are serious spiritual conditions that can only be resolved with a renewed mind and the Word of God.

There is a way out of every situation—or a way to make up for it. When life throws its punches, God showers His mercy. Purchase a journal or scrapbook and use it as an outlet for your emotions. Write down what you're thinking and feeling daily, then review what you've written and measure it against what the Word of God has to say. In addition, you may want to make a list of things you are thankful for or the things in life you love the most. You can include drawings, photos or magazine cut-outs to illustrate your list. When you are feeling blue, take out your journal or scrapbook and review its contents for encouragement.

Isaiah 40:29

"He giveth power to the faint; and to them that have no might he increaseth strength."

35

EATING DISORDERS

I n a society that glorifies *thinness*, an enormous amount of pressure is put on men and women to obtain the "perfect" body. Unfortunately, it is the media, and not the medical profession, that has defined what is beautiful, trendy and acceptable.

For instance, television, magazine columns and advertisements, movies and clothing designers continue to set impossible physical standards for the average woman to follow. Tall, thin and attractive models or celebrities are used to promote their products, subtly manipulating men and women into buying cosmetics, clothing, appliances, vehicles and other products they would not normally like or be able to afford. Many corporations have done a good job of capitalizing on our emotions while, at the same time, tearing down our self-image and replacing it with a faulty one.

Individuals either driven by a deep-seated need to conform to societal pressure generated by the media or who have other emotional and psychological issues are known to suffer from eating disorders such as anorexia, bulimia, and binge eating. Because these conditions usually appear in early to mid-adolescence, many believe that these illnesses and their life-threatening consequences are prevalent only among teenagers. However, studies show that it is also a serious issue among adult men and women from all walks of life.

Just the Facts

Scientists and researchers have learned that eating disorders arise from a combination of long-term behavioral, emotional, psychological, interpersonal and social factors. Following are some basic facts you should know about eating disorders and their warning signs.

1. Anorexia Nervosa.

Anorexia is the condition in which an individual experiences excessive weight loss through self-starvation. Although the majority of those who suffer from this condition are teenage girls and adult women, teen boys and adult men have also been known to engage in this behavior. This is a common psychiatric diagnosis in young women, and it has an extremely high death rate. Individuals suffering from this disorder refuse to maintain body weight that is considered minimally normal for their height, body frame, age and lifestyle. They accomplish this goal by literally starving themselves.

> *Those who struggle with eating disorders usually begin their journey of dieting, bingeing and purging as a way to cope with painful emotions.*

The body is unable to function properly when it doesn't receive the nutrients it needs. In an effort to maintain optimal energy levels, it will slow down all of its processes. This can result in serious medical conditions such as heart failure due to a slowed heart rate, as well as low blood pressure, osteoporosis, muscle loss, severe dehydration, fainting and fatigue. The body will also completely cover itself with a downy layer of hair in an effort to keep warm.

Symptoms of anorexia include a fear of becoming overweight, feeling fat in spite of dramatic weight loss, preoccupation with body weight and shape and loss of the menstrual cycle. There are also several warning signs to watch for:

- Drastic weight loss
- Continual denial of hunger
- Excuses to avoid meals and situations involving food
- Excessive and rigid exercise regimen
- Loss of involvement with friends and normal activities
- Primarily concerned with dieting and weight loss

2. Bulimia Nervosa.

Bulimia occurs when individuals secretly engage in a cycle of binge eating followed by purging. The bulimic, mostly high school and college females, eats incredibly large amounts of food in relatively short periods of time, and then gets rid of the food by vomiting, using laxatives or over-exercising.

Often these individuals appear to have an average body weight, which makes it easy for their behavior to go unnoticed. However, these people tend to develop complex schedules or rituals that allow them the opportunity to engage in private bingeing and purging sessions. Warning signs include:

- The disappearance of large amounts of food in short periods of time
- Frequent trips to the rest room immediately after meals
- The smell and signs of vomiting
- Swelling in the cheeks or jaw area
- Involvement in an excessive and rigid exercise program

People with eating disorders who receive early diagnosis and intervention are most likely to recover.

The effects of this eating disorder are extremely harmful. Recurring binge-and-purge sessions have a tremendous impact on the digestive system. The body suffers from dehydration and loss of potassium and sodium, which can lead to heart failure and death. There is also a potential for gastric rupture, inflammation and rupture of the esophagus, tooth decay and staining from stomach acids, constipation and chronic irregular bowel movements.

3. Binge Eating (also known as Compulsive Overeating).

This condition does not involve purging. It is characterized by frequent episodes of uncontrolled overeating. These individuals also engage in sporadic fasts or repetitive diets that result in feelings of shame or self-hatred.

Researchers are still trying to determine just how prevalent binge eating really is. They have found that women binge more often than men and both appear to be of normal or heavier than average weight. However, there are some cases where the body weight can range from normal to severe obesity. Another interesting fact uncovered by researchers is that many of these individuals have a history of depression and struggle with anxiety and loneliness.

Warning signs:

- Hoarding of food
- Hiding food and wrappers
- Eating in secret (alone)
- Feeling a lack of control during the episode
- Consuming large amounts of food without feeling hungry
- Eating rapidly

As with the other two eating disorders, bingeing has its own set of health issues like heart disease, high blood pressure, high cholesterol, secondary diabetes and gallbladder disease.

Talk it Out

You may wonder how to approach someone who struggles with an eating disorder. My advice is that you express your concerns in a loving and supportive way while being honest and respectful. But be sure to do it early on. Do not wait until your friend or relative begins to show signs of physical damage.

Choose a private and relaxed setting for your discussion. You want to remain calm and caring while pointing out the specific things you've noticed about their behavior. Always use "I" statements. For example, "I'm concerned about you because you constantly refuse to eat." Or, "I feel frightened whenever I hear you vomiting." These statements are non-confrontational and will not put the person on the defensive.

Avoid making accusations by using "You" statements such as, "You have to eat something or you are going to get sick!" "You must be out of your mind!" Or, "You are definitely out of control!" Statements like these add to their feelings of guilt and shame.

You can avoid the struggle of trying to conform to a "standard" image by accepting who you are.

Most importantly, don't be discouraged when they become angry with you and deny that there is a problem. Just continue to show your love, support and understanding. If they won't listen to your concerns for their well-being, then you may need to involve someone else. This is especially true in the case of an adolescent or teenager.

Getting a parent, teacher, minister or counselor involved is the best thing you could ever do for that individual.

Once a person has begun their battle with any of these eating disorders, professional help is needed. You may think you are helping by saying things like, "If you'd just stop and begin to eat right, everything would be fine!" However, statements like that will do little to bring about a change in a person's behavior. It isn't that simple. Those who struggle with eating disorders usually begin their journey of dieting, bingeing and purging as a way to cope with painful emotions. They also see it as a way to be in control of their life. However, these destructive acts cause damage not only to their physical health, but also to their self-esteem.

> *If you or someone you know is struggling with an eating disorder, arm yourself with knowledge, compassion and the Word of God.*

Enjoy Life

It may be difficult at times to look in the mirror and like what you see; however, it *is* possible. Try to incorporate one or more of the following into your daily routine.

- Appreciate everything your body can do.
- Keep a list of 10 things you like about yourself, and read it often.
- Carry yourself with confidence, knowing that true beauty comes from the inside.
- Surround yourself with positive people.
- Wear comfortable clothes that make you feel good about yourself.
- Put your time and energy to work by volunteering to help others.

For more information on eating disorders, contact the national Eating Disorders Awareness and Prevention (EDAP) association at (206) 382-3587 or visit their Web site: *www.edap.org*.

When it comes to any life-threatening condition, it is vital to seek and receive professional help. People with eating disorders who receive early diagnosis and intervention are most likely to recover.

Strategies for Prevention

In this chapter, I have presented a list of warning signs by which parents can recognize changes in the eating behaviors of their sons and daughters. Become familiar with the signs. Be *proactive* instead of *reactive* should you notice your child displaying any of the behaviors or symptoms associated with eating disorders. Listed here are some strategies for prevention and early intervention.

• Be aware that athletic activities may put a weight restriction on your child that ultimately puts him or her at risk for developing an eating disorder. This is especially true for gymnasts.
• Explain to your children how the media has shaped cultural attitudes surrounding the "ideal" or "perfect" body and teach them not to allow anyone to emphasize body size or shape as an indication of their worth or identity.
• Confront the parents of those who tease your children about their weight.
• Explain to your children the importance of self-acceptance.
• Teach them the dangers of trying to alter one's body shape through excessive dieting, the value of proper exercise and the importance of eating three well-balanced meals a day.
• Be a good example for your children by eating sensibly and participating in a regular exercise program.

God made you and likes you just the way you are.

Emphasize the Truth

This whole matter of trying to become what society says is beautiful, and the emotional and psychological challenges and dangers a person goes through to accomplish that goal, has damaged the spirit and self-image of many people.

You can avoid the struggle of trying to conform to a "standard" image by accepting who you are. When you understand that God has created you perfectly in His image, it won't matter what someone else may think of your outer appearance. In fact, He made you just the way you are for a purpose—He likes you that way! You will always be beautiful or handsome in His sight. Psalm 139:13-16 in the *New King James Version* says:

> *For you formed my inward parts; You covered me in my mother's womb. I will praise You, for I am fearfully and wonderfully made; Marvelous are Your works, And that my soul knows very well. My frame was not hidden from You, When I was made in secret, And skillfully wrought in the lowest parts of the earth. Your eyes saw my substance, being yet unformed, And in Your book they all were written, The days fashioned for me, When as yet there were none of them.*

When a person succumbs to the deception that he or she can have a perfect body and then engages in destructive eating habits to change their body shape, they are really telling God, "You didn't do a good job when You made me, so now I'll have to make some alterations."

There is nothing wrong with trying to control your weight and wanting to look good on the outside. You *should* be mindful of your weight, particularly for health reasons. The proper way to watch your weight is by eating healthy foods, exercising regularly and drinking plenty of water. It will take hard work and determination, but consistency will get you there. While destructive eating habits will most likely produce the desired results, it will cost you your health and maybe even your life.

The Ideal You

Eating disorders are the result of distorted self-perception. Often the individual compares him or herself to an impossible and faulty standard of beauty or fitness. They forget that everyone's genetic makeup is unique—metabolisms vary, and what works for one person may not work for another. In addition, they are not seeing themselves from a heavenly perspective.

The key to effectively overcoming an eating disorder is not by professional counseling or medical attention—although those things do help to flesh out other root causes and correct any side effects present—but the Word of God. The Bible is full of scriptures that speak of God's love for you (1 John 3:1; 1 John 4:19; 1 Peter 2:9-10; 1 Peter 5:7;

Titus 3:1-8). The best thing to do is to study those scriptures, meditate on what they say, and speak them aloud daily over your life.

By transforming the way you think about yourself, you will forever change how you see yourself. Begin today to renew your mind with the truth of God's Word. It won't be long before you'll see a difference in your attitude toward your body!

Loving and accepting yourself for who you are is vital to a healthy, well-balanced lifestyle. Of course slight modifications in diet and exertion are always welcome, as they assist your body in performing at optimal levels. However, if you don't learn to love yourself as you are, you'll *never* think you look good! Change first occurs in the heart. Renew your mind according to the truth of God's Word, and be at peace with yourself.

If you or someone you know is struggling with an eating disorder, arm yourself with knowledge, compassion and the Word of God. Focus on the positive and ask for help. It's always there when you need it. In addition, keep in mind the old saying, "Beauty is in the eye of the beholder." Whether you have an eating disorder or not, look into the mirror every day and say, "I love and cherish who God made me to be. I'm absolutely beautiful in God's eyes and He loves me unconditionally!"

Eating disorders are life-threatening conditions that can be overcome through counseling, medical attention and by meditating on the Word of God.

Take a moment to evaluate the way you think about yourself. Are you constantly complaining about your figure or weight? Do you compare yourself to impossible "supermodel" standards of perfection? Is anyone worried about your weight or current fitness program? If you said yes to any of these questions, seek help from a friend, minister, teacher or parent. Discuss your fears or concerns with them and adjust your thinking so you can see your body in a better light. You may also wish to contact a nutritionist or personal trainer for assistance in putting together a dietary and exercise regimen that is just right for you.

2 Corinthians 4:16

"For which cause we faint not; but though our outward man perish, yet the inward man is renewed day by day."

36

CHILD ABUSE

W hen God said to use the rod of correction to drive foolishness out of children (Proverbs 22:15), He was not advocating abuse. Discipline and correction should be based on love. Unfortunately, one of the most tragic occurrences is the violence that children suffer at the hands of caregivers. The use of corporal punishment as a means of discipline was never intended to go to the extreme that it has.

Best described as "intentional acts resulting in physical or emotional harm," *child abuse* is one of the leading causes of death in young children. Thousands of children are killed each year and thousands more suffer permanent physical and mental disabilities. Abuse occurs in all levels of society, regardless of income, race, religious background or ethnicity. However, studies show that it is most prevalent among groups who live below the poverty level. Researchers have found that something as simple as having basic necessities is what often separates abusers from non-abusers.

Child abuse can generally be divided into four categories: physical, sexual, emotional/verbal and neglect. If you see any of the following signs of abuse, call local authorities immediately so both the adult and child receive help. Don't hesitate by thinking that you're going to cause trouble or that it's none of your business; if you don't intervene, who will? Do the right thing for the child and the caregiver, and get them the help they need.

1. Physical abuse.

This type of abuse involves deliberate acts of violence that wound or kill, such as beating, kicking, biting, burning and shaking. Bruises, broken bones or burn marks are generally visible. At times the child may deny any maltreatment, and instead make excuses for his or her injuries, or for the abuser.

2. Sexual abuse.

Some adults will use children to satisfy their sexual desires. This is also known as *pedophilia*. Fondling, intercourse, incest, sodomy and rape are some of the awful acts perpetrated against children. In some cases, they are even exploit-

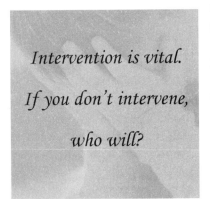

Intervention is vital.

If you don't intervene,

who will?

ed through prostitution or featured in pornographic movies and magazines.

A child can display both physical and psychological signs of sexual abuse. A medical professional can usually detect the physical signs, such as genital irritation, absence of the hymen in young girls, presence of the abuser's seminal fluid or pubic hair, and so on. Pregnancy and venereal disease in a child are the most probable physical indicators since they require intercourse.

Some early psychological signs are abnormal behavior, such as violent tendencies, as well as an unusual interest in sexual organs. Long-term effects include depression and low self-esteem. Experts believe that this type of maltreatment is the most unreported due to the secrecy or "code of silence" that often exists in these cases.

3. Emotional abuse.

Emotional abuse is characterized by acts of verbal and mental maltreatment such as belittling or confinement in dark spaces, like a closet. Since there is no outward evidence of abuse, in many cases it is not easily detected. The two most common acts of emotional abuse are the parent's failure to meet the child's need for affection and psychological care. However, there are other acts that constitute this type of neglect such as the child witnessing spousal abuse and allowing youngsters to use drugs or alcohol.

4. Neglect.

The most common form of maltreatment is neglect. Every child is entitled to provisions such as food, clothing, shelter and medical attention. The failure of a parent or caregiver to adequately provide for their child's basic needs constitutes physical neglect. Other areas include improper supervision and protection from hazardous materials and dangerous situations. Abandonment, expulsion from the home or not allowing a runaway to return home are also acts of neglect.

Acts of educational neglect include allowing the child to skip school, failure to enroll the child in school at the mandatory school age and not providing for a special educational need. This kind of neglect causes children to fall behind both academically and socially. They ultimately miss out on the social development that the classroom setting and interaction with peers adequately provides.

Why?

According to researchers, child abuse generally stems from a number of economic, social and environmental influences. Factors such as poverty and the impact of social and cultural forces surrounding the family also prove to be causes. Isolation is yet another factor to consider. When a parent who is already at risk for becoming an abuser is left alone to raise children without the support of friends and relatives, the danger increases. And since no one is around to spot the abuse when it happens, it could go undetected for years.

Because abuse has such devastating effects on the intellectual, physical, social and psychological development of children, the road to recovery can be long and difficult. The scars are deep and can last a lifetime. Victims are at high risk for becoming abusers themselves. In severe cases, psychiatric disorders like depression, excessive anxiety or multiple personality disorder may develop. There is also an increased risk of suicide among the more severe cases.

The most common form of maltreatment is neglect.

Usually children who have been abused by their caregivers must deal with mixed feelings about their own self-worth and do not easily trust others. Infants, toddlers and preschoolers display insecure attachments to their parents, while older children find it difficult to form close ties with others. New experiences are threatening to older boys and girls, and they are not as curious or ready to learn as their peers are. As teenagers, they often commit delinquent acts, which may later develop into more serious criminal activity.

Counseling is usually the method of treatment recommended. Although counselors cannot replace the parental bonding that children need to grow and develop, they *do* provide the opportunity for children to develop a trusting relationship with an adult. Sessions are conducted in a safe environment where there is no threat of danger to the child. Group counseling is especially good for children who have been sexually abused. This setting reduces their feelings of shame and the sense of feeling different from other children.

Where to Go

Many people are familiar with the term child abuse, but don't know much about it or don't know where to go for help or for more information. Following are the names, Web addresses and telephone numbers of organizations who can provide you with answers to your questions.

United States

- **Childhelp USA** - 1-800-4-A-CHILD (1-800-422-4453)
  National Child Abuse Hotline – staffed 24 hours a day
- **Child Abuse Prevention Network** - *www.child-abuse.com*
- **National Clearinghouse on Child Abuse and Neglect**
  (703) 385-7565 or *www.calib.com/nccanch*

Canada

- **Canadian Society for the Investigation of Child Abuse (CSICA)** - 403-289-8385 or *www.csica.zener.com*
- **National Clearinghouse on Family Violence Canada**
  www.hc-sc.gc.ca

United Kingdom

- **National Society for the Prevention of Cruelty to Children (NSPCC)** -
  +44 020 7825 2500 or *www.nspcc.org.uk*

South Pacific and Asia

- **The National Association for the Prevention of Child Abuse and Neglect (NAPCAN)**
  +61 2 9211-0224 or *www.napcan.org.au*
- **Doctors for Sexual Abuse Care (DSAC)** - +64 9 376-1422 or E-mail: *dsac@ihug.co.nz*
- **Against Child Abuse** - +852 2351 6060 or *www.aca.org.hk*

South Africa

- **Childline South Africa**
  24-hour toll free number: 08000 55555

It breaks my heart when I hear about children who suffer beatings, neglect and sexual abuse at the hands of those who are supposed to protect and nurture them. I also hurt for the abuser. As a pastor and a Christian, I cannot hate the person committing the act. I realize that, first and foremost, there are demonic forces at work in their life, motivating them to do what they do to others.

Child abuse is cyclical. Most abusers are former victims of abuse who had insecure, fearful and dangerous relationships with their own parents. As a result, they did not learn how to form warm, secure family ties, which caused their *own* children to suffer. Having had poor role models for parents, abusers don't know how to be good parents them-selves. Many times they have unrealistic and very high expectations of their children and become frustrated when these expectations are not met. This frustration and a sense of their own failure often lead to abuse. This is known as a *generational curse*—a destructive tendency that is passed from one generation to the next.

Most abusers are former victims of abuse

The good news is that a generational curse *can* be broken. It doesn't have to go to the next generation. The cycle can end with the abuser. Parents or adults who are at risk of becoming abusive, or who have experienced abuse themselves, must make a *conscious* effort to seek professional help. Fortunately, there are many types of social programs available. How well these programs work is entirely up to the caregiver. He or she must first recognize that there is a problem and then be willing to change. Of course, this is easier said than done; but it *can* be done over time.

I often tell my congregation, "Change isn't change until you've changed." It's insane to want different results while doing the same things. Change begins with a decision and continues with the constant application of newly-learned principles. Consistency, coupled with sheer determination and willpower, is the key to breakthrough.

Help Is Available

There are a variety of programs designed to prevent child abuse or intervene on behalf of a child. They identify high-risk parents and provide parental-skills training, counseling, education and social support. Trained social workers or nurses provide this support by visiting the home on a regular basis.

If you are currently abusing a child, STOP right now and seek professional assistance immediately. Don't be afraid to ask for help. Professionals are more than willing to help those who want to help themselves. Even if you feel that you are on the verge of becoming an abuser, do something *now* before you cross over and do something that you will regret for the rest of your life. Therapy or counseling will help you get to the root of the problem and deal with it—once and for all.

Before I became a minister, I was a therapist in a clinic. I had a system called the *flush theory*. I believe that people are affected by what is happening on the inside. The first thing they must do is identify what's going on inside of them, and then flush it out. Once it is flushed out, it no longer has the ability to affect them. My flush system *always* worked.

Clean From the Inside Out

Perhaps you suffered abuse as a child and find yourself on the verge of doing the same thing with your own children. Or you may have already begun to abuse them and want to stop, but don't know how. Flushing your "system" with the Word of God is the only truly successful way to prevent or stop child abuse. This is done by the renewing, or transformation, of your thought process. Negative thoughts lead to negative actions. In other words, what you think about the most is what you will do.

The key to mind renewal is to replace the negative, destructive thoughts in your mind with the positive, constructive thoughts found in Scripture. Abuse is inevitable when you don't understand the purpose for something. Dig into the Bible and find scriptures that reveal God's purpose for children, the appropriate methods of correction, and your responsibilities as a caregiver. Write them down on a sheet of paper and memorize them by speaking them aloud over your life daily. Although you may not see results right away, be assured that it is working. Over time, you will see a difference in your reactions and behaviors.

The Power of Forgiveness

If you are someone who has experienced abuse, it is vital to your mental and emotional well-being that you forgive your abuser and let him or her go. You cannot free yourself from past hurts when you hold on to them by harboring resentment and unforgiveness. The only person you are hurting is yourself. You can't move forward to a promising future while you are stuck in the past.

Release the abuser from your mind and heart by making a decision to do so. You may want to say aloud that you are choosing to forgive them. For example, you could say something like, *"I forgive* [name] *for* [physically, sexually, emotionally] *abusing* [or neglecting] *me. I make a quality decision to release* [name]. *I will no longer be angry or bitter toward them. Neither will I continue to live in fear. I am a new person, whole in every way."* Then let God's love for *you* become the force of love toward those who have hurt you.

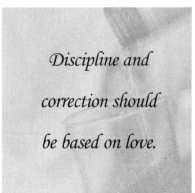

Discipline and correction should be based on love.

While forgiving others is important, it is equally important that you forgive *yourself* for whatever part you feel you may have contributed to the abuse. Many times victims tend to blame themselves for the actions of others. But self-forgiveness is harmful because it prevents you from achieving wholeness and living your life to the fullest.

Whatever your case may be, don't take yourself on a guilt trip. The past is the past. There's nothing you can do to change it. You can't go back and live it over. But you *can* live for today and believe for a fresh start. You *can* look to the future and believe for God's highest and best!

*   *   *   *   *

Although it seems as though child abuse is an incurable epidemic, that is not the case. As in everything else in life, it is a learned behavior that can be changed over a period of time. Individuals desiring a better life for themselves and the children in their care are often able to stop damaging and destructive practices and develop healthier outlooks and behaviors.

The key to overcoming abuse is *prevention* and timely *intervention*. Professional counseling, anger-management training, the development of healthy caregiving skills and forgiveness, coupled with the consistent application of biblical principles, can and will change even the bleakest of circumstances.

Acts of abuse are merely the manifestation of a deeper, more serious condition existing on the inside.

Use the information in this chapter to help you determine if you or someone you know is being abused. Contact local authorities if necessary. If you are a parent or caregiver, review the parenting principles in part three of this book, *Family Planning and Children*, to assist you in enhancing your skills.

Ephesians 5:15-17, NIV

"Be very careful, then, how you live—not as unwise but as wise, making the most of every opportunity, because the days are evil. Therefore, do not be foolish, but understand what the Lord's will is."

Recommended
Resources / Bibliography

RECOMMENDED RESOURCES/ BIBLIOGRAPHY

The following is a sampling of the resources we recommend to assist you in broadening your knowledge regarding the topics covered in this book. Although the majority of them are biblically-based, some of them are not. Be sure to measure the information contained in each one against the truths outlined in the Word of God.

Part I: Before the Ring

Abraham, Ken. *Unmasking the Myths of Marriage: Things Your Mother Never Taught You About Marriage.* Tarrytown: Revel Books, 1990.

Bright, Bill et al., *Seven Promises of a Promise Keeper.* Dallas: Word Publishing, 1999.

Burkett, Larry. *How to Manage Your Money.* Chicago: Moody Press, 2000.

Burkett, Larry and Taylor, Michael E. *Money Before Marriage: A Financial Workbook for Engaged Couples.* Chicago: Moody Press, 1996.

Butler II, Keith A. *God's Plan for the Single Saint.* Southfield: Word of Faith Publishing, 1999.

Cole, Edwin Louis. *Maximized Manhood.* Revised Edition. New Kensington: Whitaker House, 1991.

Coleman, William L. *The Engagement Book: Preparing for the Love of a Lifetime.* Wheaton: Tyndale House, 1980.

Coleman, William L. *Before the Ring: Questions Worth Asking.* Grand Rapids: Discovery House, 1991.

Dobson, James C. *Love for a Lifetime: Building a Marriage That Will Go the Distance.* Sisters: Multnomah, 1983.

Dollar, Taffi. *The Portrait of a Virtuous Woman: Fulfilling the Will of God for Your Life and Empowering Those Around You.* Nashville: Thomas Nelson, 2000.

Eager, George B. *Love, Dating and Marriage.* Valdosta: Mailbox Club Inc., 1987.

Fryling, Alice and Robert. *A Handbook for Engaged Couples.* Revised Edition. Downers Grove: InterVarsity Press, 1996.

Hardin, Jerry D. and Sloan, Diane C. *Getting Ready for Marriage Workbook: How to Really Get to Know the Person You're Going to Marry.* Nashville: Thomas Nelson, 1992.

Harris, Joshua. *I Kissed Dating Goodbye.* Sisters: Multnomah, 1997.

Jones, Debby and Kendall, Jackie. *Lady In Waiting: Developing Your Love Relationships.* Shippensburg: Destiny Image Publishers, 1995.

Littauer, Florence. *Personality Plus: How to Understand Others by Understanding Yourself.* Grand Rapids: Baker Book House, 1992.

Mack, Wayne A. and Mack, Nathan A. *Preparing for Marriage God's Way.* Tulsa: Virgil Hensley Publishing, 1986.

Meyer, Joyce. *How to Succeed at Being Yourself.* Tulsa: Harrison House, 1999.

Myles, Munroe. *Singles 101: Keys to Wholeness and Fulfillment.* Lanham: Pneuma Life Publishing, 1999.

Muzzy, Ruth and Hughes, R. Kent. *The Christian Wedding Planner.* Wheaton: Tyndale House, 1991.

Parrott, Drs. Les and Leslie. *Saving Your Marriage Before It Starts.* Grand Rapids: Zondervan, 1995.

Parrott, Drs. Les and Leslie. *Relationships*. Grand Rapids: Zondervan, 1998.

Prokopchak, Steve and Mary. *Called Together: A Marriage Preparation Workbook*. Nashville: Thomas Nelson, 1994.

Rainey, Dennis. *Building Your Marriage*. Little Rock: Group Publishing, 2000.

Rauniker, Don. *Choosing God's Best: Wisdom for Lifelong Romance*. Sisters: Multnomah, 1998.

Trent, John. *The Making of a Godly Man Workbook: A Guide to Help Men Live Out the Seven Promises*. Colorado Springs: Focus On the Family Publishing, 1997.

Warren, Neil Clark. *Finding the Love of Your Life: 10 Principles for Choosing the Right Partner*. Colorado Springs: Focus On the Family Publishing, 1992.

Williamson, Martha. *Inviting God to Your Wedding and Keeping Him In Your Marriage*. New York: Harmony Books, 2000.

Wilson, P.B. *Knight In Shining Armor*. Eugene: Harvest House, 1995.

Wright, H. Norman. *Before You Say "I Do:" A Marriage Preparation Manual*. Eugene: Harvest House, 1997.

Part II: Marriage Enrichment

Avanzini, John and McNaughton, Deborah. *Have a Good Report: Christian Credit Repair*. Fort Worth: John Avanzini Ministries, 1991.

Boone, Wellington. *Your Wife Is Not Your Momma: How You Can Have Heaven In Your Home*. New York: Doubleday, 1999.

Bundschuh, Rick and Gilbert, Dave. *Dating Your Mate: Creative Ideas for Those Who Are Married or Those Who Would Like to Be*. Eugene: Harvest House, 1987.

Burkett, Larry. *Financial Guide for Couples*. Colorado Springs: Chariot Victor Books, 1993.

Chapman, Gary. *The Five Love Languages: How to Express Heartfelt Commitment to Your Mate*. Chicago: Northfield Publishing, 1992.

Dobson, James C. *Love Must Be Tough*. Dallas: Word Publishing, 1996.

Dobson, James C. *Straight Talk to Men and Their Wives*. Dallas: Word Publishing, 1980.

Dobson, James C. *What Wives Wish Their Husbands Knew About Women*. Wheaton: Tyndale House, 1988.

Dobson, James C. *Night Light: A Devotional for Couples*. Sisters: Multnomah, 2000.

Dollar, Creflo A. *No More Debt! God's Strategy for Debt Cancellation*. Atlanta: Creflo Dollar Ministries, 2000.

Dollar, Creflo A. *The Covenant Connector: How to Get Connected to the Promises of God Through the Tithe*. Atlanta: Creflo Dollar Ministries, 1997.

Gray, John. *Men Are From Mars, Women Are From Venus: A Practical Guide for Improving Communication and Getting What You Need in Relationships*. New York: Harper Collins, 1992.

Harley, Williard. *His Needs, Her Needs: Building an Affair-Proof Marriage*. Tarrytown: Revel Books, 2001.

Harvey, Donald R. *The Spiritually Intimate Marriage*. Tarrytown: Revel Books, 1991.

Hendrix, Harville. *Keeping the Love You Find: A Personal Guide*. New York: Pocket Books, 1992.

Hendrix, Harville. *Getting the Love You Want: A Guide for Couples*. New York: Harper Collins, 1988.

LaHaye, Tim and Beverly. *The Act of Marriage*. Grand Rapids: Zondervan, 1998.

LaHaye, Tim and Beverly. *The Act of Marriage After 40*. Grand Rapids: Zondervan, 2000.

Lucado, Denalyn et al., *Promises, Promises: Understanding and Encouraging Your Husband*. Gresham: Vision House Publishing, 1996.

Omartian, Stormie. *The Power of a Praying Wife*. Eugene: Harvest House, 1997.

Smalley, Gary. *If Only He Knew: Understanding Your Wife*. Grand Rapids: Zondervan, 1982.

Smalley, Gary. *How to Become Your Husband's Best Friend*. Grand Rapids: Zondervan, 1985.

Smalley, Gary. *The Language of Love*. New York: Pocket Books, 1995.

Storey, Duane and Kulkin, Sanford. *Body and Soul*. Sisters: Multnomah, 1995.

Young, Ed. *Romancing the Home: How to Have a Marriage That Sizzles*. Nashville: Broadman & Holman, 1993.

Wheat, Ed and Wheat, Gaye. *Intended for Pleasure: Sex Technique and Sexual Fulfillment in Christian Marriage*. Tarrytown: Revel Books, 1997.

Wright, Norman H. *Communication: Key to Your Marriage*. Ventura: Regal Books, 2000.

Part III: Family Planning and Children

Battle, Jacqueline. *God's Purpose for Virginity*. Chicago: Cornerstone Publishing, 1992.

Burkett, Larry. *Family Financial Workbook: A Practical Guide to Budgeting*. Chicago: Moody Press, 2000.

Burkett, Larry. *Money Management for College Students*. Chicago: Moody Press, 1998.

Chapman, Gary. *The Five Love Languages of Children*. Chicago: Northfield Publishing, 1997.

Chapman, Gary. *The Five Love Languages of Teenagers*. Chicago: Northfield Publishing, 2001.

Dobson, James C. *Parenting Isn't for Cowards*. Dallas: Word Publishing, 1997.

Dobson, James C. *Life On the Edge: A Young Adult's Guide to a Meaningful Future*. Dallas: Word Publishing: 2000.

Dobson, James C. *Preparing for Adolescence*. Ventura: Regal Books, 1999.

Dobson, James C. *The Strong-Willed Child*. Wheaton: Tyndale House, 1992.

Dobson, James C. *The Fundamentals of Child Discipline*. Dallas: Word Publishing, 1995.

Dobson, James C. *The New Dare to Discipline*. Wheaton: Tyndale House, 1996.

Dobson, James C. *The New Hide or Seek: Building Confidence In Your Children*. Tarrytown: Revel Books, 2001.

Dollar, Taffi L. *How to Train Up a Child Without Breaking His Spirit*. Atlanta: Creflo Dollar Ministries, 1999.

LaHaye, Tim and Beverly. *Raising Sexually Pure Kids*. Sisters: Multnomah, 1998.

Mize, Jackie and Mize, Terri. *Supernatural Childbirth*. Tulsa: Harrison House, 1997.

Omartian, Stormie. *The Power of a Praying Parent*. Eugene: Harvest House, 1995.

Reisser, Paul and Dobson, James C. *The Focus On the Family Complete Book of Baby and Childcare*. Wheaton: Tyndale House, 1997.

Wagner, Jan. *Raising Safe Kids In an Unsafe World: 30 Simple Ways to Prevent Your Child From Being Lost, Abducted or Abused*. Austin: Yello Dyno Publishing, 1996.

Part IV: The Secret to a Happy Family

Copeland, Germaine. *Prayers That Avail Much: 3 Volumes In 1*. Tulsa: Harrison House, 1997.

Copeland, Germaine. *Prayers That Avail Much for Children*. Tulsa: Harrison House, 1996.

Field, David. *Family Personalities*. Eugene: Harvest House, 1988.

Hickey, Marilyn. *Building Blocks for Better Families*. Denver: Marilyn Hickey Ministries, 1998.

Meyer, Joyce. *Battlefield of the Mind*. Tulsa: Harrison House, 1996

Miller, Steve and Becky. *Memory Verse Games for Kids*. Eugene: Harvest House, 1997.

Price, Frederick K. C. *Marriage and Family*. Tulsa: Harrison House, 1988.

Treat, Casey. *Renewing the Mind: The Key to Transformation*. Tulsa: Harrison House, 1993.

Treat, Casey. *Renewing the Mind: The Foundatiom of Your Success*. Tulsa: Harrison House, 2000.

Wright, H. Norman. *Raising Kids to Love Jesus*. Ventura: Regal Books, 1999.

Internet Sites

Disney Online – Family Fun
www.family.go.com

Focus on the Family
www.fotf.org

The Mayo Clinic
www.mayoclinic.com

Part V: Making a Go of It

Conway, Jim. *Adult Children of Legal or Emotional Divorce: Healing Your Long-Term Hurt*. Downers Grove: InterVarsity Press, 1990.

Dollar, Creflo A. *The Color of Love.* Tulsa: Harrison House, 1997.

Hickey, Marilyn. *Divorce Is Not the Answer.* Green Forest: New Leaf Press, 1985.

Munroe, Myles. *Single, Married, Separated and Life After Divorce.* Shippensburg: Destiny Image Publishers, 1992.

Parrott, Drs. Les and Leslie. *Saving Your Second Marriage Before It Starts.* Grand Rapids: Zondervan, 2001.

Wright, H. Norman. *Before You Remarry.* Eugene: Harvest House, 1999.

Internet Sites

Administration on Aging (AOA)
www.aoa.dhhs.gov

American Association of Retired Persons (AARP)
www.aarp.org

American Psychological Association (APA)
www.helping.apa.org – keyword(s): stepfamily

The Blended Family
www.blendedfamily.com

TheFamily.com
www.thefamily.com – keyword(s): seniors, stepfamily

The Learning Network
www.familyeducation.com – keyword(s): seniors, stepfamily

ParentsPlace.com
www.parentsplace.com – keyword(s): stepfamilies

Suite101.com
www.suite101.com – keyword(s): seniors, stepfamily

Stepfamily Association of America (SAA)
www.saafamilies.org

Part VI: Life on the Edge

Alsdurf, James and Phyllis. *Battered Into Submission: The Tragedy of Wife Abuse in the Christian Home.* Downers Grove: InterVarsity Press, 1989.

Cantrell, Leslie A. *Into the Light: A Guide for Battered Women.* Revised and Expanded Edition. Indianapolis: Kidsrights, 1994.

Carroll, Charles, R. *Drugs in Modern Society.* Third Edition. Madison: Brown & Benchmark Publishers, 1993.

Cohen, Mary Anne. *French Toast for Breakfast: Declaring Peace With Emotional Eating.* Carlsbad: Gurze Books, 1995.

Dollar, Creflo A. *S.O.S. Help! My Flesh Needs Discipline.* Atlanta: Creflo Dollar Ministries, 1998.

Dollar, Creflo A. *Lasciviousness: The Result of Neglect.* Atlanta: Creflo Dollar Ministries, 1994.

Hall, Lindsey. *Bulimia: A Guide to Recovery.* Carlsbad: Gurze Books, 1992.

Hickey, Marilyn. *Breaking the Generational Curse.* Denver: Marilyn Hickey Ministries, 1999.

Hickey, Marilyn. *Breaking the Generational Curse, Part 2.* Denver: Marylin Hickey Ministries, 1996.

Hickey, Marilyn. *Breaking Generational Curses.* Tulsa: Harrison House, 2001.

Huch, Larry. *Free at Last: Breaking the Cycle of Family Curses.* Minneapolis: Albury Publishing, 2000.

Lemberg, Raymond and Cohen, Leigh. *Eating Disorders: A Reference Sourcebook.* Westport: Oryx Press, 1999.

Meyer, Joyce. *Beauty for Ashes: Receiving Emotional Healing.* Tulsa: Harrison House, 1994.

Savelle, Carolyn. *Conquering the Spirit of Offense.* Crowley: Jerry Savelle Publications, 1998.

Sherrer, Quin and Garlock, Ruthanne. *A Woman's Guide to Breaking Bondages.* Ann Arbor: Vine Books, 1994.

Sledge, Tim. *Making Peace With Your Past: Help for Adult Children of Dysfunctional Families.* Nashville: Lifeway Press, 1992.

Strom, Kay Marshall. *In the Name of Submission: A Painful Look at Wife Battering.* Sisters: Multnomah, 1986.

Wright, Norman H. *Crisis Counseling – What to Do and Say During the First 72 Hours: A Practical Guide for Pastors, Counselors and Friends.* Ventura: Regal Books, 1999.

Internet Sites

Alcoholics Anonymous
www.alcoholics-anonymous.org

American Association of Suicidology
www.suicidology.org

Center for Mental Health Services
www.mentalhealthnih.gov

Eating Disorders Awareness and Prevention, Inc.
www.edap.org

MSNBC
www.msnbc.com – keyword(s): addiction, alcoholism

Narcotics Anonymous
www.na.org

National Clearinghouse on Child Abuse and Neglect
www.calib.com

National Coalition Against Domestic Violence
www.ncadv.org

National Depressive and Manic-Depressive Association
www.ndmda.org

National Women's Health Information Center
www.4woman.gov

APPENDIX A

Five Steps to Complete Salvation

1. Recognize and admit that you are a sinner (Psalm 51:5).

2. Repent of your sins (1 John 1:9).

3. Confess Jesus Christ as Lord and Savior (Romans 10:9,10).

   "Father, in the name of Jesus, I recognize and admit that I am a sinner. I repent of my sins and I make a 180° turn away from sins to You by changing my heart, mind and direction. I confess with my mouth that Jesus is Lord, and I believe in my heart that You raised Him from the dead. I invite You to come into my life, Lord Jesus, and I thank You that I am saved. Amen."

4. Receive baptism by water (Matthew 3:6) and the baptism in the Holy Spirit with the evidence of speaking in tongues (Acts 2:3,4, 38; Acts 8:14-17).

5. Pray, read and obey the Word of God daily (1 John 5:3).

ABOUT THE AUTHORS

Dr. Creflo A. Dollar is the pastor and founder of World Changers Church International, a non-denominational church located in College Park, Georgia.

Dr. Dollar received the vision for World Changers Ministries (WCM) in 1981 while a student at West Georgia College. God instructed him to teach the Body of Christ the Word of God with simplicity and understanding. In February of 1986 WCM held its first worship service with only eight members at Kathleen Mitchell Elementary School in College Park. Attendance grew rapidly, as a result, the ministry relocared to a modest-sized chapel, then later moved to its present location - the 8,500 seat World Dome.

A world-renowned author, Dr. Dollar has written several books on a variety of topics, including debt-cancellation, healing, prosperity, prayer and victorious living. Many of his past works, including *The Anointing to Live, Understanding God's Purpose for the Anointing* and *The Divine Order of Faith* have been added to the curriculum of several Christian colleges across the United States. His latest release, *The Image of Righteousness*, has received tremendous acclaim, both nationally and internationally.

Dr. Dollar received his Doctorate from Oral Roberts University in 1998 and serves on the Board of Regents. In addition to being a successful businessman and entrepreneur, he is also the publisher of *Changing Your World* magazine, an inspirational monthly publication.

* * * * *

Taffi L. Dollar is the Executive Director of World Changers Ministries, the President and CEO of Arrow Records and the overseer of the Women's Fellowship.

A native of Atlanta, Taffi obtained a bachelor's degree in Mental Health and Human Services from Georgia State University. She accepted Jesus Christ as Lord while attending a Bible study headed by Dr. Creflo A. Dollar on the campus of West Georgia College.

An aficionado of gospel music in all of its various forms, Taffi established Arrow Records in 1998, a dynamic, Christian-based record company located in College Park, Georgia. With its motto, "Music That Pierces the Heart," this rising star in the music industry has already produced several award-winning albums, including *From the Heart of God*, which features the *Changing Your World* Mass Choir.

* * * * *

Both Creflo A. Dollar and Taffi L. Dollar can be seen and heard worldwide through the *Changing Your World* Broadcast and conventions. Recognized for their cutting-edge revelation and humorous, pragmatic approach, the Dollars' teachings have enabled thousands to experience financial breakthrough, restoration and healing in their lives as a result of applying the simple, biblical principles outlined in their messages.

With satellite offices in Australia, the Republic of South Africa and the United Kingdom, they are truly setting the standard for excellence in ministry and making a mark in the lives of millions that can never be erased!